DEATH, RESURRECTION,
AND HUMAN DESTINY

PREVIOUSLY PUBLISHED RECORDS OF BUILDING BRIDGES SEMINARS

The Road Ahead: A Christian-Muslim Dialogue,
Michael Ipgrave, Editor (London: Church House, 2002)

Scriptures in Dialogue: Christians and Muslims Studying the Bible and the Qur'ān
Together, Michael Ipgrave, Editor (London: Church House, 2004)

Bearing the Word: Prophecy in Biblical and Qur'ānic Perspective,
Michael Ipgrave, Editor (London: Church House, 2005)

Building a Better Bridge: Muslims, Christians and the Common Good,
Michael Ipgrave, Editor (Washington, DC: Georgetown University Press, 2008)

Justice and Rights: Christian and Muslim Perspectives, Michael Ipgrave,
Editor (Washington, DC: Georgetown University Press, 2009)

Humanity: Texts and Contexts: Christian and Muslim Perspectives,
Michael Ipgrave and David Marshall, Editors
(Washington, DC: Georgetown University Press, 2011)

Communicating the Word: Revelation, Translation, and Interpretation in
Christianity and Islam, David Marshall, Editor
(Washington, DC: Georgetown University Press, 2011)

Science and Religion: Christian and Muslim Perspectives, David Marshall, Editor
(Washington, DC: Georgetown University Press, 2012)

Tradition and Modernity: Christian and Muslim Perspectives, David Marshall,
Editor (Washington, DC: Georgetown University Press, 2013)

Prayer: Christian and Muslim Perspectives, David Marshall and Lucinda Mosher,
Editors (Washington, DC: Georgetown University Press, 2013)

For further information about the Building Bridges process, please visit:
http://berkleycenter.georgetown.edu/resources/networks/buildingebridges

Death, Resurrection, and Human Destiny

Christian and Muslim Perspectives

A record of the eleventh Building Bridges Seminar
Convened by the Archbishop of Canterbury
King's College London and Canterbury Cathedral
April 23–25, 2012

DAVID MARSHALL and LUCINDA MOSHER, Editors

GEORGETOWN UNIVERSITY PRESS
Washington, DC

Library of Congress Cataloging-in-Publication Control Number: 2014005922

⊗ This book is printed on acid-free paper meeting the requirements of the American National Standard for Permanence in Paper for Printed Library Materials.

21 20 19 18 17 16 15 14   9 8 7 6 5 4 3 2 First printing

Printed in the United States of America

Contents

Participants

Muhammad Abdel Haleem
King Fahd Professor of Islamic Studies, School of Oriental and African Studies, University of London

Asma Afsaruddin
Chair and Professor of Islamic Studies, Department of Near Eastern Languages and Cultures, Indiana University

Ahmet Alibašić
Lecturer, Faculty of Islamic Studies, University of Sarajevo, Bosnia and Herzegovina

Richard Burridge
Dean of King's College London and Professor of Biblical Interpretation

Gavin D'Costa
Professor of Catholic Theology, University of Bristol, UK

Valentin Dedji
Minister in Charge, St Mark's Methodist Church, Tottenham, London

John J. DeGioia
President, Georgetown University, Washington, DC

Brandon Gallaher
Postdoctoral Fellow in Theology, Regent's Park College, University of Oxford, UK

Lucy Gardner
Tutor in Christian Doctrine, St. Stephen's House, University of Oxford, UK

Feras Hamza
Assistant Professor of Middle Eastern Studies, American University in Dubai

Harriet Harris
University Chaplain, University of Edinburgh

Musharraf Hussain
Chief Executive, Karimia Institute, Nottingham, UK

Michael Ipgrave
Bishop of Woolwich, Church of England

Daniel A. Madigan
Director of Graduate Studies, Department of Theology, Georgetown University, Washington, DC

Dennis McAuliffe
Associate Professor of Italian, Bryn Mawr College, Pennsylvania

Jane Dammen McAuliffe
President, Bryn Mawr College, Pennsylvania

Ibrahim Mogra
Chairman, Mosque and Community Affairs Committee, Muslim Council of Britain

M. M. Dheen Mohamed
Associate Dean for Academic Affairs, College of Sharia and Islamic Studies, Qatar University

Sajjad Rizvi
Associate Professor of Islamic Intellectual History and Director of Education, University of Exeter, UK

Geoffrey Rowell
Bishop of Gibraltar in Europe, Church of England

Recep Şentürk
Director General and Dean of Graduate Studies, Alliance of Civilizations Institute, Fatih Sultan Mehmet Vakif University, Istanbul

Reza Shah-Kazemi
Research Associate, Institute of Ismaili Studies, London

Philip Sheldrake
Senior Research Fellow, Cambridge Theological Federation, UK

Ayman Shihadeh
Senior Lecturer in Islamic Studies, School of Oriental and African Studies, University of London

Mona Siddiqui
Professor of Islamic and Interreligious Studies and Assistant Principal for Religion and Society, University of Edinburgh

Martin Lukito Sinaga
Study Secretary, Theology and Church Program, Lutheran World Federation, Geneva

Miroslav Volf
Director, Yale Center for Faith and Culture and Henry B. Wright Professor of Systematic Theology, Yale Divinity School, New Haven, Connecticut

Rowan Williams
Archbishop of Canterbury, Church of England

Tim Winter
Shaykh Zayed Lecturer in Islamic Studies, University of Cambridge, UK

N. T. Wright
Professor of New Testament and Early Christianity, University of St. Andrews, UK

Acknowledgments

Many thanks are due to all those whose hard work made possible the smooth running of the seminar recorded in this volume. Particular mention should be made of Richard Burridge, Clare Dowding, and their colleagues at King's College London, and of Toby Howarth and Tess Young at Lambeth Palace. The extremely generous support for Building Bridges provided over many years by Georgetown University has been essential to the flourishing of this project. Particular thanks, as ever, go to the president of Georgetown University, John J. DeGioia, and to Tom Banchoff, director of the Berkley Center for Religion, Peace, and World Affairs. Once again, it has been a pleasure working with Richard Brown and the staff of Georgetown University Press.

Introduction

DAVID MARSHALL

In his final year as Archbishop of Canterbury, Dr. Rowan Williams convened the eleventh annual Building Bridges seminar for Christian and Muslim scholars, on the theme of "Death, Resurrection, and Human Destiny." The seminar lasted from April 23–25, 2012; the first day was dedicated to public lectures at King's College London while the second and third days consisted of private sessions at the Canterbury Cathedral Lodge for the group of some thirty invited seminar participants.

This record of the seminar closely follows the structure of its three days. The Preface draws on comments made by Rowan Williams in introducing the seminar. He begins by reviewing ten years of Building Bridges, noting two distinctive features of this approach to Christian–Muslim dialogue. First, it has not sought a high public profile but rather has been concerned to develop a community of scholars whose aim has been "to model a patience in dialogue that is fundamentally oriented towards getting to know one another's hearts." Second, Building Bridges has emphasized the study of scripture because "what actually changes things and moves us forward is watching somebody else engaging at depth with their own sacred texts and with their own tradition." Turning to the theme of this seminar, Williams notes that, in a culture that finds it hard to discuss death, it is important for Muslims and Christians, who "share the vocabulary of death, resurrection, and judgment," to "talk to each other with honesty and with openness about our mortality" and so "contribute to the health of the society and the world around us."

Part I of this volume ("Surveys") consists of edited versions of the three pairs of lectures given on the seminar's opening day, with each of the lectures by a Christian followed by a response from a Muslim, and vice versa. The first two essays focus on scripture. After a brief survey of the relatively few references to resurrection in the Old Testament, N. T. Wright argues that early Christianity "was not nearly as interested in 'life after death' as the modern world has been. . . . The emphasis is on the present: Jesus is raised, therefore he is the world's true Lord, and therefore we have a job to do." Christians were in fact concerned with " 'life after life after death': the ultimate resurrection, *after* a period of being bodily dead." Wright illustrates his reading of the New Testament with detailed comments on the response of Jesus to the Sadducees' question about the afterlife (Mark 12:18–27) and passages from I Corinthians 15, Romans 8, and Revelation 21–22. The essence of the biblical hope is that "the creator God will rescue his whole creation from all that defaces and corrupts it, and this act of restorative justice, long promised in scripture, has been accomplished through the death and resurrection of Jesus, Israel's Messiah." Mona Siddiqui's essay focuses chiefly on the Qur'ān while also drawing in some wider Islamic perspectives. She emphasizes the vivid imagery with which the Qur'ān conveys the reality of an afterworld and an afterlife and also draws attention to the contrast between the Qur'ānic eschatology and the fatalistic determinism of the pagan Arabs, who typically responded with incredulity to Muḥammad's proclamation. Siddiqui refers to the development in Islamic tradition of certain aspects of the Qur'ān's eschatology, such as its brief references to *barzakh*, which came to be understood as both the time and the place of waiting between death and resurrection. She also notes how the Qur'ān's references to an eschatological role to be played by Jesus are greatly developed in the later tradition. Her concluding emphasis is on the Qur'ān's message of hope in the divine mercy.

With the essays by Asma Afsaruddin and Geoffrey Rowell we move from scripture to tradition. Afsaruddin draws on the ḥadīth corpus, works of exegesis (*tafsīr*), and ethical or edifying literature to give some impression of the "richly textured tapestry" that records how Muslims "have conceptualized life after their earthly existence." Topics covered in this wide-ranging survey include the need for constant remembrance of death; the mysteries of death and the grave (including discussion of the two angels, Munkar and Nakīr, and of *barzakh*); the intercession of the Prophet; the topography of the next world; and the "exalted status assigned by the tradition to martyrs, especially military martyrs." Afsaruddin concludes that the materials surveyed "encode . . . the fundamental human hope that the mercy of the Almighty will envelop us all, erase all the failings that make us so fallibly human, and allow us to reach our fullest potential in the presence of the Divine." Geoffrey Rowell's overview of the Christian tradition proceeds in chronological order from the Creeds and the Fathers through medieval developments and the Reformation to the modern era. He concludes by noting the centrality of the resurrection of Jesus to the Christian hope, but in the course of his essay he emphasizes the diversity, across time and ecclesial traditions, of Christian eschatological thinking and associated devotional practice. For example, he comments on the "different theologies and maps of Christian hope" of the Eastern and Western traditions. Rowell also notes the influence on Christian eschatology of surrounding culture, whether Gnostic and Platonist thought in the early period or, in more recent centuries, the impact of the Enlightenment.

The third pair of essays address the theme of "dying well" or "the good death" in Christian and Islamic perspective; here, especially with the essay by Harriet Harris, the focus also shifts to the modern world and to "actual" practice, rather than what "should" be believed and practiced. Harris considers Christian approaches to death in the West today, a context that is simultaneously "secularized" and "multifaith." Although explicit teaching on the need for readiness for death may now be much rarer than it was, Christians still absorb something of an "art of dying" through their worship and discipleship. Harris gives particular attention to the growth of the hospice movement, noting that "hospice care . . . involves an explicit philosophy that death is neither to be postponed nor hastened, and is the area in our culture where we are most attentive to dying." She also discusses euthanasia before concluding with some observations on new approaches to Christian ministry around death in the changing context of the modern Western world. In his wide-ranging essay, Sajjad Rizvi interacts with a variety of perspectives on death, both from within the Islamic tradition and beyond it. A central section of the essay focuses on three Islamic narratives of sacrifice and martyrdom that illustrate exemplary approaches to death: the stories of Abel, Abraham and his son, and, discussed at greatest length, Ḥusayn at Karbala. The story of Ḥusayn prompts a number of observations about distinctively Shīʿī beliefs and practices. It is "through their ritual mourning of Ḥusayn" that believers "grasp the nature of the good life and the good death." Rizvi concludes with some reflections on how euthanasia might be approached in the light of the thought of Mullā Ṣadrā. Part I concludes with "Reflections" by Rowan Williams, an edited version of comments made by him at the end of the day of public lectures, in which he explores six themes or thematic clusters that emerged from the day's proceedings.

Part II ("Texts and Commentaries") offers a record of the two days of private sessions held at Canterbury. These sessions focused on a sequence of Christian and Islamic texts chosen for their relevance to the seminar's themes: first scriptural texts, then texts from two medieval classics, then contemporary texts illuminating current funeral practice among Muslims and Christians. In each case the text is given first, followed by an essay by a seminar participant. The biblical text chosen is I Corinthians 15, St. Paul's most sustained discussion of the resurrection; Richard Burridge then offers detailed commentary on this chapter. From the Qur'ān a selection of passages is followed by comments by Muhammad Abdel Haleem.

Moving to the medieval period, we focus first on a choice of passages from *The Remembrance of Death and the Afterlife*, Book XL of al-Ghazālī's *Revival of the Religious Sciences*. Tim Winter provides a brief overview of al-Ghazālī's life and work before introducing the *Revival* and this, its final book. Winter concludes that "even in this terrifying book about God's wrath and judgment, we are regularly and discreetly reassured that mercy will have the last word." Next we explore the eschatology of one of the great works of medieval Christianity through a selection of passages from Dante's *The Divine Comedy*, following his progression from *Inferno* through *Purgatorio* to the vision that concludes *Paradiso*. Dennis McAuliffe explains the structure and some key features of Dante's masterpiece before commenting on the selected passages.

The final two selections of texts were included to illuminate current funeral practice among Muslims and Christians in England. *Journey to the Afterlife: A Muslim Funeral Guide*, written by one of the seminar participants, Musharraf Hussain, is a booklet (published in 2010) that combines practical advice and religious guidance and is designed to meet the needs of a local Muslim community in Nottingham in recent years. The passages included discuss matters such as washing the body of the deceased, the proper way of conducting funeral prayers, and offering condolences. In his accompanying essay, Hussain elaborates on these and other features of Muslim practice around the time of death, at many points drawing out aspects of the Muslim understanding of and approach to death. There follows a selection of texts related to funerals from the Church of England website. Along with the funeral liturgy most widely used in the Church of England today, this section includes materials providing information and guidance of various kinds. Michael Ipgrave's essay comments on certain points within this selection of texts while also offering wider observations on issues such as the diversity of contemporary funeral practice and recent historical change, for example, in relation to cremation.

The volume contains four further pieces. "Conversations in Canterbury" offers an overview of some of the main points emerging in the seminar's private sessions, both in small groups and in plenary. In his afterword, Rowan Williams draws together some concluding thoughts on the seminar as a whole. The "Personal Reflections" offer brief responses from a number of the participants to a question posed before the seminar: "In your experience, what resources has your faith given you for responding to the deaths of others and/or the prospect of your own death?" Finally, in this volume recording the tenth and final Building Bridges seminar chaired by Archbishop Rowan Williams, it is appropriate to offer an overview and analysis of the whole project up to this point. This is provided by Lucinda Mosher in her concluding essay "A Decade of Appreciative Conversation: The Building Bridges Seminar under Rowan Williams."

Note on Translations of the Bible and the Qur'ān

When not indicated otherwise in the notes, the translations of the Qur'ān in this volume are either from M. A. S. Abdel Haleem, *The Qur'an: A New Translation* (Oxford: Oxford University Press, 2010), or are the author's own translation, and translations of the Bible are either from the New Revised Standard Version or are the author's own translation.

Preface

ROWAN WILLIAMS

I want to begin by expressing deep gratitude to King's College London, from the Principal to the Dean and the Dean's colleagues and staff to all those who have helped to make us so welcome here. As the Principal, Professor Trainor, has said, this is a place naturally equipped for the kind of dialogue that we have sought to pursue; it's a very great pleasure to be able to have the public part of our proceedings here in this historic setting.

A public word of thanks is also due to Georgetown University, to President DeGioia and his colleagues, for the extraordinary support that they have given over the years to Building Bridges. Since very early on in the life of this project, our association with Georgetown has been deeply significant in focusing and resourcing our work. That connection has become deeper and deeper over the years, and as the whole project moves into a new phase, with Georgetown taking a still more leading role in the organization of these seminars, I want to thank President DeGioia very much indeed for the wonderful privileges that our link with Georgetown has brought.

The initial impetus behind Building Bridges was the events of 9/11. In the months following that appalling catastrophe, my predecessor, Archbishop Carey, believed it necessary to draw together as many as possible of the representatives of Christianity and Islam who were willing to engage seriously with each other about mutual understanding and cooperation in a very fragile global situation.

So the first, relatively brief, Building Bridges seminar was held at Lambeth Palace in January 2002. And on that basis, it was thought that Building Bridges ought to move to a regular and perhaps rather more searching level—that is, that seminars should involve longer, more extended conversation, making considerable use of study and discussion in small groups, and that we should seek to draw together as many scholars and people of intellectual influence in the

Christian and Islamic worlds as we could on an annual basis, to explore themes of common interest.

So, just over a year later, in April 2003, the first extended Building Bridges seminar was held in Doha, in Qatar. Subsequent seminars have been held in a variety of locations, in Christian and in Islamic contexts, in academic settings and in settings more obviously in the midst of dialogue on the ground, for example in Sarajevo and in South East Asia.

In the last ten years, dialogue between Christians and Muslims has become, one might almost say, *fashionable*. The question is bound to arise: what is distinctive about what *we* do in Building Bridges? I want to note two things. The first is that we have not sought a high public profile. While there are plenty of people who work at that level, and there are plenty of people who address the political and geopolitical issues, there are perhaps fewer groups that seek to build lasting and intimate relationships among themselves, and that seek to give priority to the study of each other's scriptures. So we have not sought a high public profile; we have not sought to make statements and issue communiqués. We have sought understanding of a particular kind. And by keeping a very strong core of regular participants so that we get to know each other quite closely, we have attempted to model a *patience* in dialogue that is fundamentally oriented toward getting to know one another's hearts.

That takes me to the second distinctive point, which I have already noted in passing. We have focused our attention very, very strongly on shared study, both of our sacred texts, the Bible and the Qur'ān, but also of texts from our traditions. We have therefore tried to watch each other engaging with our sources. It's easy enough to comment at a distance on how other people use their sources; easy enough, perhaps, to make a sketchy survey of other people's sources and texts and think you understand them. But what actually changes things and moves us forward is watching somebody else engaging at depth with their own sacred texts and with their own tradition.

So we have modeled our meetings on that principle. We engage with what we believe God has given us to engage with, in holy text and in tradition. And we invite our neighbours and friends to watch us doing that, and to learn a bit about how to share in that as best they can. That focus on sacred texts means that a great deal of our work together in discussion is text-based. We have tried to avoid large generalities, so that we can come back again and again to the specifics of what we believe God is saying to us in the texts with which our tradition engages.

Our practice has been to conduct part of our discussion in public, with distinguished scholars addressing a larger audience so that the wider public has an opportunity to engage with our discussion. We then go into our more private sessions, mainly spent in small groups, where we exchange our comments and our reflections on texts. I'm happy to say that on this occasion, after our day of public lectures at King's College, we shall be holding our private sessions in Canterbury. So that is the method—the philosophy, if you like—of the Building Bridges seminars. And from the seminars that we have held so far, there has issued a series of publications, which together offer a very rich resource of shared reflection.

We have sought to address matters of shared interest and concern for Christians and Muslims. That is, we have sought to come at contemporary, pressing geopolitical questions, not from the point of view of headlines but from the point of view of those concerns that are deeply rooted in our hearts as people of faith. So over the years we have looked not only at the definitions of some of the key terms in our different traditions—what prophecy means, for example. We have also looked at issues of poverty and justice and at questions around tradition and modernity. Last year we had a particularly searching and enriching series of sessions on prayer in our two traditions. This year we turn our attention to eschatology: death, resurrection, and human destiny.

Both Islam and Christianity have a distinctive approach to issues around death and resurrection. They share the vocabulary of death, resurrection, and judgment. They share a sense of human destiny as historically shaped—shaped around the address and engagement of God the Creator. So it is to be expected that we will have something to say to one another about these questions of death and destiny.

We believe, as do, I think, all people of faith, that in a culture that is still uncharacteristically reticent—shy, you might say—of addressing questions of death and destiny, the more we talk to each other with honesty and with openness about our mortality, the better we shall contribute to the health of the society and the world around us. We are living in a culture in which, strangely, *mortality* is still one of the subjects least easy to discuss and think through in public. We behave and we speak as if we were not only individually immortal but also corporately or socially and politically immortal. We behave not only as if our individual lives were somehow magically protected from hurt—ideally, anyway—but also as if our human environment were magically protected from hurt. The religious conviction that we are not only mortal but also answerable for what we do with our mortal span is one of the things that gives us a due sense of proportion and humility, in our relation not only to our own lives and aspirations but to our entire material environment.

Far from being matters of a narrowly religious import, the themes we shall be discussing over these coming days thus have wide implications for the health of our human race in its environment. We are grateful for the opportunity to open this discussion up in the presence of a large audience, so I welcome all of you who are here today and hope that today will be a stimulus and an enrichment both for those who call themselves people of faith and for those who don't; and that we may emerge with a fuller sense of our humanity as well as how that humanity is to be transformed by the touch of God.

PART I

Surveys

Death, Resurrection, and Human Destiny in the Bible

N. T. WRIGHT

Introduction

The classic Christian belief about God's ultimate destiny for his human creatures is the resurrection of the body. Many are therefore surprised to discover that belief in resurrection hardly features in the Old Testament at all. By the time of Jesus it was, in fact, a topic of controversy among different Jewish parties, with the conservative Sadducees rejecting it, the more radical Pharisees embracing it, and other Jewish groups and individuals remaining ambiguous or opting for some form of Platonism.[1]

The controversy between Pharisees and Sadducees highlights a key element in the biblical vision of life beyond the grave, and of God's ultimate purpose for his human creatures. The present world is the good Creation of the God of justice and mercy. Resurrection is the point at which God's Creation and God's justice meet; together these themes affirm that the present world, and what humans do in it, matters. Resurrection was always an implicitly political doctrine. That was the main reason for the first-century Jewish controversy.

The ancient Israelite vision of God's world and his people was not, after all, so very different from that of the later Christians and Rabbis, even though there was no developed vision of what happened after death. The ancient Israelites believed that after death God's people were laid to rest in "Sheol," a shadowy subterranean location.[2] They were "asleep with their ancestors"; but the nature of that sleep and the chance of anything beyond it were not discussed. This was not because the earlier biblical writers were at a more "primitive" stage in which questions of "life after death," so important in the modern West, had not yet impinged but because they laid powerful emphasis on the goodness of the this-worldly creation of land, family, seasons, and harvests, and on the importance of a human and earthly justice that reflected and embodied God's own concern for things to be put right, especially in relation to the poor and needy. It was

3

out of that passion for God to put things right that the biblical doctrine of resurrection began to emerge.

Resurrection in the Old Testament

Resurrection itself appears first in the Old Testament as a metaphor. Hosea and Ezekiel both speak of Israel's God raising people up; these passages, originally metaphors for national restoration after disaster, were interpreted already by the first century in terms of actual resurrection.[3] Many other texts were similarly interpreted. "When your days are fulfilled and you lie down with your ancestors," promises YHWH to David, "I will raise up your offspring after you . . . and I will establish his kingdom" (II Sam. 7:12).[4] The early Christians took the verse as a prophecy that confirmed their view that Jesus's resurrection established him as the Davidic Messiah.[5]

Then there is the sudden strange passage in Isaiah, promising the abolition of death itself:

> And he will destroy on this mountain the shroud that is cast over all people, the sheet that is spread over all nations; he will swallow up death for ever . . . . (Isa. 25:7–8a.)
>
>   Your dead shall live, their corpses shall rise. O dwellers in the dust, awake and sing for joy! For your dew is a radiant dew, and the earth will give birth to those long dead. (Isa. 26:19)

These passages echo the most famous Old Testament prediction of resurrection: Daniel 12. Set at the time of the revolt led by Judas Maccabaeus against the Syrian tyrant Antiochus Epiphanes in the 160s BC, the book offers hope for persecuted Jews, reaching a climax in the promise of ultimate deliverance:

> Many of those who sleep in the dust of the earth shall awake, some to everlasting life, and some to shame and everlasting contempt. Those who are wise shall shine like the brightness of the sky, and those who lead many to righteousness, like the stars forever and ever. (Dan. 12:2–3)[6]

This was the passage that strengthened resurrection faith among subsequent Jewish generations, and that was dismissed by the Sadducees as a late innovation. The Maccabean period also gave rise, of course, to some of the most explicit expressions of ancient Jewish resurrection faith, notably in II Maccabees.[7]

The Early Christians and Jesus

It was to the book of Daniel that the early Christians went, as well, to understand who Jesus was and what he had accomplished in his life, his death, and his resurrection. Nobody was expecting a crucified Messiah. There is, however, massive, incontrovertible evidence that after his death Jesus's first followers did indeed come to regard him as Israel's Messiah, but this is inexplicable unless they believed that God had raised him bodily from the dead. It is not my present task to argue that this was true, though of course I think it was.[8] My task is to show the remarkable way in which this belief colored and shaped the New Testament's vision of life beyond the grave and of God's ultimate destiny for his human creatures.

The first Christians put together their knowledge of Jesus with their fresh reading of the Old Testament scriptures to claim not just that in Jesus there was a new ethic or spirituality, nor even that in Jesus there was a new and definite hope for life after death. Their claim was that, in and through Jesus, Israel's God had become king of the whole world. With Jesus's resurrection, then, the early Christians believed that the world was, as it were, under new management, though the style of that management was unlike anything imagined before. When Paul concludes his greatest argument, he quotes Isaiah 11 to this effect, referring to Jesse, the father of King David, and seeing the coming Messiah as his "root," the one who sustains his whole family: "There shall be the root of Jesse, the one who rises up to rule the nations; the nations shall hope in him" (Rom. 15:12).[9] Rising and ruling go together.

This is important not just as background but also as formative context. Early Christianity was not nearly as interested in "life after death" as the modern world has been. In none of the four gospels, nor in the first chapter of Acts, does Jesus's resurrection cause anyone to speculate about their own ultimate future. The emphasis is on the present: Jesus is raised, therefore he is the world's true Lord, and therefore we have a job to do. Jesus's resurrection does of course point to the future, which his people may one day share, but that is not seen as its primary purpose. Jesus's resurrection is about what Jesus's whole public career was about: God's kingdom arriving, however paradoxically, "on earth as in heaven." An overconcentration on "life after death" in its various forms is, I think, a medieval corruption, distracting attention from the horrible parody of God's kingdom on earth offered by the ill-named Holy Roman Empire.

The early Christians were in fact not nearly as interested as we today are in "life after death," the condition or location of people immediately after they died. That was, to be sure, a topic of discussion in the first century, but the New Testament has very little to say about it. They were much more interested in "life after life after death": the ultimate resurrection, after a period of being bodily dead. Like Jesus in the tomb prior to Easter, there would be a two-stage sequence, and it was the final stage that mattered far more.

Fascinatingly, Jesus himself had very little to say on all this—another indication that the question of life after death was not, in itself, the central point of his aim and mission. We have a couple of incidental references to God's new world, and to the righteous shining like stars within it.[10] There is then the brief discussion with the Sadducees.[11] This passage is often misunderstood, and we must look at it more closely.

The Sadducees pose a trick question to Jesus, apparently undermining the very idea of resurrection. The Levirate law of marriage indicated that when a husband died childless, his brother should marry the widow to raise up children for the dead man. Supposing this happens seven times over; which brother will be the husband in the resurrection?[12] This was not simply an abstract theological question. "Resurrection" was part of radical Pharisaic belief, looking for Israel's God to overturn the present order (represented by the aristocratic Sadducees) and to replace it with his own kingly rule. Jesus's dramatic action in the temple, in which he acted out symbolically God's coming judgment on that temple and its destruction, seemed to have indicated that he too believed in just such a drastic turnaround. So what did Jesus think about the resurrection? Was he too among the revolutionaries?

Since the Sadducees were suspicious of the later biblical books (not least the revolutionary Daniel), the challenge was to demonstrate the doctrine from the Pentateuch.[13] But before Jesus answers them exegetically, he clarifies a vital point. This is where the greatest misunderstandings occur.

It has been assumed in Western Christianity that the ultimate aim is to leave this present world and to "go to heaven." Even the word "resurrection" itself, which in the first century always referred to new bodily life, is seen by many as denoting its opposite, namely disembodied immortality. For Jesus and his first followers, as for the Pharisees, belief in "resurrection" meant belief in a two-stage postmortem reality—such as we find also, I understand, within classic Islamic belief. One did not go straight from death into new bodily life. After death there would be a period of being physically dead. But if there was resurrection to come, that could not be the whole story. People used to say that Greeks believed in immortality while Jews believed in resurrection, but that is highly misleading. Some Greeks (not all) followed Plato in looking for an ultimate disembodied immortality. Some Jews—namely, the Pharisees and perhaps the Essenes—believed in a resurrection that would be to an immortal physicality, a new sort of body beyond the reach of death. There must then be some kind of continuity between bodily death and bodily resurrection. They had various ways of expressing this continuity. The Apocryphal book called The Wisdom of Solomon speaks of "the souls of the righteous" as being "in the hand of God," and of being "at peace" (Wisdom 3:1–3). As John Polkinghorne once put it, God will download our software onto his hardware until he gives us new hardware again so that we can run the software for ourselves. But this state is temporary. A few verses later, Wisdom declares that "in the time of their visitation they will shine forth, and will run like sparks through the stubble. They will govern nations and rule over people, and the Lord will reign over them for ever" (Wisd. of Sol. 3:7–8). This, as I and others have argued, must indicate the hope of resurrection in God's kingdom of ultimate justice.[14]

The intermediate state could be spoken of in different ways, indicating that there was no dogmatic concern in the early period to tidy the matter up. Some, it seems, could speak of the continuance of a "spirit" or an "angel," as when the frightened group of believers assumes that Peter has been killed in prison so that his voice outside the door must be the voice of his "angel."[15] If they used the word "soul," that by no means indicates that they were buying in to the Platonic belief in a preexistent and automatically immortal element in the human makeup.

This brings us back to the point of confusion in the discussion between Jesus and the Sadducees. In Mark's version, Jesus's answer goes like this:

"Where you're going wrong," replied Jesus, "is that you don't know the scriptures, or God's power. When people rise from the dead, they don't marry, nor do people give them in marriage. They are like angels in heaven. However, to show that the dead are indeed to be raised, surely you've read in the book of Moses, in the passage about the bush, what God says to Moses? 'I am Abraham's God, Isaac's God and Jacob's God'? He isn't the God of the dead, but of the living. You are completely mistaken." (Mk. 12:24–27)

What is Jesus saying here? He is insisting that when the dead are raised they will not marry because they will be like the angels in heaven.[16] The point of this is not that resurrection life will be disembodied and (in that sense) "spiritual" but that it will be unending, immortal, and hence will no longer need marriage and procreation. Jesus is firmly locating the resurrection within a new physical world in which death itself will have been defeated. Resurrection is not reincarnation, coming back again and again into yet another decaying body within the same world. It means going on, after a period of rest in God's presence, into the new Creation, and being equipped with a body appropriate for that new world. Jesus does not say, then, that the dead will become angels in heaven but that in this respect only they will be like them.

The other necessary clarification of this passage is that, like many Rabbinic discussions, it stops before the argument is explicitly concluded. As in a chess game, you stop when the crucial move is made, without playing out the final sequence. Jesus quotes Exodus 3:6, where God says to Moses "I am the God of Abraham, the God of Isaac and the God of Jacob," and declares that since God is not the God of the dead but of the living, this means that Abraham, Isaac, and Jacob are alive to God, or in God's presence. This does not mean that the three patriarchs have already been resurrected. It means that, like the righteous in Wisdom 3, they are alive in God's presence as they await the day when they will be bodily raised. Their present disembodied existence in God's presence is not their final destination. This is where we remind ourselves of the ancient Israelite belief: what matters is not to get out of God's world but to celebrate it and for God to remake it. When God puts the world to rights, he will not abandon his Creation but restore it. Jesus's action in the temple, the wider context of this discussion, was indeed the sign of God's eschatological judgment, just as Jesus's whole public career was the embodiment of God's eschatological kingdom, God returning to his people in that blazing mixture of rescuing love and sorrowful wrath that the prophets had long foretold.

Those who wrote and first read the synoptic gospels would have been in no doubt what resurrection meant. Each gospel ends not with Jesus's body mouldering in the grave while his soul (or spirit, or angel) goes marching on into a timeless Platonic eternity but with Jesus being bodily raised, leaving an empty tomb behind him, with his crucified body now transformed into a new type of physicality, which we realize in awe is the very start of the new Creation. That is why the resurrection stories in the gospels are so strange. Something genuinely new has been launched upon the world.

Resurrection in the Rest of the New Testament

What we then find in the rest of the New Testament is truly remarkable. In traditional cultures, people faced with death reach for traditional categories, sayings, and rituals. Radical change does not happen just because of someone's interesting speculation. But right across the first Christian century we find clear, innovative teaching: God will remake his Creation and raise his people from the dead to share in it—indeed, to rule over it—transforming them into newly embodied immortal humans after their time of being dead. This is incomprehensible without the Jewish background, but no Jews had said it like this before. It is only explicable on the basis of Jesus's resurrection.

The point, once again, is that we are not simply talking about a future reality. It has already begun with Easter; Christians already share this new life in the mystery of baptism and in the strikingly different way of life to which they are committed. Precisely because the biblical view of resurrection is about new Creation, and because this began with Jesus and specifically with Easter, its focus can never simply be on a world beyond this one. As I said, the ultimate future does not occupy the place in early Christianity that it came to occupy in the Middle Ages and in subsequent Western Christianity. If God is putting the world to rights once and for all, and if this has been inaugurated with Jesus himself, then the central Christian task is not simply to prepare for "life after death" but to work for that same loving, restorative justice in the present world.

The New Testament hope, then, is founded on two things: the ancient biblical vision, and the surprising realization (and hence redefinition) of that in Jesus himself. The ancient vision was of Creation set free from violence, war, pain, and suffering.[17] Israel's God would return in power and restore his Creation, vindicating his faithful, suffering people. This vision inspired the hugely popular book of Daniel, which was drawn on by Jesus himself as a key element in his self-understanding. And this vision, reworked around Jesus himself, finds fresh expression in the New Testament.

(I should stress, before we glance at some texts, that like all expressions of future hope for a new world, their language is like a symbolic signpost. That does not mean there is not a reality to which this signpost points; only that, as with symbols on a map, we should not mistake them for realistic photographs of that future.)

Out of dozens of possible passages, I highlight three that can hardly be omitted. The first passage is from I Corinthians 15, which is discussed in some detail elsewhere in this volume. Paul, faced with questions about the future resurrection, contextualizes them within a fresh vision of the ultimate future. Drawing on Genesis, Daniel, and the Psalms, he sketches the role of Jesus as the truly human one through whom the creator is now ruling the world, and as the Messiah of Israel through whom God is defeating all his enemies, including, ultimately, Sin and Death, seen as cosmic powers larger than the sum total of individual sins and individual deaths. This is Paul's Jesus-shaped reworking of the Jewish apocalyptic scenario in which God overthrows all evil powers and establishes his kingdom on earth as in heaven:

> But in fact the Messiah has been raised from the dead, as the first fruits of those who have fallen asleep. For since it was through a human that death arrived, it's through a human that the resurrection from the dead has arrived. All die in Adam, you see, and all will be made alive in the Messiah.
>
> Each, however, in proper order. The Messiah rises as the first fruits; then those who belong to the Messiah will rise at the time of his royal arrival. Then comes the end, the goal, when he hands over the kingly rule to God the father, when he has destroyed all rule and all authority and power. He has to go on ruling, you see, until "he has put all his enemies under his feet." Death is the last enemy to be destroyed, because "he has put all things in order under his feet." But when it says that everything is put in order under him, it's obvious that this doesn't include the one who put everything in order under him. No: when everything is put in order under him, then the son himself will be placed in proper order under the one who placed everything in order under him, so that God may be all in all. (I Cor. 15:20–28)[18]

This spectacular passage raises all kinds of theological questions, but for our present purposes I focus on four points only. First, the event for which many Jews had longed had arrived. Jesus's resurrection was not simply a strange quirk or bizarre miracle. It was "the resurrection from the dead."[19] But this event had split into two moments, one of which had already happened, one of which was still to come. The Messiah leads the way; his people will follow: "Each in proper order."

Second, therefore, Paul's focus is not on "life after death," the state that immediately follows human death. He focuses on the final stage in the two-stage postmortem reality. At the end of the chapter, he allows for an exception: any still alive when the Lord returns will not die and be raised; they will be "changed" (I Cor. 15:51–52), transformed into incorruptible physicality. For them, there will be only one moment of change. All others will have two moments of change: bodily death resulting in life after death (however we describe it) and then, after that, bodily resurrection into the new body. There is no hint of anyone other than Jesus himself being already raised to new bodily life. All others are still waiting.

Third, Paul has nothing to say here about the intermediate state, about "what happens when we die," except for this one word: "sleep." The Messiah is the first fruits of those who have "fallen asleep" (v. 20) in the exception just mentioned, "we won't all sleep" (v. 51). That echoes a regular biblical image for death, notably in Daniel 12:2.[20] When Paul speaks of it, however, he is not answering our modern questions about the location or state of the dead. He is using a regular biblical metaphor as a heuristic tool to denote the first stage in the two-stage progression.[21] One other mention of the "intermediate state" comes in Philippians 1:23, when Paul says he would prefer to leave the present life and be with the Messiah "because that would be far better." I do not think he would have said that if he thought the Christian dead were unconscious.

This "far better" but still intermediate state then corresponds, for Paul, to the hints in Luke and John: the dying brigand will be "with Jesus in Paradise" today—in other words, before Jesus's resurrection on the third day. And Jesus promises his followers a place of rest and refreshment when they follow him through death, even though the further reality of final resurrection still awaits.[22] And, just as there is no hint of anyone other than Jesus being yet raised from the dead, there are no grades or distinctions among the Christian dead. They are all in the same place and the same state, and will all be raised together at the last.

Fourth, corresponding to the two-stage postmortem reality that believers may expect, there is a two-stage reality of God's kingdom. At the moment, Jesus is ruling the world (this idea is of course much misunderstood and so much mocked, but Paul really means it). One day that task will be complete, and God will be all in all. As the prophets said, the earth shall be full of the knowledge and the glory of the Lord, as the waters cover the sea.

This leads us to the second of our three main passages. In Paul's letter to the Romans, full of rich teaching on resurrection, the argument of the first half of the letter reaches a spectacular climax in chapter 8:

> This is how I work it out. The sufferings we go through in the present time are not worth putting in the scale alongside the glory that is going to be unveiled for us. Yes: creation itself is on tiptoe with expectation, eagerly awaiting the moment when God's children will be revealed. Creation, you see, was subjected to pointless futility, not of its own volition, but because of the one who placed it in this subjection, in the hope that creation itself would be freed from its slavery to decay, to enjoy the freedom that comes when God's children are glorified.
>
> Let me explain. We know that the entire creation is groaning together, and going through labour pains together, up until the present time. Not only so: we too, we who have the first fruits of the spirit's life within us, are groaning within ourselves, as we eagerly await our adoption, the redemption of our body. We were saved, you see, in hope. But hope isn't hope if you can see it! Who hopes for what they can see? But if we hope for what we don't see, we wait for it eagerly—but also patiently. (Rom. 8:18–25)

Creation itself, says Paul, will be set free from its slavery to decay: God (in other words) will do for the whole cosmos what he did for Jesus at Easter, having first done this for "those who belong to the Messiah" (Rom. 8:9–11). New bodily life for Jesus leads to new bodily life for his people, and then a renewed physical existence for the cosmos. Christians are then caught in between the one and the other: already "belonging to the Messiah," and sharing his resurrection life (6:1–14; 8:1–17) but still sharing, too, the groaning of all Creation as the present body yearns for transformation.[23] This passage indicates more fully than elsewhere that for Paul the vision of final resurrection is not centered so much on the state of bliss we are promised but on the vocation of the truly human people to be "kings and priests," ruling the created order on God's behalf and summing up the worship of all Creation. This, indeed, is probably what he means by "the glory" that redeemed humans will share: it is not a general promise of spectacular, perhaps illuminated, existence, but more specifically the promise of dominion, sovereignty, over the world. Paul has already spoken of this coming "reign" in Romans 5:17. Now, picking up the theme from Genesis 1–2 and Psalm 8, that humans are supposed to be in charge of God's world, he declares that when redeemed humans are given this "glory," then Creation itself will share the freedom that will result. To put it the other way: Creation has been longing for the wise stewardship of obedient humanity. It was "subjected to futility" because God had purposed that it would only come into its proper fulfilment when the humans who were supposed to be looking after it were themselves redeemed. In the resurrection, that will at last be granted. This scene thus looks back to Romans 1:18–31, where Paul describes the chaos of the world consequent upon human sin. This is how that problem is to be solved at last.[24]

Our third and final passage is the last great scene in the Bible: Revelation 21 and 22. We start with 21:1–14:

> Then I saw a new heaven and a new earth. The first heaven and the first earth had passed away, and there was no longer any sea. And I saw the holy city, the new Jerusalem, coming down out of heaven, from God, prepared like a bride dressed up for her husband. I heard a loud voice from the throne, and this is what it said: "Look! God has come to dwell with humans! He will dwell with them, and they will be his people, and God himself will be with them and will be their God. He will wipe away every tear from their eyes. There will be no more death, or mourning or weeping or pain any more, since the first things have passed away."
>
> The one who sat on the throne said, "Look, I am making all things new." And he said, "Write, because these words are faithful and true." Then he said to me, "It is done! I am the Alpha and the Omega, the beginning and the end. I will freely give water to the thirsty, water from the spring of the water of life. The one who conquers will inherit these things. I will be his God and he shall be my son. But as for cowards, faithless people, the unclean, murderers, fornicators, sorcerers, idolaters and all liars—their destiny will be in the lake that burns with fire and sulphur, which is the second death."
>
> Then one of the seven angels who had the seven bowls filled with the seven last plagues came over and spoke to me. "Come with me," he said, "and I will show you the bride, the wife of the lamb." Then he took me in the spirit up a great high mountain, and he showed me the holy city, Jerusalem, coming down out of heaven from God. It has the glory of God; it was radiant, like the radiance of a rare and precious jewel, like a jasper stone, crystal-clear. It has a great high wall with twelve gates, and twelve angels at the gates, and names inscribed on the gates, which are the names of the twelve tribes of the children of Israel. There are three gates coming in from the East, three gates from the North, three gates from the South and three gates from the West. And the wall of the city has twelve foundation-stones, and on them are written the twelve names of the twelve apostles of the lamb. (Rev. 21:1–14)

Note first that, instead of the closing vision many Western Christians imagine, of the "saved" being taken up from earth to heaven, Revelation insists that the "new Jerusalem" will come down from heaven to earth. This marks the rejection of all forms of Gnosticism: the present Creation is good and to be renewed. The "new heaven and new earth" are not "new" in the sense of an entire Creation made afresh out of nothing. The rest of the book makes it clear that they are a fresh Creation made out of the old one. The "oldness" that passes away (21:1) is, once again, the decaying corruptibility of the present world; when God deals with that, the new world can emerge. In Romans 8 the imagery used was that of a woman in labor pains, about to give birth; this time the image is of a wedding. It will be the marriage of heaven and earth, the coming together of the twin halves of Creation. God from the beginning made "heaven and earth" to be the mutually compatible spheres of his Creation; now they will be joined forever. God will now dwell permanently with humans (21:3). They will have been raised from the dead (20:4–13) and will inhabit the new, enormous city.

But there are surprises for anyone who comes with a normal Western expectation of what the ultimate future will be like. Many imagine that in God's new Creation there will simply be "the saved," those who belong to God and the Lamb. Earlier chapters of Revelation seem to support this by saying that all others will be thrown in the lake of fire.[25] But as the picture develops a somewhat different sight emerges:

> I saw no temple in the city, because the Lord God the Almighty is its temple, together with the lamb. And the city has no need of sun or moon to shine on it, for the glory of God gives it light, and its lamp is the lamb. The nations will walk in its light, and the kings of the earth will bring their glory into it. Its gates will never be shut by day, for there will be no night there. They will bring the glory and the honour of the nations into it. Nothing that has not been made holy will ever come into it, nor will anyone who practices abomination or who tells lies, but only those who are written in the lamb's book of life.
>
> Then he showed me the river of the water of life. It was sparkling like crystal, and flowing from the throne of God and of the lamb through the middle of the street of the city. On either bank of the river was growing the tree of life. It produces twelve kinds of fruit, bearing this fruit every month; and the leaves of the tree are for the healing of the nations. Nothing accursed is there any more. Rather, the throne of God and of the lamb are in the city, and his servants will worship him; they will see his face, and his name will be on their foreheads. There will be no more night, and they will not need the light of a lamp or the light of the sun, because the Lord God will shine on them, and they will reign forever and ever. (Rev. 21:22–22:5)

The city appears complete and self-contained; but then we are told that "the nations will walk in its light, and the kings of the earth will bring their glory into it" (21:24). What is more, the tree of life will grow beside the city's river, "and the leaves of the tree are for the healing of the nations" (22:2). Despite the terrible warnings of cataclysmic judgment that catch our attention in Revelation, there is a sense that in God's new world, Jesus's followers will play the crucial role but that this role will itself be healing and restorative. Judgment is necessary not simply as a way of punishing the wicked but also so that God's new world will be free of any possibility of future corruption. Mysteries remain, to be sure. Despite the apparently final judgment of chapters 19 and 20, many will still be "outside" the city (22:15). Nobody could accuse Revelation of teaching universal salvation (that all will eventually be saved).[26] But there does seem to be a larger hope than simply the rescue of all professing Christians from future judgment. In much of the Bible, salvation is not simply God's gift to his people but his gift through his people to the world. Perhaps that is what Revelation is hinting in its closing chapters, confusing once more the comfortable categories of Western Christianity and challenging us to probe further.

Conclusion

Time presses; many urgent matters have been omitted. One such might be the origin of death itself. Some in the Christian tradition have spoken as though there was no death at all in the original creation while others, sensitive to issues of biological origins, have allowed for bodily death as part of the original and normal God-given life cycle but have stressed that the advent of sin gives a whole new dimension to death, which is then dealt with in the events concerning Jesus. In other words, "immortality" was not part of the original Creation; it was a further gift to be given ("the Tree of Life" in Genesis), the chance of which was forfeited by the original humans—this would then be the point Paul is making in Romans 5:12—but which is given freely through Jesus the Messiah. The question of why Paul intensified the normal earlier Jewish view of human sinfulness seems best addressed in terms of his reflection on the crucified Messiah: if that is the "solution" God has provided, the "problem" must be even worse than we had imagined.[27]

I have tried in this essay to highlight the biblical hope for humanity in terms of the larger hope within which the question is framed. The Creator God will rescue his whole Creation from all that defaces and corrupts it, and this act of restorative justice, long promised in scripture, has been accomplished through the death and resurrection of Jesus, Israel's Messiah. When, therefore, humans come to share the life of Jesus through faith and baptism, they are caught up into that larger project. They are thereby assured of their own ultimate "life after life after death"—that is, resurrection—and of a time of rest and peace "with Christ" or "in the hand of God" in between bodily death and that final resurrection life.

Later Christianity developed various parodies of this two-stage postmortem reality. The myth of purgatory is the most obvious of these. Granted, present Christian existence still includes groaning, rebellion, and failure, but the early Christians believed that the moment of death itself would deal with all that: the one who has died, Paul declares, is free from sin (Rom. 6:7). In another passage, he declares that "the day" (of judgment) will come like a fire and burn up everything in the Christian's life and work that has not been of God (I Cor. 3:10–15). That is the basis for the teaching of Pope Benedict, that "purgatory" will be that moment of fiery judgment, immediately upon death, when all that is evil is burnt away.[28]

But the early Christians were not simply waiting to see how the "last day" would work out. Their confidence in Jesus as Messiah and Lord was naturally worked out in the works of love, mercy, and justice that, here and now, anticipated that new day. Paul closes his long resurrection chapter by insisting that the work we do in the present "will not be worthless" (I Cor. 15:58). All that is done in the present, in Christ and by the Spirit, will somehow last into God's new world. More powerful still is the famous passage in which Paul lays to rest any sense of uncertainty about the future. Christians in every generation have clung on to these verses for their vision of God's all-powerful love:

What then shall we say to all this?
    If God is for us, who is against us?
        God, after all, did not spare his own son; he gave him up for us all!
        How then will he not, with him, freely give all things to us? . . .
            No: in all these things we are completely victorious through the one who loved us. I am persuaded, you see, that neither death nor life, nor angels nor rulers, nor the present, nor the future, nor powers, nor height nor depth nor any other creature will be able to separate us from the love of God in King Jesus our Lord. (Rom. 8:31–32, 37–39)

Notes

1. For these and other details, see the relevant sections of N. T. Wright, *The Resurrection of the Son of God*, vol. 3 of *Christian Origins and the Question of God* (London: SPCK; and Minneapolis: Fortress Press, 2003).

2. From where they might be, though ought not to be, summoned back; see the famous story at I Samuel 28:3–25.

3. See Hosea 6:2; Ezekiel 37.

4. We might compare Psalm 16:9–11.

5. E.g., Romans 1:3–4.

6. This also echoes Isaiah 53.

7. II Maccabees 7 tells the grisly story of the seven martyred brothers and their mother, with their regular refrain of affirming that God will restore their bodies.

8. See *Resurrection of the Son of God*; also my *Surprised by Hope: Rethinking Heaven, the Resurrection, and the Mission of the Church* (London: SPCK; and San Francisco: HarperSanFrancisco, 2007).

9. While Old Testament quotations in this essay are from the New Revised Standard Version, New Testament quotations are from Tom Wright, *The New Testament for Everyone*, 18 vols., published in the United States as N. T. Wright, *The Kingdom New Testament* (London: SPCK; and San Francisco: HarperOne, 2011).

10. Matthew 19:28 (the verse also refers to Daniel 7:9f); 13:43 (referring to Dan. 12:3).

11. Matthew 22:23–33; Mark 12:18–27; Luke 20:27–40. On this, see *Resurrection of the Son of God*, 415–29.

12. Deuteronomy 25:5–10.

13. To whom they had appealed by citing the Levirate law: Mark 12:19 and parallels.

14. Wisdom chapter 5 makes clear that this will mean resurrection, not simply a continuation of their present disembodied immortality (see *Resurrection of the Son of God*, 162–75). Indeed, the notion of resurrection requires a temporary disembodied immortality and should not therefore be played off against the idea; just as resurrection itself will be, for Wisdom as for Paul (I Cor. 15:54), an embodied immortality or perhaps an immortal embodiment. No room for Platonism here.

15. Acts 12:15; see the similar hints in Acts 23:6–9, on which, see *Resurrection of the Son of God*, 132–34.

16. Matthew 22:30; and Mark 12:25. In the Lukan parallel (20:35–36) they are "equal to angels," *isangeloi*.

17. See, e.g., Isaiah 2:2–5, 11:1–9, 65:17–25; Micah 4:1–5; Psalms 96, 98; and many other related passages.

18. For a full treatment of this passage, see *Resurrection of the Son of God*, 333–38.

19. Cf. Acts 4:2.

20. It is used elsewhere in the New Testament as well: e.g., Matthew 27:52; John 11:11–14, where the ambiguity of "sleep" is exploited; Acts 7:60, 13:36; I Corinthians 7:39, 11:30, 15:6 and 18, I Thessalonians 4:13–15 (on which, see below); II Peter 3:4.

21. There are two other striking passages where he does similar things: I Thessalonians 4:13–15 and Philippians 3:20–21, about which we cannot now speak.

22. Compare Luke 23:43 with Luke 24:1–49; and John 14:2–3 with John 5:24–29.

23. See Philippians 3:11–14.

24. See also Romans 4:18–22, where this is anticipated in the case of Abraham.

25. Revelation 20:11–15.

26. Some have imagined, on the basis of Romans 5:12–21 in particular, that Paul believed that all would be saved; this, however, is difficult to sustain in view of Romans 2:1–16 and passages like I Corinthians 6:9–10; Galatians 5:21; Ephesians. 5:3–5; Philippians. 3:19; Colossians 3:6; II Thessalonians 1:5–10, 2:9–12.

27. See, e.g., Galatians 2:21. I have written somewhat further on the question of sin and death in N. T. Wright, *Evil and the Justice of God* (London, SPCK; and Downers Grove, IL: InterVarsity Press, 2006); and on Romans 5 in my commentary on Romans in Robert W. Wall, J. Paul Sampley, and N. T. Wright, *New Interpreters Bible*, vol. 10, *Acts–First Corinthians* (Nashville, TN: Abingdon Press, 2002).

28. See Joseph Ratzinger, *Eschatology: Death and Eternal Life*, vol. 9 of Johann Auer and Joseph Ratzinger, *Dogmatic Theology*, English trans. (Washington, DC: Catholic University of America Press, 1988), 218–33, and my discussion in *Surprised by Hope*, 178–83. As I say there (178), Ratzinger, along with Rahner, has detached the concept of purgatory from the concept of an intermediate state, and has broken the link that, in the Middle Ages, gave rise to the idea of indulgences and so provided a soft target for Protestant polemic. This represents a considerable climb-down on the part of an avowedly conservative Roman Catholic from the doctrine of Aquinas, Dante, and Newman.

Response to N. T. Wright

REZA SHAH-KAZEMI

This brief response to Professor Wright's essay centers on his statement:
"It has been assumed in Western Christianity that the ultimate aim is to
leave this present world and to 'go to heaven.'" Wright claims this is a simplifi-
cation of the "two-stage postmortem reality," which, he rightly says, is also
expressed in classical Islamic theology. However, there is no contradiction in
Islamic or, I would argue, Christian theology between asserting the reality of
the resurrection of the body at the end of this cycle of time and affirming the
belief that, at death, the sanctified soul goes to heaven immediately. Dying and
going to heaven is indeed our ultimate aim, whether we are Muslim or Christian. We may therefore take Jesus at his word when he promises the good thief:
"Today thou shalt be with me in Paradise" (Luke 23:43). Similarly, we can take
literally the many promises of the Prophet Muḥammad regarding the immediacy of entry into heaven for martyrs and saints upon physical death; and one
can interpret the following important ḥadīths to mean that the heavenly or
hellish state begins immediately upon death for every soul: "Death is the Resurrection: whoever dies, his resurrection has come." "The grave is either one of
the chasms of hell or one of the Gardens of heaven."[1]

By no means would I deny the resurrection of the body at the Final Hour.
Rather, I would argue, on the one hand, that the "grave" signifies a trajectory
that leads, for the majority, to Judgment at the Final Hour, and, on the other,
that Heaven can be conceived not simply as a "place" awaiting us at the end of
some chronological continuum but as a dimension of being that exists in a
mode of time transcending terrestrial temporality, a location transcending terrestrial space, and partaking of a substance scarcely imaginable for the human
mind. "My Kingdom is not of this world" (John 18:36) because "the Kingdom
of God is within you" (Luke 17:21). Heaven can thus be conceived as both
transcending the world metaphysically and penetrating the world ontologically.

The Qur'ān refers not only to the saved ("those of the right hand") and the
damned ("those of the left hand") but also to the "foremost," *al-sābiqūn*, who

are brought nigh to God, *al-muqarrabūn* (56:8–14). The implication here is that the generality of saved souls do have to wait until the general resurrection and final judgment before attaining the plenary paradisal condition—prefigured to some degree by their already heavenly condition in the "grave," the intermediary state or *barzakh*; but the "foremost" can be considered to be granted the divine "nearness" in Paradise immediately upon death, in a celestial mode of duration outside of the framework of terrestrial time, in a spiritual body appropriate to its celestial ambiance. The Prophet—together with all the prophets—is understood to be in this state, here and now, contrary to what is stated by Wright in relation to Moses, who is deemed to be not in Paradise but still awaiting the day when he will be bodily raised.

On a related note, I wonder whether Wright's focus on Jesus's resurrection and its eschatological implications deflects our attention away from Jesus's own teachings on the deepest mysteries of the human condition and, therefore, human destiny, the theme of our seminar. In the Gospel of John, Jesus tells his disciples that if they keep to his teachings, they shall know the Truth, and the Truth shall make them free (8:31–32). This ultimate truth, or what is called in Islam the *ḥaqīqa*, is a spiritual truth that can save us here and now—not only in the Hereafter. The question I would pose to Wright is this: does not the stress on the bodily resurrection in the Kingdom, in an indeterminable future, diminish our capacity to assimilate the burning actuality and irresistible immediacy of the spiritual kingdom, accessible here and now? In other words, is a fully consummated soteriology not being overshadowed by an anticipated eschatology?

My reading of the New Testament focuses far more on the Gospels than on the letters of St. Paul—on what in Muslim terms would be called the *risāla*, or revealed message of Jesus himself. I would argue that it is from the point of view opened up by the content of this message—that is, the *ḥaqīqa* or ultimate truth—that the full, metaphysical, and not merely eschatological meaning of Jesus's resurrection can be more fully appreciated. It is in the light of his own esoteric teachings, I propose, that we can appreciate the relationship between liberation in this world and life in the Hereafter. What these teachings appear to be saying is this: not only do the souls of the sanctified go directly to Heaven after death, they are also in Heaven, in a certain sense, here and now. For the Kingdom of God, as already noted, is "within you" (Luke 17:21). If the kingdom is within you, it is because you are in the kingdom; you are in it because you are encompassed and penetrated by it ontologically, whether you know it or not.

Here I would argue that Jesus's transfiguration, which is not mentioned by Wright, is of immense significance: he gives his disciples a glimpse of the Kingdom within himself, his already celestial nature; that is, he exteriorizes through visible light what is hidden "within" him in the depths of his spirit, showing them, in the words of Meister Eckhart, the "archetypal body" that all of us have.[2] For, according to Eckhart, all that God gave Jesus, He has given to Eckhart, who emphasizes that this "all" excludes nothing: "neither union nor holiness."[3] This is why Eckhart can encourage us all to yearn for the birth of the Word in our own souls, the Birth that constitutes perfect beatitude—the very substance of Paradise.

Jesus's transfiguration can be understood from a mystical point of view as a revelation of the *ḥaqīqa*, the spiritual reality, proper to the heart. The Kingdom of God, Paradise in the plenary sense, is already accessible because it is already fully present in the heart. Thus, for al-Ghazālī, "the Science of the Hereafter" and "the Science of the Heart" are one and the same thing. The Prophet tells us that the heart is "the throne of the All-Merciful" ('*arsh al-Raḥmān*); and God tells us that neither His heaven nor His earth can contain Him, but the heart of His believing slave does contain Him.[4] Likewise, we have this esoteric saying of Imām 'Alī: the hearts of the saints are already in Paradise, their bodies, only, are at work in this world.[5] In such spiritual teachings we are given a dazzling vision of the hierarchical states of being unfolding within the center or heart of human consciousness, a vision that accords with Jesus's injunction to lay up our treasures in heaven, not earth, and where our treasure is, there will our heart also be (Matt. 6:19–20). We have here a vision of deliverance that surpasses the terrestrial coordinates of time and space, an intuition that spiritual depth is equivalent to celestial height, a sense that the chronological flow of outward time is arrested and transformed into the ontological space of the kingdom within.

Notes

1. For both of these ḥadīths see Al-Ghazālī, *The Remembrance of Death and the Afterlife* (Kitāb dhikr al-mawt wa-mā ba'dahu), Book XL of *The Revival of the Religious Sciences* (Iḥyā'

'ulūm al-dīn), translated with an introduction and notes by T. J. Winter (Cambridge: Islamic Texts Society, 1989), 127.

2. On the "archetypal body," see Franz Pfeiffer, trans., *Meister Eckhart* (London: John M. Watkins, 1947), 15.

3. M. O'C. Walshe, trans. *Meister Eckhart: Sermons and Treatises* (Longmead, UK: Element Books, 1979), 1:xlviii.

4. For discussion of both of these sayings, see Seyyed Hossein Nasr, "The Heart of the Faithful Is the Throne of the All-Merciful," in James S. Cutsinger, ed., *Paths to the Heart: Sufism and the Christian East* (Bloomington, IN: World Wisdom, 2002), 32–45.

5. For discussion of this and other similar sayings, see Reza Shah-Kazemi, *Justice and Remembrance: Introducing the Spirituality of Imam 'Alī* (London: IB Tauris, 2006), 55.

Response to Reza Shah-Kazemi

N. T. WRIGHT

I am grateful both for Dr. Shah-Kazemi's sensitive and probing response and for the chance of a brief counterresponse. As often in theology, it is a matter of balance. I eagerly agree that the promise of final bodily resurrection, as part of the new Creation, should not detract from the promise, to all believers, of finding themselves immediately after death in the presence of Jesus himself. That, as St. Paul says, will be "far better" (Phil. 1:23). Shah-Kazemi implies at one point that this will itself be a form of "resurrection," but the New Testament does not and would not say that. Resurrection will be part of the ultimate new Creation, which is why Jesus's own resurrection, the climax of all four gospels, is so explosive: God's promised future bursting in upon our unprepared present time.

If we take "heaven" to denote "the place where God is," or "the state in which people enjoy God's immediate presence," then I agree that "going to heaven" (or, if you prefer, "Paradise") is indeed a strong part of Christian teaching. The reason I regularly find it necessary to stress that this is only the first stage of a two-stage reality is because many modern Western Christians have not even heard of this, leaving them to assume that "resurrection" is simply a fancy metaphor for "going to heaven when we die." This undermines the resurrection's radical reaffirmation of the goodness of Creation, distorts the nature of Christian mission, and risks colluding with death itself. Thus, "dying and going to heaven" cannot be the Christian's ultimate aim but only the penultimate one.

Likewise, I eagerly agree that in the teaching of Jesus himself, as of the whole New Testament, heaven and earth do indeed overlap and interlock, and that through the presence, teaching, and, above all, the death and resurrection of Jesus, this overlap can become a present reality in the lives of believers. This idea translates the ancient Temple theology into Christian categories, providing the groundwork of both Christian spirituality and sacramental theology. However, most scholars would not read Luke 17:21 to mean that. The Greek phrase in question ("the kingdom of God is *entos hymōn*") does not denote an internal or "spiritual" reality, but rather has an active sense: not only "the kingdom of God is 'in your midst,'" but also something like "and it's up to you what you do about it."

What is more, the saying in John 18:36 should not be translated "my kingdom is not of this world," as though to imply that the "kingdom" is a detached, other-worldly reality. The Greek and the context together make it clear. "My kingdom," says Jesus, "is not *from* this world"; in other words, his kingdom comes from somewhere else, but it remains emphatically *for* this world ("on earth as in heaven," you might say). Jesus contrasts his sort of kingdom-for-the-world, which comes through suffering love, with other kinds. "If my kingdom was from this world," he continues at once, "my servants would fight."

I welcome, of course, the stress on Jesus's teaching. But his teaching about the renewal of the heart, and about fresh inner illumination, cannot be detached from the larger context of his announcement of God's inbreaking kingdom; and this, as he steadily makes clear, will come about only through his death and resurrection. That is Jesus's "revealed message" in all four gospels. Whatever one makes of the Transfiguration, it is not linked explicitly to questions of "life after death," which is why, writing on those topics, I did not mention it. The idea that it might reveal an Eckhartian "archetypal body" that "all of us have" is, I think, foreign to the teaching of Jesus and the New Testament. This is not to deny the constant promise of transformation by the Spirit, already in the present and ultimately (in the resurrection) in the future.

And of course, to reemphasize, I fully and enthusiastically agree that part of the whole point of the New Testament is that what we are promised in the ultimate future has come rushing forward into the present in Jesus himself and in the gift of his Spirit. Balancing out the "already" and the "not yet" of all that is a much-loved pastime of Christian theologians, and it is good to share that delicate and evocative discussion with our Muslim friends.

Death, Resurrection, and Human Destiny
Qur'ānic and Islamic Perspectives

MONA SIDDIQUI

Most of us would agree that love and death are the biggest stories in our lives. Both consume our beings in different ways for, as one popular poem expresses it, "One takes your heart, the other takes its beat." Yet, while we think frequently about love and death, they both come to us uninvited and we find ourselves ready for neither, certainly not for death.

The question of what happens to us beyond death is one of the most engaging issues for humankind and forms a key theme in both Christianity and Islam. Whether it is understood as part of a cyclical process in that we return as another incarnation, or as a transitional moment in that we pass from one world to another, death comes as a rupture in life as we know it. Notwithstanding the medical technology that has changed the point at which we pronounce death biologically so that science seems to be constantly pushing back the time of death, by death I simply mean the end of our physical life as we experience it on this earth. In this essay I explore primarily the Qur'ānic perspectives on death, resurrection, and the afterlife and their impact on us individually. It is God, the ultimate authority, the Creator of all, working in the linear flow of time, who determines our existence and our demise. Although the Qur'ān repeatedly mentions a life beyond this earthly existence and events of the Eschaton, the relationship between humankind, resurrection, and death is a rich didactic theme in the Islamic tradition, capturing the imagination of scholars throughout history. Thus, at various points I have also drawn upon wider Islamic sources for a more comprehensive reflection on death, what happens in the grave, resurrection, and the afterlife. However, this essay only provides a glimpse into some of the key Qur'ānic and extra-Qur'ānic concepts; it is by no means an exhaustive account of the various themes and terms.

According to the Qur'ān, death is the one event affecting all life—"Every soul will taste death" (29:57)—but it is also the event through which human life enters into another stage of its destiny. In Islam, this transformation of earthy life is real and ordained by God. It begins in the grave but we have no definitive sense of where it ends. We may not comprehend fully what a future life after death means, but the events in an afterworld form one of the central motifs of the Qur'ānic narratives, with the result that belief in the Day of Judgment and the afterlife became a fundamental article of faith. The ethical teachings of the Qur'ān are to be understood in the light of the reality of the Day of Judgment for the whole of human history is a movement from Creation to the Eschaton. However, neither the time of our own death nor the time of the Day of Judgment is known to us. If God determines the lifespan of the individual, he also determines the duration of humanity as a whole upon the earth. These are among many secrets known only to God, who is intimately but not openly tied to the lives of his creatures, never revealing himself directly to humankind. God retains the element of secrecy by speaking only through inspiration or from behind a veil: "It is not granted to any mortal that God should speak to him except through revelation or from behind a veil, or by sending a messenger to reveal by His command what He will" (42:51). The secrecy motif is presented throughout the Qur'ān in various ways: God hides and reveals; God knows the secrets of our hearts but human beings do not know the secrets of God. In this way, the moment of our death is also known only to God, even though it is the angel of death, 'Izrā'īl, who takes our soul from us at the actual moment of death. It is said that 'Izrā'īl, who is not mentioned by name in the Qur'ān but is alluded to as the "angel of death" (32:11), acts only as God's instrument and does not himself know who is to die. It is said that forty days before a person's death "a leaf falls from a tree, and an angel records the deed and informs Death. Death is sometimes seen as an independent entity, but more often is personified in the terrifying angel 'Izrā'īl."[1]

It should be borne in mind here that Qur'ānic references to soul and spirit (*nafs* and *rūḥ*) resulted in various theological and philosophical conclusions over what exactly stayed in the grave and what was taken by God. The most common view held by classical Islam and in general still underlying much of contemporary thought is that the *nafs* and *rūḥ* inhabit or infuse the material body, *badan*, and this substance, regardless of the degree of spirituality that one chooses to ascribe to it, is taken by God at some point after death.[2]

The relationship between our life in this world and in the afterworld lies in accepting that, although our body is mortal and our time on this earth is finite,

God has decreed another place for us. This is a place in time that has yet to occur and is often depicted in terms of Paradise and Hell or the Garden and the fire. This life, which remains unseen, is often imagined in physical imagery that vividly conveys the reality of an afterworld and an afterlife.[3] These overlapping images of a life beyond this earthy life are frequently mentioned in the Qur'ān, reminding us of the interdependence of this life and the next. This other world can be imagined, but it is not imaginary. The Qur'ān reflects this through such verses as: "The life of this world is nothing but a game and a distraction; the Home in the Hereafter is best for those who are aware of God. Why will you [people] not understand?" (6:32).

While the pre-Islamic Arabs may have believed in some kind of transformation after death, there is not much evidence that they believed in an afterlife within a distinct place and time beyond this world. Yet fundamental to the Qur'ānic message is that there does exist another world to which we do not just migrate but rather to which we progress in stages from this world. Transcendence is layered, a concept depicted beautifully in the story of Muḥammad's Night Journey (Isrā') and Ascension to the Heavens (Mi'rāj). This story is mentioned only briefly in the Qur'ān: "Glory to Him who made His servant travel by night from the sacred place of worship to the furthest place of worship" (17:1).[4] It is, however, embellished in greater detail in the ḥadīth literature, which includes details of Muḥammad's ascension through the heavenly layers and meetings with past prophets. The mystical story serves as a metaphor of the journey of the human soul in its spiritual growth in life.

The basis for understanding the nature of other worlds is the vision of life after death as a "living" journey of accountability to God, not only as a glorious meeting with God. Once ejected from the celestial dwelling (2:36–38), humankind must endeavor to gain an even higher salvation. To acquire or be rewarded with such a salvation demands above all faith in God and good works. In mainstream Muslim thought, there is a harmonious link between the temporal and the eternal (al-dunyā and al-ākhira) in that our actions here will determine our ultimate destiny. Life in the Garden and the Fire follows life on earth, but because the Garden and the Fire act as metonymies for reward and punishment. They do not exist solely as distant realms; rather, they provide a guiding force in a believer's life.[5] Furthermore, the Qur'ān talks in some dramatic detail of the fires of hell and the glories of heaven as if they are spatially real, and repeats in different ways the notion that heaven and hell have a purpose. We will know of their purpose once we reflect more fully on the purpose of this life: "We were not playing a pointless game when We created the heavens and earth and everything in between; We created them for a true purpose, but most people do not comprehend" (44:38–39).

Death and the afterlife are connected by the themes of resurrection and the Day of Judgment. The Day itself is one of the highest unknowns of the Islamic faith, known to no one except God, not even his prophets: "People ask you about the Hour. Say 'God alone has knowledge of it.' How could you [Prophet] know?" (33:63). Despite providing a cohesive narrative of God's message in human history, even prophecy is limited, for the mission of the prophets ends with their deaths; it is God's revelation that lives on. The Prophet had difficulty in persuading the Meccans and the Medinese of the reality of life after death, that the day would come when the dead would rise and stand in front of the unseen, unknowable but merciful Creator: the two great eschatological moments of Resurrection (*qiyāma*) and Gathering in the presence of God (*ḥashr*). The view of death of the pagan Arabs focused on the physical reality of "decayed bones," which they could not imagine returning to life. However, this incredulity is repeatedly challenged in the Qur'ān. One of its most detailed treatments of the physicality of nature, and of life springing and developing from the absence of life, occurs in the following passage:

> People, [remember,] if you doubt the Resurrection, that We created you from dust, then a drop of fluid, then a clinging form, then a lump of flesh, both shaped and unshaped: We mean to make [Our power] clear to you. Whatever We choose We cause to remain in the womb for an appointed time, then We bring you forth as infants and then you grow and reach maturity. Some die young and some are left to live on to such an age that they forget all they once knew. You sometimes see the earth lifeless, yet when We send down water it stirs and swells and produces every kind of joyous growth: this is because God is the Truth; He brings the dead back to life; He has power over everything. There is no doubt that the Last Hour is bound to come, nor that God will raise the dead from their graves. (22:5–7)

These are constant themes in the Qur'ān, addressed to an audience familiar with death as a final end, not as any kind of new consciousness. "Part of the fatalistic determinism of the pre-Islamic Arabs was their sense that each human life is for a fixed term or *ajal*. It is immutably set; on the appointed day one's life comes to an end."[6] This fatalistic determinism, reflected in the notion of *ajal*, meant there was no place for divine intervention. What made the Qur'ānic message radical was that it offered the fatalistic Bedouins the message of hope, of another life beyond the hardships of their own existence. The Qur'ān quotes the pagan Arabs as asserting: "There is only our life in this world; we die, we live, nothing but time [*dahr*] destroys us" (45:24). It is this sentiment that is rejected in the Qur'ān. "This idea of an *ajal* is repeated in the Qur'ān, both for individuals (6:2, 7:34, 16:61, 20:129) and for nations (10:49, 15:4–5). Here, however, the emphasis is not on an impersonal determinism but on divine prerogative; God ascertains the life-spans of persons and of communities, and in His hands lies the fate of all that He has brought into being."[7]

The Qur'ān contains its own paradigms of fated humanity and free humanity, a tension that occupied the formative *kalām* scholars careful to absolve God of wrongdoing against humans. Against the background of Meccan skepticism about the physical resurrection of the body, the Qur'ān reminds us that just as God created us from nothing, so he can bring us back to life after death. More importantly, there is a purpose to this resurrection—it is the point through which one will eventually come to meet God; if you deny resurrection, you deny God. Death then becomes the doorway to eternal life, after which there is no return to earth. As the Qur'ān says: "Lost indeed are those who deny the meeting with their Lord until, when the Hour suddenly arrives, they say, 'Alas for us that we paid no regard to this!'" (6:31). It is the divine weighing up of good deeds with bad deeds that forms the rationale of the Day of Judgment, even though divine justice remains a powerful mystery: "Every soul is held in pledge for its deeds, but the Companions of the Right will stay in Gardens and ask about the guilty. 'What drove you to the Scorching Fire?' and they will answer, 'We did not pray; we did not feed the poor; we indulged with others [in mocking the believers]; we denied the Day of Judgment until the Certain End came upon us'" (74:38–47).

At times there is almost a sense of urgency in the Qur'ān. At each instant we are drawing nearer to the climax of time and history, when all will be brought into the presence of the Creator. The unreality of time as a specific duration is demonstrated on the day of resurrection, when our time on earth will seem an extremely short period: "He will say: 'How many years were you on earth?' and they will reply, 'We stayed a day or a part of a day'" (23:112–13); "On the day He gathers them together, it will be as if they have stayed [in the world] no longer than a single hour" (10:45). It is not made clear in the Qur'ān why our time on earth will seem so short, or even whether that means we will remember anything of our time on earth. The Qur'ān is not concerned with human memories, for however strong are our ties of love in this life, they are only part of our destiny and not our ultimate destiny.

The Qur'ān mentions in different ways, often thematically overlapping, the concept of life immediately after death, the period between death and the day of resurrection, signs of the End Times here on earth, and images of the various abodes of the afterlife. It is said that around a third of the Qur'ān is eschatological in character. Its eschatological passages are dominated by two ideas—damnation and forgiveness at God's final judgment. Yet, in addition to the Qur'ān's emphasis on the final resurrection and the Day of Judgment, we also find three references to *barzakh*, an enigmatic term that literally means a barrier or limit. The primary reference is: "When death comes to one of them, he cries, 'My Lord, let me return so as to make amends for the things I neglected.' Never! This will not go beyond his words: a barrier [*barzakh*] stands behind such people until the very Day they are resurrected" (23:99–100). *Barzakh* came to be understood by Muslims as the period straight after death, the period in the grave and the time that separates the dead from the living, a time of suspension between death and final resurrection. But its significance also lies in the inability during this period of the dead to return to the earth, to return to this life in any way until the day of resurrection. While there are no references to *barzakh* in the canonical ḥadīth traditions, "it came to be understood as simultaneously the *time* every individual must wait between death and resurrection and the *place* or abode of that waiting."[8]

In the hierarchy of Creation, *barzakh* is a more intense reality than this earthly life, a prelude to a final reckoning. While there remained a diversity of opinion as to whether and how the body could be resuscitated and united with the soul in the grave, over time there developed a general view that this time in the grave was not simply a state of stillness but rather of reckoning and judgment. In the time and place of *barzakh*, the soul will be questioned about good and bad deeds and faithfulness to God. The two angels responsible for this task are often identified as Munkar and Nakīr, who, while not mentioned in the Qur'ān, appear frequently in the narratives of the grave. The theologian and philosopher al-Ghazālī defends belief in this interim period in the grave and the certainty of the questioning: "And the kinds of punishment vary with the times, and so the interrogation of Munkar and Nakīr takes place at the moment of being deposited in the grave and chastisement is after it."[9] Yet, in more recent times, the poet philosopher Muḥammad Iqbāl defined *barzakh* as a state of "psychic unhingement" for the human ego in which the person can take stock of past achievements and future possibilities; it is not "merely a passive state of expectation; it is a state in which the ego catches a glimpse of fresh aspects of Reality and prepares himself for adjustment to these aspects."[10]

Although the verses dealing with the various signs of the coming of the Hour (*sāʿa*) are scattered throughout Qur'ān, it is God's subversion of the natural order that forms the most dramatic sign of the imminence of the Day of Judgment. Cosmic disintegration will signal the physical end of the world and the nearness of resurrection. The dramatic Qur'ānic imagery foresees this day as one when the laws of nature will be suspended and humankind will be called upon to answer for how they have lived. The Qur'ān announces:

> When the sun is rolled up, when the stars are dimmed, when the mountains are set in motion, when pregnant camels are abandoned, when wild beasts are herded together, when the seas boil over . . . when the sky is stripped away, when Hell is made to blaze and Paradise brought near: then every soul will know what it has brought about. (81:1–6, 11–14)
>
> On the Day of Resurrection, the whole earth will be in His grip. The heavens will be rolled up in His right hand . . . the Trumpet will be sounded, and everyone in the heavens and earth will fall down senseless except those God spares. It will be sounded once again and they will be on their feet, looking on. The earth will shine with the light of its Lord. (39:67–69)

Muslim commentators of both the classical and modern periods have debated whether the resurrected body is the same as the earthly body or is of another physical form. Some claim that if the heavens and the earth have changed, then the human form cannot remain exactly the same. Others argue that our present physical form is suitable only for this earthly life and that, while resurrection is not simply about spiritual resurrection, we cannot be certain in what physical form we will rise in our second creation. What kind of individuality is necessary for the final working out of human action is something we cannot know. Furthermore, it seems that whether or not the whole of Creation comes to an end before the final judgment, the events around the End Times, resurrection, and our final destiny are more significant for humankind than for the rest of the natural world. The role of the natural world is primarily to act as a witness to our actions, as suggested by the Qur'ān in a haunting, poetic passage: "When the earth is shaken violently in its [last] quaking, when the earth throws out its burdens, when man cries: 'What is happening to it?' on that Day, it will tell all" (99:1–4). Dramatic as this concept is of the natural earth telling her stories about man's deeds, the verse reminds us first and foremost of our individual accountability to our Creator. Nature is not a silent or neutral field; she sees, hears, and feels. Our ultimate destiny lies with the mercy and grace of God, but human freedom means freedom to do wrong to ourselves and to one another; in all of this nature is a witness to our actions.

The various Islamic sources do not seem to yield a consistent picture outlining the exact sequence of events leading up to the resurrection and God's judgment. However, after the various signs heralding the Day of Judgment and after passing through several stages, people will ultimately know their fate before God. One of the clearest descriptions in the Qur'ān of our ultimate destiny is contained in the concept of a record of our deeds in this life: "On that Day you will be exposed and none of your secrets will remain hidden. Anyone who is given his Record in his right hand will say, 'Here is my Record, read it. I knew I would meet my Reckoning,' and so he will have a pleasant life in a lofty Garden with clustered fruit within his reach. . . . But anyone who is given his Record in his left hand will say, 'If only I had never been given any Record and knew nothing of my Reckoning. How I wish death had been the end of me'" (69:18–27). The fate that follows for the two categories of people is expressed largely within the Qur'ānic descriptions of heaven and hell. Damnation in hell is described in terrifyingly graphic detail with blasts of smoke, boiling water, and unquenchable thirst awaiting those who have rejected God, while the tree of Zaqqūm provides them with deadly fruit (22:19–22, 37:62–68). Conversely, sensual images of rivers of milk and honey, pure, nonintoxicating wines, silken couches, jewel-encrusted thrones, black-eyed houris, and youths described as "pearls well guarded" dominate the popular imagination of heavenly delights (47:15, 52:17–20, 24). Whether such images are to be understood literally or allegorically, Islamic thought is not apologetic about the heavenly fulfillment of physical human desires. This has been the case even when Christian polemicists have accused Muslims of being obsessed with the flesh and of not understanding that in the next life such physical pleasures do not matter for the children of God.

One of the most intriguing signs of the End Times is the appearance of Jesus. For Muslims, Jesus is not just a prophet, he is also a chosen Messenger from God, the miracle-worker, the *rūḥ-Allāh* or "spirit of God," one of the key prophets in the long history of prophecy, the one preceding Muḥammad, the one lifted up by God at the point of crucifixion, but also the one who will act as a witness on the Day of Judgment. Despite a variety of views found in classical Islamic sources on the issue of Jesus's death, the standard Islamic teaching is that Jesus escaped death, that God raised him body and soul to heaven, and that God will send him back to earth in the End Times. A sequence of three Qur'ānic verses have become the focus of much of the exegetical speculation as to what happened to Jesus on the cross and the significance of his appearance on the Day of Judgment:

> And [the Jews] said, "We have killed the Messiah, Jesus, son of Mary, the Messenger of God." (They did not kill him nor did they crucify him, though it was made to appear like that to them; those that disagreed about him are full of doubt, with no knowledge to follow, only supposition; they certainly did not kill him—No! God raised him up to Himself. God is almighty and wise. There is not one of the People of the Book who will not believe in [Jesus] before his death, and on the Day of Resurrection he will be a witness against them.) (4:157–59)[11]

Only in one other verse is there a possible link between Jesus and the eschaton. Verse 43:61 is translated by Abdel Haleem as "This [Qur'ān] is knowledge of the hour," but he also notes the alternative translation: "[Jesus] gives knowledge of the hour." Assuming the latter interpretation, this verse has been understood as meaning either that Jesus has knowledge of the apocalyptic hour or that the apocalyptic hour will not arrive before Jesus returns to earth. If the Qur'ān alludes to Jesus as having knowledge of the coming of the hour, it does not provide any details about Jesus's role as witness on that day, or what he will do or say. Rather, such details were fleshed out by the Qur'ān commentators (*mufassirūn*), who were convinced that Jesus would return to this world in the eschaton primarily to kill the antichrist, al-Dajjāl, and destroy all religions other than Islam. In his analysis of the various understandings of Jesus's crucifixion in the Qur'ān, Gabriel Reynolds quotes from Ibn Kathīr the kind of description that became commonly associated with Jesus's role in the Eschaton: "Christ will kill those in error, destroy crosses, and kill swine. He will enforce the *jizya*, meaning he will not accept it from any of the people of the religions. He will not accept anything but Islam or the sword." Reynolds continues: "Later Ibn Kathīr concludes that this verse is a report of the manner in which Christ will punish the Jews 'for their grave insults of him and his mother [see 4:156] and the Christians for the way they venerated him by claiming that he was something he was not, lifting him up in the face of [the Jews] from the station of prophethood to the station of lordship. He is far above what these people say.'"[12]

The Qur'ānic Jesus developed into a central character of Muslim eschatology. But Muslim exegetes saw his return to fight against evil and restore justice in a particularly Islamic way; Jesus's return does not signify for them good news in the Christian sense. In Islamic understanding, the eschatological function of Jesus Christ is to fulfill a divinely ordained prophetic mission that will pave the way for the Day of Judgment. Jesus becomes a sign that this Day is impending, but his role is that of a Muslim prophet who, like all prophets, will eventually die. Conversely, in Christianity, Jesus Christ is the primary source of the eschatological hope and his death on the cross is central to Christian thought and to the Christian doctrine of salvation. Here, God has intervened in the mystery of Christ's suffering, crucifixion, and resurrection, allowing for love to walk this earth and transform human existence. Wolfhart Pannenberg writes: "The real riches of salvation owned by Christians are participation through the Spirit of love in the life of God revealed in Jesus Christ." He adds that the "forgiveness of sins as a subject of Christian devotionalism" is not "isolated from the resurrection hope guaranteed through communion with Christ."[13] However, Muslims and Christians know that the word of God always points to something more profound than what scripture alone records, and it seems to me that, for all that has been said about him, the Qur'ānic Jesus still remains a mystery. He is unique and intrinsic to the drama of End Times, even if his salvific role remains ambiguous.

The dominant Qur'ānic theme regarding human destiny is that God's mercy or wrath awaits us all. God, in his compassion, may forgive every person in the end in response to "an atom's weight of good" (99:7), but we must base our lives on the constant endeavor to be morally aware and to do good deeds. We are responsible for our own deeds, and we are alone in death carrying into the grave and into the next life only ourselves and our actions. This theme is expressed poignantly in al-Ghazālī's *Letter to a Disciple*. Al-Ghazālī writes of Ḥātim al-Aṣamm, who said:

I observed mankind and saw that everyone had an object of love and infatuation which he loved and with which he was infatuated. Some of what was loved accompanied him up to the sickness of death and some [even] up to the graveside. Then all went back and left him solitary and alone and not one of them entered his grave with him. So I pondered and I said: the best of what one loves is what will enter one's grave and be a friend to one in it. And I found [it to be] nothing but good deeds! So I took them as the object of my love, to be a light for me in my grave, to be a friend to me in it and not leave me all alone.[14]

Although death and the afterlife are central themes in the Qur'ān and in Islam, there is another message that weaves itself in and out of the images of heaven and hell, between this world, *al-dunyā*, and the next world, *al-ākhira*. It is the message of hope in divine mercy. The fundamental human condition is to have been created weak and strong, both discerning and ignorant, open to temptation but, through repentance (*tawba*), able to return to God. God, for his part acting in accordance with his merciful nature, will forgive. This continuous dynamic at the heart of the relationship between God and humankind is reflected in two similar traditions: "If you had not sinned, God would have created a people who would and would have pardoned them"; and "If you had not sinned, I would have feared of you what is more evil than sins. It was said: And what is that? He [Muḥammad] said: Pride."[15]

It was after all pride and arrogance (*istikbār*) that led Iblīs to disobey God and so become the "accursed Satan." Although the Qur'ān talks of doing good in the hope of a future reality, it is our present reality that is transformed first by the good that we do. The Qur'ān repeats that salvation is for those who have both submitted and done good works, thus indicating that the pleasures of heaven are not just for people who believe in God but also for those who act rightly and justly in the here and now. The human journey is the struggle to do right in spite of all the wrong we do. This is why divine mercy is such a powerful theme in the Qur'ān; it is the attribute of a God eagerly desiring his Creation to turn to him always, at any time, and from any distance: "Say, 'My servants who have harmed yourselves by your own excess, do not despair of God's mercy [*raḥmat Allāh*]. God forgives all sins: He is truly the Most Forgiving, the Most Merciful [*al-ghafūr al-raḥīm*]'" (39:53).

Al-Ghazālī quotes a tradition in which a believer implores God to keep him away from sin. God's response is, "All my believing servants ask this from me. But if I should keep them away from sin, upon whom will I bestow my blessings and to whom will I grant forgiveness?"[16] God expects—indeed, wants—human beings to commit sin so that he can forgive; herein lies a mutual dependency between the divine and the human, a dependency that does not limit God nor imply need on God's part, but that allows him constant opportunities to show the full magnitude of his love. God demands unswerving loyalty to his unique being but in return his mercy knows no bounds. In those Qur'ānic verses and ḥadīths that speak so profusely about God's mercy, we find a radical Islamic doctrine of eternal hope; there is no room for nihilism in Islam. In humankind's wretched but eternal need for God lies the recognition that hope is alive in this world and in the next. Most importantly, to paraphrase Kipling, our souls will not be squandered. Faith in a just God is not an illusion or a projection of one's own dreams or fears. God is real, our sins are real, and divine forgiveness is real. The most dramatic aspect of the Islamic perspective on death, resurrection, and the afterlife is not the potent images of heaven or hell but the ultimate vision of God. However we make this journey to God when we die, and in whatever form, in this life we must always be conscious of and guided by the Qur'ānic verse: "We belong to God and to Him we shall return" (2:156).

Notes

1. Nerina Rustomji, *The Garden and the Fire* (New York: Columbia University Press), 2008, 40.

2. See Jane Smith and Yvonne Haddad, *The Islamic Understanding of Death and Resurrection* (Oxford: Oxford University Press, 2002), 36.

3. For a full analysis of images of the afterworld and afterlife, see Rustomji, *The Garden and the Fire*.

4. "The sacred place of worship" and "the furthest place of worship" are generally understood in the Islamic tradition as Mecca and Jerusalem, respectively.

5. Rustomji, *The Garden and the Fire*, 41.

6. Smith and Haddad, *Islamic Understanding of Death*, 5

7. Ibid.

8. Ibid., 8.

9. William McKane, *Al-Ghazālī's Book of Fear and Hope* (Leiden: Brill, 1962), 66.

10. Muhammad Iqbal, *The Reconstruction of Religious Thought in Islam* (Lahore: Ashraf Press, 1999), 120.

11. For an extensive description of both classical and modern Islamic exegesis on these and other Qur'ānic verses related to the crucifixion, see Todd Lawson, *The Crucifixion and the Qur'ān: A Study in the History of Muslim Thought* (Oxford: Oneworld, 2009).

12. Gabriel Said Reynolds, "The Muslim Jesus: Dead or Alive?" *Bulletin of SOAS* 72, no. 2 (2009): 237–58, at 249.

13. Wolfhart Pannenberg, *The Apostles' Creed* (London: SCM, 1972), 160, 163.

14. Abū Ḥāmid al-Ghazālī, *Letter to a Disciple: Ayyuhā'l-Walad*, bilingual English–Arabic ed., trans. with an introduction and notes by Tobias Mayer (Cambridge: Islamic Texts Society, 2005), 28.

15. Both are cited in McKane, *Al-Ghazālī's Book of Fear and Hope*, 17.

16. Abū Ḥāmid al-Ghazālī, "Kitāb al-khauf wa'l-rajā'," in *Iḥyā' 'ulūm al-dīn*, vol. 4 (Damascus, n.d.), 132.

Response to Mona Siddiqui

JANE DAMMEN McAULIFFE

In reflecting upon Dr. Siddiqui's insightful essay, I am drawn to several key elements. The first is the way she links death and love—"One takes your heart, the other takes its beat"—which quickly expands into the linking of love and forgiveness, and love and Creation. In an especially striking statement, Siddiqui underscores these connections: "God expects—indeed, wants—human beings to commit sin so that he can forgive." Each person, in other words, is a process of continuous divine Creation, a constant interaction between Creator and created. In a book of Lenten lectures, Archbishop Rowan Williams makes a similar point about divine interaction with human frailty: "God does not come to 'humanity' in the abstract; forgiveness engages with a particular past."[1] Siddiqui returns to this theme to close her lecture, citing Qur'ān 2:156, a verse usually quoted at Muslim funerals: "To God do we belong and to him do we return."

A second element upon which Siddiqui's presentation focuses is the transition between death and afterlife understood as a sequence of stages, a journey. Frequently likened to Muḥammad's Night Journey and Ascension, this transition has been the subject of much theological speculation. Qur'ānic attention to the event of death itself is somewhat limited. Verse 56:83 visualizes the soul of the dying person as coming up to the throat, while 6:93 speaks of angels reaching out to request the soul: "When the wrong-doers reach the pangs of death and the angels stretch their hands out (saying): 'Deliver up your souls.'" The subsequent periods, such as the time in the grave before physical resurrection, are elaborated largely in ḥadīth. The Qur'ān has much more to say about the events of the Last Day, often resorting to quite dramatic depiction, such as the extraordinary sound imagery of the earth shaking and the trumpet blaring. These and other "Signs of the Hour" (i.e., the apocalyptic events that precede the resurrection and judgment) constitute the undoing, reversal, or deconstruction of the first Creation.

A third theme that Siddiqui weaves through her presentation is that of divine secrecy, such as her assertion that God "is intimately but not openly tied to the lives of his creatures." The disjunction between divine and human knowledge has long been a subject of Muslim philosophical and theological speculation— God knows our hearts but we do not know God's—and the Qur'ān frequently points to the hour of a human's death as a clear instance of divine omniscience versus human ignorance. Yet, 3:7, a key locus of hermeneutical reflection, has prompted interpretation suggesting that some people have been graced with a special, deeper kind of knowledge and understanding.[2] This verse, among others, served as a prooftext for discussions about varying levels of intellectual and spiritual attainment and the consequent exposure to religious teachings appropriate to each level.

Stepping back a bit from the specifics of Siddiqui's presentation, my own rereading of the relevant Qur'ānic passages left me struck anew with the surprisingly contemporary tone of Muḥammad's preaching about death and resurrection. It would not be a stretch to compare his *jāhiliyya* audience to Schleiermacher's "cultured despisers." Many in Mecca mocked the idea that life could be breathed into dead bones ("That is their reward because they disbelieved Our revelations and said: 'When we are bones and fragments shall we, forsooth, be raised up as a new creation?'" [17:98–99]), rather clinging to a fatalistic notion of time and destiny (*dahr*, 45:24; 76:1). Opposition to Muḥammad proved to be particularly vehement on three points: his denial of tribal deities, his preaching of the End Times and the Day of Judgment, and his insistence that God raises the bodies of the dead to new life.

N. T. Wright makes a similarly vigorous defense of analogous New Testament claims as he points to "two thousand years of sneering skepticism toward the Christian witness" on bodily resurrection.[3] According to Wright, the post-Enlightenment rejection of the reality of Jesus's resurrection (and our own) allows us to believe "that we have now come of age, that God can be kicked upstairs, that we can get on with running the world however we want to, carving it up to our advantage without outside interference."[4] One finds an echo here of Muḥammad's inveighing against the entrenched economic and political interests in the Ḥijāz. Early Meccan preaching clearly links resurrection and judgment with human accountability before God, a disquieting challenge to the pronounced inequity that the Prophet saw operating in his own society.

Another striking feature of the Qur'ān is the strong sense of place in its representations of postdeath events. A recent book on Muslim understandings of heaven and hell argues that "Islamic eschatology provides an after*world*, while Christian eschatology focuses on an after*life*."[5] The author cites Ibn al-Jawzī's (d. 1200) depiction of human life as a progression of places: "You will merely be transferred from one house to another, from the womb to the world, from this world to the grave, from the grave to the Judgment, from the Judgment to eternal existence in either the Garden or the Fire."[6] The terms "garden" and "fire" themselves conjure palpable, physically charged spatial images, depictions that are further developed by the description of the geography, material culture, and environmental furnishings of these eternal abodes. But the eschatological places and spaces are neither static nor passive. For example, much happens in the grave. The dead feel the pressure and constriction of the tomb; they undergo the questioning of Munkar and Nakīr; and they are aware of the liminality of their intermediate state (*barzakh*).[7]

A final comment on the connection between resurrection and Creation can conclude this response. In the Qur'ānic understanding, life is a continual process of Creation and recreation. God brings life out of death at every instant and bodily resurrection is yet another instance of this.[8] Creation is both universal and particular; God calls the world and humankind into existence as a whole but also the individual in his or her mother's womb. The Qur'ān speaks of two births and two deaths (2:28 and 40:11). While these verses are variously understood, a common interpretation points to death before life in this world and death when our time on earth has ended. Parallel to this would be birth as an infant entering the world and rebirth on the day of resurrection.

Notes

1 Rowan Williams, *Resurrection: Interpreting the Easter Gospel*, rev. ed. (Cleveland, OH: Pilgrim Press, 2002), 37.

2. "He it is Who hath revealed unto thee (Muhammad) the Scripture wherein are clear revelations—they are the substance of the Book—and others (which are) allegorical. But those in whose hearts is doubt pursue, forsooth, that which is allegorical seeking (to cause) dissension by seeking to explain it. None knoweth its explanation save Allah. And those who are of sound instruction say: We believe therein; the whole is from our Lord; but only men of understanding really heed." Mohammed Marmaduke Pickthall, trans., *The Glorious Koran*

(London: George Allen & Unwin, 1976), 62. This translation reflects the dominant interpretation that puts a full stop between "Allah" and "those who are of sound instruction." The alternative exegesis to which I refer would be translated as ". . . save Allah and those of sound instruction. [They] say: We believe . . . ."

3. N. T. Wright, *Surprised by Hope: Rethinking Heaven, the Resurrection, and the Mission of the Church* (New York: HarperCollins, 2008), 68.

4. Ibid., 75.

5. Nerina Rustomji, *The Garden and the Fire: Heaven and Hell in Islamic Culture* (New York: Columbia University Press, 2009), xvi.

6. Ibid., xviii, quoting from Abū al-Faraj ibn al-Jawzī, *Kitāb al-quṣṣāṣ wa-mudhakkirīn*, ed. and trans. Merlin Swartz (Beirut: Dar El-Machreq, 1986), 171.

7. *An* intermediate state between life in this world (*al-dunyā*) and the next world (*al-ākhira*).

8. "Who will bring life to these bones when they have rotted away? Say, 'He will revive them who brought them into being" (36:78–79). "He brings out the living from the dead, and brings out the dead from the living, and he gives life to the earth after it is dead. And thus you shall be brought out [from the dead]" (30:19).

Death, Resurrection, and Human Destiny in the Islamic Tradition

ASMA AFSARUDDIN

I slamic tradition is defined here as consisting of extra-Qur'ānic sources—the ḥadīth corpus, containing the statements of the Prophet Muḥammad; the *tafsīr* or exegetical works; and ethical or edifying literature that provides moral counsel and guidance for the educated Muslim. Since these genres include a prodigious amount of material and it would be impossible to do full justice to it, I will restrict my discussion to selective primary sources and attempt to provide a broad overview of some of the major themes included under the topics of death, resurrection, and human destiny, particularly in the premodern literature.

Theology of Death, Resurrection, and the Afterlife

The constant remembrance of death is a frequent *topos* in Islamic edifying literature and pious works in general. The well-known figure of piety and abstemiousness from the eighth century ʿAbd Allāh b. Mubārak (d. 797) wrote a treatise titled in Arabic *Kitāb al-Zuhd*. The word *Zuhd* is notoriously difficult to translate pithily into English. Variously rendered as "piety," "abstemiousness," and "God-consciousness," *zuhd* is all this and more. It is above all a moral and ethical imperative that encourages the believer to live his or her life in this world as a preparation for the more glorious life in the presence of the Almighty in the next. The pious, abstemious person realizes that death is both the joyous gateway to the Hereafter and the sober reminder of the true purpose of our earthly life that heightens our spiritual awareness and God-consciousness. Ibn al-Mubārak records a report from the famous Companion ʿAbd Allāh ibn ʿAbbās, who counseled: "If you should see a man close to death, give him good tidings so that he may meet his Lord with a happy disposition. But while he lives, awake in him fearful reverence for his Lord, the Mighty and Exalted."[1]

Another early pious figure, the jurist Nuʿaym b. Ḥammād (d. 843), emphasizes that the preparation for our eternal life in the next world revolves around constant remembrance of death, which protects us from the useless distractions of life. He cites a ḥadīth in which the Prophet remarks, "Increase your remembrance of that which extinguishes worldly frivolities—that is to say, Death."[2]

Death is a sober reminder that our worldly possessions and friendships do not travel with us into the next world. In another ḥadīth, the Prophet is quoted as observing: "Three things follow the deceased—two of them return and only one remains. His family, wealth, and actions follow him—however, his family and wealth come back and only his deeds remain."[3] Appreciation of the fleeting nature of our worldly attachments enhances our awareness of death and the eventual meeting with our Creator. Even though—in our modern, somewhat deracinated world—reflection on death is regarded as rather morbid and unhealthy, the great Muslim scholars, like their Christian counterparts, saw such contemplative practices as nurturing one's inner, spiritual life and as representing the pathway to true wisdom and happiness. The famous Muslim mystic and theologian Abū Ḥāmid al-Ghazālī (d. 1111) addresses the student of the mysteries of God in the following manner: "Know, beloved, that we cannot understand the future world, until we know what death is: and we cannot know what death is, until we know what life is: nor can we understand what life is, until we know what the spirit is."[4] Al-Ghazālī further remarks that not all of the things and accoutrements of this world are blameworthy; rather happiness consists in finding pleasure in the right things and in the right attributes because they lead to happiness in the next world. Thus, he says,

> Delight in knowledge, delight in worship, delight in prayer and delight in communion with God are things of this world, but still they are for the sake of the future world. It follows, therefore, that the pleasures of the world are not all of them blamable, but only those which entail punishment in the future world, or which are not in the path to paradise, and so the apostle declares, "The world is a curse and that which is in it is a curse, except the remembrances of God and that which is the object of His love."[5]

Death and the Grave: Pondering Its Mysteries

What happens at the time of death, in the grave, and during the Resurrection are topics that find scanty reference in the Qur'ān itself. However, the ḥadīth, exegetical literature, and pious edifying works occasionally provide us with details about such matters. Once again, al-Ghazālī describes for us the process of the soul departing from the human body. The soul is attended by four angels who announce to the dying person that they had been responsible for his food, his drink, his breath, and his term of life, all of which are now coming to an end.[6] While death in general is an agonizing experience for the human being, al-Ghazālī comments, "The good soul slips out like the jetting of water from a waterskin, but the profligate's spirit squeaks out like a skewer from wet wool."[7]

An anonymous work titled *Kitāb aḥwāl al-qiyāma* (*The Book of the Circumstances of the Resurrection*) provides graphic descriptions of the momentousness of death and its terrifying aspects. The angel of death, called ʿIzrāʾīl, appears in an awe-inspiring form to the dying person. When the latter asks, "Who are you?" ʿIzrāʾīl answers: "I am the angel of death, who makes your children orphans and wife a widow."[8] When the soul of the pious individual slips out, two or four angels clad in white garments and with faces gleaming like the sun approach it, bearing clothes and sweet-smelling embalming fluid with which to wrap it. In some accounts, it is the angel Gabriel who accompanies the ascending soul. The trip to the highest level of Paradise mirrors the Prophet Muḥammad's Night Journey, for at each level the ascending soul encounters bygone communities. Finally, the soul and its angelic escorts reach the highest pavilions and the heavenly lote tree (*sidrat al-muntahā*), the level that is the closest to God. Here the Almighty welcomes the righteous soul briefly, commands the angel to inscribe his or her name in the heavenly registers, and returns the soul to the body. Fewer details are available concerning the unrighteous individual. Al-Ghazālī says that in such a case, ʿIzrāʾīl will deliver the evil soul to the guardians of hell, who clothe it in a hair shirt. The angel supervising these guardians is called Daqyāʾīl, who attempts, like al-Ghazālī, to rise through the heavenly layers with the soul but is prevented from doing so. Daqyāʾīl then casts away the soul and it returns to the body. All of these events are described as happening so quickly that the soul returns to the body while it is still being prepared for burial.[9]

Islamic tradition maintains that—once placed in the grave—the deceased is visited by two angels, Munkar and Nakīr, who ask questions about the person's faith. These angels are not mentioned in the Qurʾān, but in the popular tradition they have become an almost ubiquitous feature of posthumous life in the grave. Their interrogation represents a preliminary assessment of an individual's worldly record of faith and deeds before the Day of Resurrection and the final, definitive divine judgment on that day. The tradition also informs us that the faithful will be spared the pressure of the grave that will afflict the wrongdoers. Typically, accounts of the ordeals in the grave are tempered by reminders of God's mercy and forgiveness, so as to instill hope in the reader.[10]

The tradition therefore came to recognize an intermediate stage between death and resurrection, *barzakh*, that very broadly may be understood to correspond to the Catholic notion of purgatory. The term is used in the Qur'ān primarily in the sense of an obstacle (55:20; 23:100), either a moral or a concrete one, which in the exegetical and eschatological literature becomes reinterpreted as a physical barrier between this world and the next, or between the grave and the Hereafter.[11] As the equivalent of purgatory, *barzakh* in the extra-Qur'ānic tradition represents an intermediate world where the soul experiences both pleasure and pain before the Day of Resurrection.[12] The Qur'ānic concept of the A'rāf in 7:46, usually translated as "the Heights," presented another challenge to the interpreters and may be usefully compared to the Christian concept of limbo. This verse suggests a third realm inhabited by souls who have completed the judgment process but have not been deemed fully suited either for heaven or for hell. A majority of the exegetes are of the opinion that this state of abeyance is earned by those whose good deeds exactly balance their bad deeds.[13]

Extra-Qur'ānic sources state that, after the divine judgment, both the saved and the condemned will have to cross a bridge (*ṣirāṭ*). The righteous cross it easily and swiftly into the promised Garden of Bliss; the unrighteous find the passage perilous and slippery and fall off into the Abyss of Fire. Although the Qur'ān is adamant that each individual is accountable for his or her sins only and that no one can bear the burdens of another nor intercede for them, the tradition allows for the possibility of intercession by the Prophet Muḥammad for his community. The ḥadīth and eschatological literature mention a *ḥawḍ*, or a basin of sweet, delicious water, where the Prophet will meet the members of his community. Other accounts say that he will intercede on behalf of all humanity. All but the most egregiously sinful will be saved from damnation by the Prophet's intercession and God's mercy.[14]

The Afterlife—Paradise and Hellfire

Once again, compared to the Qur'ān, which has only cursory references to the Hereafter beyond the grave, the ḥadīth and Qur'ān commentaries provide a rich topography of the next world, particularly of Paradise. Thus, al-Bukhārī—in his famous ḥadīth compilation, Ṣaḥīḥ—records a report from the Prophet in which Paradise, usually referred to as "the Garden" (al-janna) is described as a vast realm that has eight gates and one hundred levels.[15] The highest level of Paradise is called Firdaws, and directly above that is the Throne of God. From this level of Paradise the four rivers of Paradise flow.[16] According to other ḥadīths recorded by al-Bukhārī and Muslim, the majority of the inhabitants of Paradise will come from the ranks of the weak and the poor on earth.[17] One report states that the best of women will precede the best of men into Paradise.[18] The Paradise dwellers are eternally young and their bodies pure, unsullied by earthly bodily functions.[19] Each man will be as tall as Adam, between sixty and ninety cubits;[20] as old as Jesus, thirty-three years; and as handsome as Joseph. Each woman is about eighty cubits tall and perennially young and beautiful. One report suggests that the Paradise dwellers continue to grow in beauty and fairness and their faces are radiant like the full moon.[21] The dark-eyed celestial houris, who are said to be made of light or saffron (or, according to variant accounts, musk, ambergris, and camphor) sing in mellifluous voices.[22] Handsome young men "well guarded as pearls" circulate among the heavenly denizens with refreshing drinks that do not intoxicate.[23] The least fortunate among the inhabitants of Paradise is described in some reports as having a thousand mansions made from pearls, chrysolite, and sapphire and with about seventy thousand servants in attendance.[24] As for the provisions (rizq) that the righteous will enjoy in the Hereafter, these include closeness to God, a noble status before Him, and the opportunity to engage in seemly praise of Him. Their souls will exult in the good things of Paradise, a state that will be enhanced when they are eventually reunited with their bodies.[25]

Believers praise God day and night with every breath they take and they are assured of His satisfaction with them. A few reports not found in the standard compilations state that Arabic will be the language of heaven. According to a number of accounts, the ultimate reward for the pious is the beatific vision of God, "clear as the full moon on a cloudless night"—as it is described in one account. Exactly how this beatific vision will be perceived by the heavenly dwellers has remained a matter of debate among Muslim scholars. The "sacred ḥadīth" (ḥadīth qudsī), which states that God has prepared for the believer "what no eye has seen, no ear has ever heard, nor has been grasped by the human heart," is often cited in this context to signify that the nature of the bounties awaiting the righteous in the next world defies worldly categories and description; this became the prevalent Ashʿarī position in accordance with their principle of "without asking how" (bi-lā kayf). Traditional theologians generally accepted at face value the description of heavenly pleasures contained in ḥadīths found in the authoritative collections while emphasizing their otherworldly nature. The Muʿtazilī, who are usually described as "rationalists" in English, tended to be more skeptical of such reports and downplayed the hyperbolic imagery conveyed by them. With regard to particularly the beatific vision of God, they rejected that possibility because it would smack of anthropomorphism, in their opinion.[26]

The Fires of Hell: Punishment for Sinners

Common terms in the Qurʾān for hell are Jahannam (Gehenna) and al-Nār, which simply means "the fire," the predominant feature of hell. The extra-Qurʾānic literature describes the features of hell in some detail. According to one ḥadīth, Gehenna will be brought near on the Day of Judgment, and the seventy thousand reins of Gehenna will be dragged by seventy thousand angels who constantly stoke its fires.[27] Al-Ghazālī identifies seven layers of hell, Jahannam being the worst.[28] The famous mystical philosopher Ibn ʿArabī describes Satan as both the king of hell and its shackled inhabitant, the image of which is said to have influenced Dante's conception of the imprisoned Lucifer.[29]

One report presents Heaven and Hell arguing with one another about the people who will enter them. Hell says, "All those who are tyrannical and arrogant will enter me," while Heaven declares, "All those who are weak and destitute will enter me." Then God addresses them both, and says to Hell, "You represent my punishment for those I wish to punish," and to Heaven, "You represent my mercy which will envelop those I wish to be merciful towards. And each of you will be full."[30] Clearly this report is meant to assure us that we are ultimately responsible for our actions and personally accountable to God for their consequences. Beyond belief and worship, the nature of our interactions with fellow human beings determines our status in the next world. This specific discourse transcends the assumed dichotomy between orthodoxy and orthopraxy and underscores instead the soteriological consequences of compassionate and humble behavior of the individual toward others (as well as the inverse).

The question then may be posed at this juncture: must those who reap the punishment of hell for their wrongdoing on earth remain in it forever? This is a question of perennial interest to humans, for who among us—sinners all—has not feared the tribulations of the next world? One ḥadīth recorded by Muslim in his *Ṣaḥīḥ* may appear to dash our hopes of gaining eventual redemption in the next world. According to the famous Companion Abū Saʿīd al-Khudrī, the Prophet is said to have remarked,

> On the Day of Judgment, Death will be brought forward like a spotted ram and placed between heaven and hell. Then a voice will cry out, "O people of Paradise, do you know what this is?" They will crane their necks to gaze at it, and then reply, "Yes, it is death." Then a voice will cry out again, "O people of hellfire, do you know what this is?" They too will crane their necks to scrutinize and reply, "Yes, this is death." Then the command is given that it be slaughtered. Then a voice will cry out again, "O people of Paradise. Eternity and no Death!" "And O people of hellfire! Eternity and no Death!"[31]

The prospect of spending Eternity in Paradise obviously poses no problems for us; but the prospect of spending Eternity in Hellfire is, to put it mildly, daunting. Although the ḥadīth just cited suggests that people will be assigned to the Garden or to the Fire forever, a majority of Muslim theologians are agreed that the faithful will eventually all emerge from punishment in hell and be transported to heaven. But what about the rest of sinning humanity? Some have found solace in Qurʾān 11:107, which states, "They will abide in it [the Fire] as long as the heavens and the earth endure, except for what your Lord wills," which has led to the interpretation that the fires of hell will at some point be completely extinguished.[32] The influential Ḥanbalī jurist Ibn Qayyim al-Jawziyya (d. 1350) came out strongly in favor of the position that the fires of hell will one day be completely extinguished; among the reasons he cited in favor of this position are (1) God so loves to forgive and release those who do wrong that He will do so; (2) one cannot equate divine anger with divine mercy; (3) three verses in the Qurʾān (6:128; 11:107; and 78:23) indicate that the Fire will not last forever; (4) while God keeps His promises, He need not follow through on His threats, the remission of which is an indication of divine mercy; and (5) although the Garden as heavenly compensation for one's deeds is an end in itself, the Fire is a means of purification.[33] Once humans have been purified of their sins, there would be no need for the existence of the Fire anymore.

Who Are the Reapers of the Celestial Garden?

Since the celestial Garden is the promised reward for the faithful, Muslim think-ers paid quite a bit of attention to the nature of the good deeds and the cultiva-tion of moral attributes that facilitate one's advancement toward it. The three groups mentioned in Qur'ān 4:69, described as obeying God and His messenger and thereby earning God's bounty, often provide the point of departure for such discussions, especially among Qur'ān exegetes. In addition to the prophets (al-nabīyyūn), these three groups are the truthful ones (al-ṣiddīqūn), the virtu-ous (al-ṣāliḥūn), and the witnesses (al-shuhadā').[34] The well-known Qur'ān commentator Fakhr al-Dīn al-Rāzī (d. 1210) inclines to the view that each of these categories is distinctive from the other and describes a specific type of person or group of people. Thus, the term al-ṣiddīqūn is applied to those who are habitually and most notably truthful, a noble and distinctive trait in believers.[35]

With regard to the shuhadā', al-Rāzī says that they are those who establish justice (al-qā'imūna bi-'l-qist) as is also borne out in Qur'ān 3:18. The one killed in the path of God is also a witness (shahīd) to the extent that he has exerted himself in aiding the religion of God and borne witness that it is the truth and distinct from falsehood. The shuhadā' bear witness in this world and the next, as indicated in Qur'ān 2:143.[36] Finally, the ṣāliḥūn, in brief, are those who are righteous in their belief and actions, and they are placed after the shuhadā' in moral excellence. There is thus a distinct hierarchy of moral excel-lence adumbrated in this verse, with the prophets at the top and the ṣāliḥūn at the bottom, each learning about religion from the category of people immedi-ately above them.[37] This hierarchy is also replicated in the next world so that the prophets occupy the highest level of Paradise, followed by the truthful ones, then the witnesses, and then the righteous in general.

Al-Rāzī's observation—that among the shuhadā' are those who bear witness to the truth with their lives—brings us to a special category of people in the Islamic tradition, who are deemed to be alive even after they are physically dead. This category owes its genesis to two key Qur'ānic verses: "Do not say regarding those who are slain in the path of God that they are dead; rather they are alive but you are not aware" (2:154); and "Do not consider as dead those who are slain in the path of God; rather they are alive and given sustenance in the presence of their Lord" (3:169). Exegeses of these verses have given rise to the exalted status assigned by the tradition to martyrs, especially military martyrs who are slain in the path of God.

In the famous exegete al-Ṭabarī's commentary on 2:154, we find a detailed description of the next world and an extensive taxonomy of the heavenly rewards awaiting specific categories of believers, indicating the extent to which this issue had begun to exercise the minds of exegetes. He begins by commenting that God addresses the believers and exhorts them to forsake all that constitutes disobedience to Him and to seek His help while patiently obeying Him in their striving against their enemies, and in carrying out the rest of their religious obligations. They are also commanded not to say regarding those who are slain in the path of God that they are dead (*mayyit*), for the dead are lifeless and deprived of their senses, unable to enjoy pleasures and experience bliss. Rather, "those among you and from the rest of My creation who are killed in the path of God are alive in My presence, [immersed] in life and bliss, [enjoying] a blissful existence and glorious provisions, exulting in what I have bestowed on them of My bounty and conferred on them of My generosity." Al-Ṭabarī quotes the earlier exegete Mujāhid b. Jabr (d. ca. 722), who understood this verse as referring to those who are alive in the presence of their Lord and enjoying the fruits of heaven and smelling its fragrance even though they are not actually within heaven itself.[38] According to the early scholar Qatāda b. Di'āma (d. ca. 735), the souls of the martyrs (*al-shuhadā'*) take the form of white birds (*ṭayr bīḍ*) that eat the fruits of heaven and reside in the celestial lote tree. Other scholars maintained that the souls of the martyrs take the form of green birds in heaven.[39]

But what if someone remonstrates that the generous compensation promised to the "one slain in the path of God" (*al-maqtūl fī sabīli llāhi*) is also generally applicable to any pious believer? In a number of reports, the Prophet had described the rewards reserved for all righteous believers and the punishment that the unbelievers would face. So what, if anything, asks this interlocutor, distinguishes the state of the one killed (*al-qatīl*) in the path of God from the rest of humanity—believers and unbelievers—who, according to these reports, are all alive in *barzakh* (the intermediary world after death between this one and the next), albeit in vastly different conditions?[40]

The answer to this question is as follows, continues al-Ṭabarī. The martyrs are distinguished from other believers by the fact that they alone are privy to the delicious food of heaven in *barzakh* before their resurrection and continue to savor it after their resurrection. This is how God has privileged them over everyone else. According to a report from Ibn ʿAbbās, the martyrs are near Bāriq, a river at the gate of Paradise, in a green dome (according to other versions, in a green garden or a white dome), where they are given their provision from heaven morning and night. The last part of Qurʾān 2:154 confirms that humans cannot see the martyrs and are therefore not aware that they are indeed alive. They are apprised of this only through God informing them of that.[41]

Al-Rāzī similarly comments that the majority of commentators are in agreement that those who are obedient to God attain their reward in their graves, even though their bodies are lifeless. Al-Rāzī believes that 2:154 does indicate a special status for the martyrs, although their status is lower than that of the prophets and the truthful ones. He also inclines toward the view that the martyrs enjoy their rewards spiritually, for no one will be physically resurrected until the Day of Judgment, and the disembodied soul is capable of experiencing pain and pleasure. On the Day of Resurrection, the souls will be united with their bodies, leading to a "fusion of the physical states with the spiritual."[42]

It is popularly assumed that the military martyr enjoys a privileged position compared with "ordinary" believers, especially based on some of the narratives extolling their deeds that occur in extra-Qurʾānic literature. However, one Qurʾānic verse in particular (39:10) is an important corrective to this perception. It refers to a special category of people who are described as earning God's unlimited approbation in the next world, a heavenly compensation denied to any other group of people. Despite the fact that this category of people has been singled out for Qurʾānic praise in this manner, it has not received much attention in the general literature. Verse 39:10 states: "O my servants who believe— fear your Lord! For those who do good in this world is goodness and God's earth is wide. Indeed the patient/steadfast ones [*al-ṣābirūn*] will be given their reward without measure." The exegetes are practically unanimous in their understanding that the referent in this verse is all those who, in the face of great tribulations and trials, were patient and steadfast in their earthly lives. As a consequence, they will be rewarded by admission into Paradise and enjoyment of the (unlimited) provisions within it.[43] For such a group of people, there is no reckoning in Paradise.[44] "Without measure" (bi-ghayr ḥisāb) means that no weight or proportion can be assigned to the reward that such virtuous people earn.[45]

In his exegesis of 39:10, the eleventh-century exegete al-Wāhidī (d. 1076) comments that the reference to "Those who do good" in the first part of this verse indicates those who place their belief in God's unicity and who perform good deeds, for which they reap Paradise. As for "their reward will be without measure," he quotes the early exegete ʿAṭāʾ b. Abī Rabāḥ (d. 733), who understood this statement to mean that their reward will be such "as could not be imagined by the mind nor could be described."[46] Al-Zamakhsharī (d. 1144), the prominent Muʿtazilī exegete from the twelfth century, similarly notes the high rank of the ṣābirūn in the Qurʾān, who are described as those who patiently bore the pain of separation from their homeland and their kinsfolk and other trials and afflictions on account of their obedience to God and their great virtue. The Prophet himself had remarked,

> The scales will be raised and the people of alms will be brought forward and their compensations will be given with due measure. Likewise with [the people of] prayer and pilgrimage. Then the people of [who underwent] trials will be brought in and the scales will not be raised for them nor will their record [of deeds] be unfurled. Rather their reward will be heaped upon them without measure.[47]

Upon seeing the extent of the reward of the people of trials, those who had been spared such tribulations would wish they had suffered a similar fate on earth.

The famous pious scholar Ibn Abī al-Dunyā (d. 894) records another ḥadīth in which the Prophet clearly singles out those who are patient as deserving of exceptional heavenly reward:

> When God will gather together creation [on the Day of Judgment] a caller will cry out, "Where are the people of patient forbearance" [ahl al-ṣabr]? A group of people, few in number, will rise and hasten towards Paradise. The angels will meet them and inquire, "We see you rushing towards Paradise—who are you?" They will reply, "We are the people of patient forbearance." They [sc. angels] will ask, "What did your patience consist of?" They will respond, "We used to patiently persevere in obeying God and were steadfast in not disobeying Him." Then it will

be said to them, "Enter Paradise—the best of recompense for those who have acted [well]."[48]

This paradigm of moral excellence is inclusive of all those righteous believers who strive daily in their lives in ordinary and extraordinary ways to fulfill the will of God and to bear witness to His goodness and solicitude for humanity, despite the worldly tribulations that descend upon them.

Conclusion

Clearly, Muslims have been concerned about their life in the next world as much as they have been concerned about their life in this world. The extra-Qur'ānic literature codifies this concern and gives us a window into how Muslims through the ages have woven together a richly textured tapestry that records how they have conceptualized life after their earthly existence. Ultimately, these narratives encode for us the fundamental human hope that the mercy of the Almighty will envelop us all, erase all the failings that make us so fallibly human, and allow us to reach our fullest potential in the presence of the Divine.

Notes

1. ʿAbd Allāh ibn Mubārak, *Kitāb al-Zuhd* (Alexandria: Dār Ibn Khaldūn, n.d.), 94. Unless otherwise attributed, all translations from Arabic sources, including the Qur'ān, are mine.

2. Ibid., 403.

3. Muslim, *Ṣaḥīḥ* (Beirut: Dār Ibn Ḥazm, 1995), 4:1798, #2960.

4. Al-Ghazālī, *The Alchemy of Happiness*, trans. Henry A. Homes (Albany, NY: Munsell, n.d.), 74.

5. Ibid.

6. Jane Smith and Yvonne Haddad, *The Islamic Understanding of Death and Resurrection* (Albany: State University of New York, 1981), 36.

7. Ibid., 37.

8. *Kitāb aḥwāl al-qiyāma*, ed. Maurice Wolff (Leipzig: F. A. Brockhaus, 1872), 11–12, cited in Smith and Haddad, *Islamic Understanding*, 34–35.

9. Ibid., 39–40.

10. "Munkar wa-Nakīr," in *Encyclopaedia of Islam*, new ed., ed. C. E. Bosworth et al. (Leiden: E. J. Brill, 1997), 7:576–77; and Smith and Haddad, *Islamic Understanding*, 41–42.

11. "Barzakh," *Encyclopaedia of Islam*, new ed., 1:1071.

12. Smith and Haddad, *Islamic Understanding*, 107ff; Nerina Rustomji, *The Garden and the Fire: Heaven and Hell in Islamic Culture* (New York: Columbia University Press, 2009), 40, 129.

13. Smith and Haddad, *Islamic Understanding*, 91.

14. Ibid., 80–82.

15. Al-Bukhārī, *Ṣaḥīḥ* (Cairo: al-Maṭbaʿa al-Bāhiyya al-Miṣriyya, 1933–62), 9:153.

16. Al-Tirmidhī, *Sunan*, ed., ʿAbd al-Raḥmān Muḥammad ʿUthmān (Medina: Muḥammad ʿAbd al-Muḥsin al-Kutubī, n.d.), 4:85.

17. Al-Bukhārī, *Ṣaḥīḥ*, 13:48; Muslim, *Ṣaḥīḥ*, 4:2186–87.

18. Abu Nuʿaym, *Ṣifat al-janna* (Cairo: Maktabat al-Turāth al-Islāmī, 1989), 115.

19. Muslim, *Ṣaḥīḥ* (Beirut: Dār Ibn Ḥazm, 1995), 4:1729, #18, 19.

20. "Cubit" is an approximate translation for the Arabic term "dhiraʿ." The measure that the Arabic term indicates can vary from place to place. The use of "cubit" here is not meant to be taken literally but as a trope for extraordinary appearance.

21. Muslim, *Ṣaḥīḥ*, 4:1727, #13, 14.

22. Rustomji, *Garden and the Fire*, 94–96.

23. Ibid., 91–93.

24. See the article "Garden" in *Encyclopaedia of the Qurʾān*, ed. Jane McAuliffe (Leiden: E. J. Brill, 2002), 2:284–85.

25. Al-Qurṭubī, *Al-Jāmiʿ li-aḥkām al-qurʾān* (Beirut: Dār al-Kitāb al-ʿArabī, 2001), 4:268.

26. "Garden," 2:284–85.

27. Muslim, *Ṣaḥīḥ*, 4:1731, #29.

28. Al-Ghazālī, *Iḥyāʾ ʿulūm al-dīn* (Cairo: al-Maṭbaʿ al-ʿUthmāniyya al-Miṣriyya, 1933), 4:659.

29. Asín Palacios, *Islam and the Divine Comedy*, trans. and abr. Harold Sunderland (London: J. Murray, 1926), 58, 92.

30. Muslim, *Ṣaḥīḥ*, 4:1733–34, #36.

31. Ibid., 4:1735, #40.

32. Smith and Haddad, *Islamic Understanding*, 94.

33. Ibid.

34. The verse states, "Whoever obeys God and the Messenger are with those upon whom God has conferred His bounty: prophets (*al-nabīyyīn*), veracious people (*al-ṣiddīqīn*), witnesses (*al-shuhadāʾ*), and righteous people (*al-ṣāliḥīn*). They are the best of companions."

35. Al-Rāzī further notes that some say that the *ṣiddīqūn* are the most excellent Companions of the Prophet; see al-Rāzī, *al-Tafsīr al-kabīr* (Beirut: Dar Iḥyāʾ al-Turāth al-ʿArabī, 1999), 4:135.

36. Ibid.

37. Ibid., 4:134–35.

38. Al-Ṭabarī, *Tafsīr al-Ṭabarī* (Beirut: Dār al-kutub al-ʿilmiyya, 1997), 2:42.

39. Ibid.

40. Ibid., 2:42–43.

41. Ibid., 2:43.

42. Al-Rāzī, *al-Tafsīr al-kabīr*, 2:126–28.

43. Muqātil b. Sulaymān, *Tafsīr Muqātil b. Sulaymān*, ed. ʿAbd Allāh Maḥmūd Shiḥāta (Beirut: Muʾassasat Taʾrīkh al-ʿArabī, 2002), 3:672.

44. Hūd b. Muḥakkam al-Huwwārī, *Tafsīr kitāb allāh al-ʿazīz*, ed. Balhhāj b. Saʿīd Sharīfī (Beirut: Dār al-Gharb al-Islāmī, 1990), 4:34.

45. Another verse—40:40—uses this phrase in regard to pious men and women in general who have faith and are therefore guaranteed entrance into heaven. Like the patiently forbearing in 39:10, they too will be given provisions without measure. For a discussion of the Qurʾānic *ṣābirūn* and the importance of the Qurʾānic trait *ṣabr* in the construction of moral excellence in Islamic pious literature and ethics, see my *Striving in the Path of God: Jihād and Martyrdom in Islamic Thought* (Oxford: Oxford University Press, 2013), ch. 7.

46. Al-Wāhidī, *al-Wasīṭ fī tafsīr al-qurʾān al-majīd*, ed. ʿĀdil Aḥmad ʿAbd al-Mawjūd, et al. (Beirut: Dār al-kutub al-ʿilmiyya, 1994), 3:574.

47. Ibid.

48. Ibn Abī al-Dunyā, *Al-Ṣabr wa al-thawāb ʿalayhi* (Beirut: Dār Ibn Ḥazm, 1997), 23.

Response to Asma Afsaruddin

GAVIN D'COSTA

I would like to start my response with Professor Afsaruddin's comment that "friendships do not travel with us into the next world" and her following citation from a ḥadīth: "family and wealth come back and only [the dead man's] deeds remain."

First, Sajjad Rizvi's essay in this volume speaks of the "friends of God" as being part of the afterlife, and I wonder whether this difference of emphasis (individual and God; individual and friends and God) indicates a significant difference? If not, I would appreciate further explanation, from a Muslim point of view, of the different emphases on friendships and human love enjoyed and struggled over, both prior to the final judgment and after the final judgment.

Second, I wonder if this difference of emphasis is also found in Christian accounts of these two states: after death and after the final judgment. Historically, friendship and love and the lack of love, as part of the created order, receive quite varied attention. For example, in a classic neo-Scholastic textbook, Joseph Pohle writes of the beatific vision in heaven: its primary object is the divine essence (an intuitive vision of the triune God); its secondary object is the contemplation of beautiful created objects outside of the divine essence.[1] Here, good friendships, beautiful music and art, and all those created realities that participate in the glory of the divine reality are enjoyed eternally. We see this in the passages from Dante's *The Divine Comedy* included in this volume. We see this in more radical ways in this volume's essays by N. T. Wright and Miroslav Volf, who have pressed us to think more carefully about these created realities and their participation in "heaven." Wright has called for a fuller account of all Creation's participation in the new heaven and the new earth; Volf has pointed to the suffering and lack of forgiveness that requires attention if the language of love and friendship is to have any eschatological currency.

Third, to drill a bit deeper into this issue, Afsaruddin writes of the penultimate state, the *barzakh*, which seems akin to purgatory, where the soul can earn partial expiation for its sins. There is an interesting apparent tension, as she notes, between the Qurʾān's teaching that "each individual is accountable for his or her sins only and that no one can bear the burdens of another or intercede for them" and Islamic notions of intercessory prayer. Indeed, it seems clear to me that, for much of the Islamic tradition, Muḥammad does have the power of intercession; also, according to Rizvi's essay in the present volume, Fāṭima too has this intercessory power. For me, this raises important questions. If Muḥammad has this particular power, how does he get it, and is it uniquely attributed to him? In principle, could others get it? If so, how? Again, with the Shiʿite tradition I sense that the powers of intercession between the living and the dead and between the dead and dead play a much stronger role.

Fourth, in the Christian tradition, understandings of purgatory and what goes on with regard to intercession are equally complicated and marked by powerful tensions because some Christians rejected not only the abuses regarding indulgences but also, later, the very notion of indulgences (intercessions on behalf of those who had died)—and, eventually, purgatory itself. Indeed, Wright has imaginatively suggested that, had Cardinal Ratzinger written his book on eschatology during the Reformation, a lot of strife might have been avoided! As a Catechism Roman Catholic, I hold to the following on this matter: that the intercession of the living on behalf of the dead is legitimate, that seeking intercession of the "dead"—the saints—on behalf of the living on earth and the "dead" in purgatory is legitimate, and that these doctrines are fundamentally aimed at articulating the social nature of our communal existence without denying individual agency and the power of love beyond death.

Fifth, the notion of the Heights, Aʿrāf, is very intriguing. If this is the state analogous to "limbo," where good and bad deeds are in exact balance, then two questions arise for me. If the Prophet interceded, then the balance would surely shift and tip toward good deeds. But if this happens, do those souls from the Aʿrāf then proceed to the *barzakh* to gain, through suffering, the partial expiation for sins. I cannot understand why they could not go directly to the *barzakh* rather than the Aʿrāf. I hope this is not turning poetry and ethics into "snakes and ladders"–type transactions. For the record, Roman Catholic thought speaks of two forms of limbo. There is "the limbo of the Fathers" (*limbus patrum*) for the righteous who lived before Christ (which is now empty, due to the descent of Christ into hell after his death and prior to the resurrection). There is also "the limbo of unbaptized children" (*limbus puerorum*)—although the recent catechism has dropped the word "limbo," now indicating a hope that these children, through the mercy of God, will enjoy eternal bliss. It is the limbo of the children that bears analogy with the A'rāf—where persons are neither good nor bad, compared to their being both equally good and bad. And this limbo is presupposed by Roman Catholic teaching on the necessity of baptism to overcome original sin.

Sixth, a universalist drive seems evident in Afsaruddin's essay—and, for me, this raises several questions. What are the conditions that cause someone to be one of "the most egregiously sinful" (as she puts it) whose powers cannot overcome the Prophet's intercession? Afsaruddin states that the majority of Islamic theologians believe that "the faithful" will all be eventually transported to heaven. Are "the faithful" only Muslims, or is the term inclusive of People of the Book? Might "the faithful" extend even to nontheist religions? In saying that the "mercy of the Almighty will envelop us all," Afsaruddin seems to imply "not just the faithful." But by what authority can Muslims extend their understanding of salvation in this universalist direction?

Finally, these same questions have dogged Christians. The current teaching of the Roman Catholic magisterium is interesting. It holds the necessity of baptism for salvation and that all people can be saved because God never leaves himself without witness to those who do not know the Gospel. Harmonizing these two teachings with other dogmas has been taxing.

Note

1. Joseph Pohle, *Eschatology: Or, the Catholic Doctrine of the Last Things, a Dogmatic Treatise*, 4th rev. ed. (St. Louis: Herder, 1920).

Death, Resurrection, and Human Destiny in the Christian Tradition

A ny survey of Christian belief about death, resurrection, and human destiny in the Christian tradition has to be selective by necessity. In his essay in this volume examining the biblical material, N. T. Wright reminds us of the centrality of the resurrection of Jesus Christ for Christian hope, and reminds us that the eschatological expectation of the earliest Christians did not necessarily coincide with what later generations of Christians believed. We need to note further that the later division of Christianity, between the Greek East and the Latin West, and the fracturing of Western Christianity at the Reformation, also gave rise to different theologies and maps of Christian hope. Interest in and speculation about the fate of the believer after death—what we might call individual or personal eschatology—was not always integrated with the eschatology of the end of time, and the themes of the Last Judgment and the Resurrection of the Dead. In even more recent times, Enlightenment critiques of traditional Christian eschatology (particularly the moral critique of the doctrine of hell and eternal punishment), evolutionary and scientific perspectives, biblical criticism, and consequent shifts in the disposal of the dead, particularly the rise of cremation in many parts of the Western Christian world, have led to further theological shifts.

The final clause of the Nicene Creed, the most significant conciliar creed of the early Christian centuries, has the following statement of belief: "We look forward to the resurrection of the dead and the life of the world to come." The Apostles' Creed, the old baptismal creed of the Church of Rome, concludes with a confession of faith in "the communion of saints, the remission of sins, the resurrection of the flesh, and eternal life." The same creed includes the clause confessing that Christ "descended into hell" (*descendit ad inferna*). As Kelly comments, "The belief that Christ spent the interval between His expiry on the cross and His resurrection in the underworld was a commonplace of Christian teaching from the earliest times."[1] The biblical text on which this belief is based is I Peter 3:18–19: Christ "was put to death in the flesh, but made alive in the spirit, in which also he went and made a proclamation to the spirits in prison." In Eastern Christian, art the icon of the Resurrection shows Christ trampling down the devil, who lies in chains; the broken doors of hell and their bolts and bars lie shattered beneath Christ's feet as he draws Adam and Eve, the first ancestors and representatives of the human race, from death to life. At Easter the Orthodox churches of the East sing in triumph: "Christ is risen from the dead, trampling down death by death, and to those in the tombs giving life!" The apocryphal Gospel of Nicodemus, or Acts of Pilate, which gives a detailed account of the descent into hell, gained much popular influence in the Middle Ages through play cycles about the Harrowing of Hell. "Hell" in this context is not hell in the ultimate sense of a place of punishment and exclusion from the presence of God but the "place or state where the souls of pre-Christian people waited for the message of the Gospel and whither the penitent thief passed after his death on the cross."[2] The reality of the death of Jesus meant that Christ participated fully in the death of human beings. So the North African Tertullian (ca. 160–ca. 225), wrote: "Christ our God, Who because He was man died according to the Scriptures, and was buried according to the same Scriptures, satisfied this law also by undergoing the form of human death in the under-world, and did not ascend aloft to heaven until He had gone down to the regions beneath the earth."[3]

The Apostles' Creed confesses belief in "the resurrection of the flesh and eternal life" (*carnis resurrectionem et vitam aeternam*). It is thought that the reference to "eternal life" may have been added to counter anxieties that resurrection was merely temporary. St. Cyril of Jerusalem emphasized that the words "life everlasting" pointed to "the real veritable life," which was God himself.[4] Eternal life was understood as participation in the life of God, the God who is a communion of love. The Christian hope was thus, as the Second Letter of Peter put it, that we "may become participants in the divine nature" (II Peter 1:4). As Kelly again summarizes, "in the middle ages the stress on LIFE EVER-LASTING was on the positive state of blessedness enjoyed by the redeemed. As St. Thomas Aquinas put it, the first truth about eternal life is that a man there finds union with God, Who is the reward and end of all our labours and crowns all our desires."[5]

The Apostles' Creed also confesses belief in the communion of saints (*sanctorum communio*). Although this has been interpreted as meaning a "sharing in the holy things" (i.e., the sacraments), it is far more likely that it stands "for that ultimate fellowship with the holy persons of all ages, as well as with the whole company of heaven, which is anticipated and partly realized in the fellowship of the Catholic Church on earth."[6] The Christian is baptized into the death and resurrection of Christ, and in the church shares the common life of the Body of Christ. As a hymn by the nineteenth-century English bishop Christopher Wordsworth puts it:

> God of God the One Begotten,
> Light of Light, Emmanuel,
> In whose body joined together
> All the saints forever dwell!

At the heart of the Christian Eucharist the prayers of the church on earth are joined with the prayers of "angels and archangels and . . . all the company of heaven." The Eucharist itself is seen by a very early Christian writer, Ignatius, Bishop of Antioch as "the medicine of immortality," when he writes to the Ephesians, "break the same Bread, which is the medicine of immortality, the antidote against death, and everlasting life in Jesus Christ."[7]

In the early centuries of the church, although the hope of resurrection continued as the dominant expression of Christian hope in the face of death, the influence of both Gnostic and Platonist ideas contributed to a view of human nature that exalted the soul over the body and emphasized the redemption of the soul apart from the body as the essential part of salvation. I summarized this in a survey of the development of Christian eschatology in my study of the nineteenth-century debates in England about eternal punishment and the future life:

> It was not surprising that the particular judgment of the individual soul at death became more important than the Last Judgment, and that the future of the individual was treated in isolation from that of the world. An image, such as the renewing fire of judgment, which was originally associated with the Last Day, later became linked with the particular judgment after death, and so contributed to the development of theories of purgatory: the purifying fire through which all had to

pass who wished to achieve the sanctity necessary for communion with God. The judgment at the Last Day was reduced to a declaratory judgment on the individual, when the sentence already passed at the particular judgment was made known, and to a judgment on the nations. . . . in the fifteenth-century devotional classic, *The Imitation of Christ* . . . "the coming of the Son of Man" is specifically referred to the moment of death.[8]

The Bull *Benedictus Deus* of Pope Benedict XII (1336) stated definitively that it was possible for a human being to fully experience heaven or hell immediately after death. In Western Christian eschatology, a pattern was established that could be set out as follows:

After death the departed soul immediately underwent the particular judgment, and was assigned to heaven, hell, or purgatory, there to remain, experiencing joy or pain as the case might be, until the Day of Judgment. At the Day of Judgment the resurrection took place and souls were once more united with their bodies to be assigned to heaven, to enjoy the perfection of bliss, or to hell, to suffer just punishment. The punishment suffered in hell consisted both of the deprivation of God (*poena damni*) and positive torment (*poena sensus*), and the punishment would be apt—"the pattern of a man's sins will be the pattern of his punishment," as the *Imitation of Christ* puts it.[9]

This summarizes the traditional Catholic eschatology as it developed in the Western Church, but we find other aspects in the development of Christian understanding, particularly in the Eastern Christian tradition, where the idea of purgatory was not developed. An early writer such as Clement of Alexandria sees the goal of Christian endeavor as the eternal contemplation of God, the "transcendently clear and absolutely pure, insatiable vision which is the privilege of intensely loving souls."[10] As Brian Daley explains, for Clement: "This promised life of vision will involve the transformation of our present nature, sanctification, sonship and friendship with God . . . and ultimately 'assimilation to God.' . . . Its full realization clearly lies beyond the limiting confines of this life."[11] Yet Clement also notes that "the resurrection for which we hope" is when "at the end of the world, the angels, radiant with joy, singing hymns and opening the heavens, shall receive into the celestial abodes those who truly repent, and, before all, the Savior himself goes to meet them . . . conducting them to the Father's bosom, to eternal life, to the Kingdom of heaven."[12] For

Clement, the resurrection of the body is the final realization of human "enlightenment," for Christ, the Tutor and Shepherd, "wishes to save my flesh by wrapping it in the robe of incorruptibility."[13] Clement's fellow Alexandrian, Origen, wrestled controversially with the nature of the resurrection, maintaining that the "real conflict is not between a hope in resurrection, and a belief in the immortality of the soul, but between the materialistic, popular conception of risen life current among the Christians of his day and a more spiritual one."[14] So Origen argues in *De Principiis* that "our new form of bodily existence at the resurrection will be the 'spiritual body' of 1 Cor. 15: a transfiguration of the present material body, free of the features that suit it only for life in this material world, and 'subtle, pure and resplendent . . . as the rational creature's situation demands and as its merits suggest.' "[15] The theme of transfiguration, as applied to the resurrection body of Christ and the hope of the resurrection of the dead, is underlined in Christian theology if we understand the "spiritual body" referred to by Paul in I Corinthians as referring to a body "animated by the [Holy] Spirit." Later theologians in the nineteenth century such as Frederick Denison Maurice (1805–72) strongly repudiated ideas of a resurrection equated with a "resurrection of relics."

In the West, Augustine of Hippo (354–430) was the most influential figure in the development of Latin eschatology. As Daley comments, most of Augustine's doctrine is thoroughly traditional, but what is new is its "systematic cohesion, its integration into a broad theological synthesis that is both philosophical and scriptural, speculative and pastorally practical." The key to understanding Augustine's eschatological hope, Daley argues, is

> to understand the sharp, metaphysically grounded distinction between time and eternity, between human existence now in history, with all the ambiguity of value and relationship that comes from our life as changeable spirits embodied in a finite, material universe, and the final existence we long for, released from the "distention" of space and time and united in stable knowledge and love with God, our source and our goal. . . . The resurrection will mean, in Augustine's view, the end of our existence in time as changeable, restless "fallen souls," and the confirmation of the present, historically conditioned order of loves in the changelessness of eternal beatitude or eternal self-destruction.[16]

Augustine "also distinguishes between the 'first death' of human beings, in time, which is their separation from God in sin and their consequent liability to the violent separation of soul from body in physical death, and the 'second death' of eternal damnation, to be experienced by sinners in a reunited soul and body that will never be annihilated."[17] Augustine likewise affirms the appropriateness of prayer for the departed. "There is no doubt that the dead are helped by the prayers of the holy Church, by the saving sacrifice [the Eucharist] . . . prayers for [those who have died in the communion of the body and blood of Christ] are not offered to God in vain."[18]

At the end of his survey of Christian eschatology in the early centuries, Daley notes significant areas of both agreement and disagreement among the early Christian writers. The areas of agreement are (1) a "linear" view of history; (2) the conviction that the fulfillment of history must include the resurrection of the body; (3) the prospect of God's universal judgment; (4) the prospect of a judgment pronounced by God at the end of an individual's life; (5) the reality of retributive punishment; and (6) the sense that the dead are still involved in the life of the Church. It became commonplace by the end of the fourth century, Daley writes,

> to emphasise that the heart of both beatitude and damnation is to be found in the relation of the human creature to God: made for union with God, we find our fulfilment only in a loving adherence to him, and are consumed by self-destructive agony if we choose decisively to turn away from him. The pains of hell and the joys of heaven, in sensible terms, are more and more clearly presented, in later Patristic literature, as simply the effect on the body of a person's fundamental relationship with God.[19]

Areas of difference concern (1) the time and nearness of the world's end; (2) the materiality and physical character of the resurrection; (3) the extent of eschatological salvation (from the universalist emphasis found in Origen and Gregory of Nyssa to the very restricted view of the number of the saved found in Augustine); (4) the possibility of change and progress for those whose final destiny has been determined; and, related to this, (5) the possibility of purgation from sin after death. "Whilst it is true that the notion of Purgatory as a separate, interim 'state' for some souls is first found in developed form in Western medi-aeval theology, its roots clearly lie in both the Greek and Latin Patristic tradition."[20]

The division of the Western Church at the time of the Reformation involved a recasting of Catholic eschatology as it had developed during the Middle Ages.

Martin Luther's protest against the practice of indulgences—payments in order to gain remission from the pains of purgatory—called into question not only the financial manipulations of the late medieval church but also the doctrine that underlay it. You could not earn your salvation. Justification was not by works but by faith alone—faith in Christ who had alone made satisfaction for sin. If Christ saved absolutely and entirely, then ideas of a further satisfaction to be made through suffering in purgatory were inadmissible. Ecclesiastes 11:3 ("in the place where the tree falls there shall it lie") was applied to the finality of death in relation to final judgment. It was a text summed up in a later English proverb of 1678:

> As the tree falls, so shall it lie,
> As a man lives, so shall he die,
> As a man dies, so shall he be,
> All through the days of eternity.

Requiem masses and prayers for the dead that seemed to make salvation dependent on human works and not on faith in Christ could not be countenanced. By contrast, when Pope Leo X condemned Martin Luther in the Bull *Exsurge, Domine* in 1520, one of the propositions condemned was that "purgatory cannot be proved from canonical Sacred Scripture."[21] As I have argued in my earlier study,

> Luther attempted to recover the primitive perspective with its emphasis on the importance of the Last Day, though his acceptance of death as the separation of soul and body meant that he still had to include an intermediate state in his eschatology. The soul, he argued, was, during this time, in a deep, dreamless sleep, without consciousness or perception, though yearning to be reunited with its body. Just as a man asleep is still alive, though he may appear lifeless, so the soul in this condition could be described as alive to God. But the day of resurrection would be the day of the resurrection of the whole man, and not just of the body only. By contrast John Calvin, who was more influenced by Platonism, was firmly opposed to ideas of the sleep of the soul, and even wrote a treatise, the *Psychopannychia* (1542), against it. Biblical references to death as a sleep were not to be taken literally, but as a metaphor which showed how the bitterness of death had been mitigated for the believer. The intermediate state was a period of waiting, but one in which the soul shared in the experiences of joy and sorrow, though in a temporary and provisional way.[22]

The disappearance of purgatory in the Protestant tradition left Protestants in the position that maintained that all humanity was divided into two categories, those whose ultimate destination was heaven and those whose ultimate destination was hell. This absolute alternative, which sharply separated the elect from the damned, often went hand in hand with a doctrine of predestination. At the same time, it often seemed to many to be at variance with human experience— most human beings were neither so transparently good or so transparently believing that they could be said to be destined unequivocally for heaven, nor, on the other hand, were most men and women so clearly evil that they were destined for hell. The doctrine of purgatory, whatever its demerits, corresponded more closely, at one level of experience at least, with the confused ways in which men and women lived than with the stark, absolute alternative. This makes it perhaps the more surprising that there is little evidence to show that the absence of a doctrine of purgatory contributed to a decline of belief in hell until the nineteenth century. The critiques of hell were on the grounds of the immorality of a God condemning to eternal torment those whose sins were by nature finite, particularly if those sinners by a doctrine of double predestination had been foreordained to damnation, just as the elect had been foreordained to salvation.[23]

Although Luther, in particular, and Calvin, to some extent, attempted to restore a theological importance to the Last Day, there was an increasing tendency in Protestant theology to revert to an emphasis on the day of death. The deathbed, with appropriate last words from the dying, would indicate whether the one who was dying was among the number of the elect. Suspicion of the millenarian excesses of the "Radical Reformation" doubtless also played its part, combined with the individualist character of the doctrine of justification by faith, meaning that hope in a consummation implied in a corporate salvation diminished or disappeared, with a consequent weakening of a strong sense of the communion of saints. As one scholar summarizes this Protestant trend, "the result was an individualized eschatology, the Last Judgment seen as a condemnation of the ungodly, and a direct linking of the bliss of heaven with the moment of death."[24]

In the eighteenth century, both Christians and more deist adherents of rational religion tended to be at one in affirming a belief in the immortality of the soul, and this was therefore not an aspect of Christian belief that came under attack. But in the nineteenth century, there was both increasing theological dissatisfaction with forensic understandings of salvation and unease with doctrines of hell and eternal punishment that offended moral awareness and sensibility. With the scientific revolution that called into question the biblical chronology of Creation and cast doubt on the account of human origins in the first chapters of Genesis, some of the assumed foundations of Christianity were shaken. If the redemption wrought by Christ was to redeem from the Fall of Adam, but the Fall of Adam was not an historical event, what sense could be made of traditional doctrines of salvation? If human origins lay in natural selection and evolution, what then was to be said about Adam being created by God with a uniquely immortal soul? The apocalyptic language of the Book of Revelation and the prophet Daniel, which was at the root of much of the imagery of Christian theology, particularly of eschatology, began to be seen by many as part of a mythological literary genre. It is not surprising that in the nineteenth century we find efforts to harmonize Darwinian language with the traditional language of Christian hope by the development of theological understandings of eschatology such as the doctrine of "conditional immortality"—a spiritual "survival of the fittest" that is still the preferred eschatology of the Adventist churches. Likewise, the hell of eternal torment became more and more problematical, and there were a number of defenders of an annihilationist position, which held that one should take as normative the language of the "second death" rather than taking literally the language of eternal torment in undying flame. Popular hellfire preachers, who delighted in bullying and terrifying their congregations with dreadful pictures of hell, seemed remote from a Christian understanding of the God who redeems by a love that comes down to the lowest part of our need.[25] The hell that was portrayed seemed not to be the judgment of God but the depiction of a God of cosmic cruelty. Increasingly, purgatorial ideas crept into Protestant theology, and many espoused a universalist hope. Likewise, much of the imagery of heaven was questioned, particularly when it seemed tied to an outmoded picture of a three-decker universe. The debates about eschatology raised in an acute way questions about the nature of religious language—and they continue to do so. In another direction were those who sought to bolster Christian belief in the hope of a life after death by seeking scientific support in the findings of psychical research.[26] Later, World War I, with its millions of dead, led to a new sympathy for prayers for the dead in Christian traditions that had not favored them.

If part of the history of Christian eschatology in the nineteenth century is of an increasingly immanentist, idealist, and optimistic understanding, with a decline in belief in a hell of eternal torment, then optimistic idealism in the twentieth century, with its darker history, seemed inadequate to the realities of good and evil. The Russian theologian Nicolas Berdyaev perceptively commented in his 1937 study *The Destiny of Man* that "the idea of hell is ontologically connected with freedom and personality, and not with justice and retribution. . . . Hell is necessary not to ensure the triumph of justice and retribution to the wicked, but to save man from being forced to be good and compulsorily installed in heaven."[27] The nineteenth century also saw in purely practical terms the beginnings of Christian churches adopting cremation as well as the traditional practice of burial. Associated with pagan practice, cremation was at first seen as running counter to the Christian hope of the resurrection but has become more widely accepted, first in Protestant and Anglican contexts, and then in the Roman Catholic context, though so far the Orthodox world remains committed to burial.

This all-too-rapid selective survey of aspects of Christian eschatology must return in conclusion to what is at the center of what Christians believe about death and God's future, the resurrection of Jesus Christ. As the First Letter of Peter begins: "Blessed be the God and Father of our Lord Jesus Christ! By his great mercy he has given us a new birth into a living hope through the resurrection of Jesus Christ from the dead, and into an inheritance that is imperishable, undefiled and unfading, kept in heaven for you, who are being protected by the power of God through faith for a salvation ready to be revealed in the last time" (I Peter 1:3–5).

Notes

1. J. N. D. Kelly, *Early Christian Creeds*, 2nd ed. (London: Longmans, Green, 1960), 379.

2. F. L. Cross and E. A. Livingstone, eds., "Descent of Christ into Hell," in *The Oxford Dictionary of the Christian Church*, 3rd ed. (Oxford: Oxford University Press, 1997). See also "Paradise," in ibid., where *ODCC* comments: "it has been variously interpreted as referring either to the intermediate state of the just before the Resurrection, or as a synonym of the heaven of the blessed." On the penitent thief, see Luke 23:43: "Then he [the penitent thief] said, 'Jesus, remember me when you come into your kingdom.' He [Jesus] replied, 'Truly I tell you today you will be with me in Paradise.'"

3. Tertullian, *De anima* 55, quoted in Kelly, *Early Christian Creeds*, 380.

4. Cyril of Jerusalem, *Catechetical Letters* 18, 28ff, quoted in Kelly, *Early Christian Creeds*, 388. See also Kelly's citations of Augustine and Chrysostom, 387.

5. Ibid., Kelly, *Early Christian Creeds*, 388.

6. Ibid., 391.

7. Ignatius of Antioch, *To the Ephesians*, 20, in *The Epistles of St Clement of Rome and St Ignatius of Antioch*, trans. James A. Kleist, Ancient Christian Writers (Westminster, MD: Newman Press, 1949), 68.

8. Geoffrey Rowell, *Hell and the Victorians: A Study of the Nineteenth-Century Theological Controversies Concerning Eternal Punishment and the Future Life* (Oxford: Clarendon Press, 1974), 23.

9. Ibid.

10. Clement of Alexandria, *Stromateis* 7.3.13.1, quoted in Brian E. Daley, *The Hope of the Early Church: A Handbook of Patristic Eschatology* (Cambridge: Cambridge University Press, 1991), 45.

11. Ibid.

12. Clement of Alexandria, *Who Is the Rich Man who will be Saved?*, §42, quoted in ibid.

13. Clement of Alexandria, *Paedagogos*, I.6.28.3–5; I.9.84.3, quoted in ibid.

14. Ibid., 52.

15. Origen, *De Principiis*, 2.2.2 and 3.6.4, quoted in ibid.

16. Ibid., 131–32.

17. Ibid., 136.

18. Augustine *Sermons* 172.2, quoted in ibid., 138–39.

19. Ibid., 219–21.

20. Ibid., 221–23. See also Jacques Le Goff, *The Birth of Purgatory* (Aldershot: Scholar Press, 1990).

21. Leo's Bull is reprinted in H. J. Hillerbrand, *The Reformation in Its Own Words* (London: SCM Press, 1964), 80–84.

22. Rowell, *Hell and the Victorians*, 25–26.

23. See D. P. Walker, *The Decline of Hell: Seventeenth-Century Discussions of Eternal Torment* (London: Routledge, 1964).

24. J. P. Martin, *The Last Judgement in Protestant Theology from Orthodoxy to Ritschl* (Edinburgh: Oliver & Boyd, 1963), 15–16.

25. An example of such a preacher is the Catholic missionary Father John Furniss, whose *Sight of Hell* in his *Books for Children* is a tour de force of sadomasochism. See Rowell, *Hell and the Victorians*, 171–73.

26. See Alan Gauld, *The Founders of Psychical Research* (London: Routledge, 1968).

27. Quoted in Rowell, *Hell and the Victorians*, 217.

Response to Geoffrey Rowell

FERAS HAMZA

B ishop Geoffrey Rowell's essay on aspects of the Christian eschatological tradition suggests three major points of interest, all of which resonate with the picture one can draw from Islam's own eschatological tradition. These three points might be aggregated as follows: (1) the afterlife landscape is rich and variegated; (2) some eschatological concepts and schemes lose emphasis over time, but some remain stable and dominate over longer historical periods; and (3) apparent tensions within eschatological schemes in both traditions persist and are seemingly sustained.

One might start on a comparative note with the theme of Christ's descent into hell to save those who could not have been witnesses to his ministry. The salvation of such individuals, traditionally identified as the righteous from earlier generations (from the Greek philosophers to the Old Testament patriarchs) is a question that is, to some extent, contingent upon the dating of the Apostles' Creed. Beyond that, it is also a question that requires some theological explanation. We know that it troubled St. Augustine even as he was inclined to accept it in some modified form. The question here, I think, is what this highly symbolic act of grace has meant for communities of Christians across history. Christ's descent into hell clearly allowed for a reconciliation between historical Christianity and the "Hellenic narrative" of Christianity's cultural history. No such reconciliation, however, was ever effected between the Muslim community and its pre-Islamic heritage. In fact, the drawing of a sharp line between the pre-Islamic time of *jāhiliyya* and the birth of Muslim history has been a major theme across Muslim literature, sacred and profane, arguably even to this day. The Prophet Muḥammad could never intercede with God in order to save his parents, both of whom died before his call to prophethood, nor indeed for that well-known surrogate father, his uncle Abū Ṭālib, who doted on his nephew throughout the persecution that his nephew Muḥammad endured during his mission to the Meccans. There is no equivalent "Descent into Hell" tradition with the Prophet Muḥammad. And yet it should be made clear that Muḥammad was never quite the ontological equivalent of Jesus. In this respect, we might add that there are numerous Muslim traditions that depict God thrusting his hand into Hell at the end of time in order to save (unidentified) individuals out of his sheer grace.

Nevertheless, I think the contrast is interesting and worth pondering for what it can tell us about the conception of "community" in both cases. Such intercessory acts are a dominant feature of both traditions. The Prophet Muḥammad is understood to have been granted an exclusive privilege of intercession on the Day of Judgment, one that he will use to save his community (*umma*). Lesser intercessory acts are no less important. Muslims are encouraged to recite passages of scripture for the dead, and there are numerous supplications structured into the daily prayers that take into account this important relationship between living and dead believers. The debates and controversies about various forms of intercession and intercessory acts in both Christianity and Islam, as well as debates concerning Purgatory, probably have more to do with establishing the boundaries of the community: the unique self-definition of God's community cannot forever be diluted by open-ended intercessory acts.

Two other points should be mentioned, both reflecting tensions regarding how to think about life after death. Again, in both religions, we can see an interest in positing two kinds of postmortem judgment, a particular judgment immediately after the moment of biological death versus a final eschatological judgment that follows the resurrection of all creatures at the end of time. To be sure, Muslim orthodoxy preferred to concentrate on the eschatological judgment; however, it could never dissolve the popular belief in some form of immediate personal judgment. Certainly, the Sufis spoke at length of a spiritual judgment taking place at the point of death. But it was not only the mystics who subscribed to such a reality. Hundreds of classical Muslim creeds described how the period in the grave was spent in a sort of preview of one's final abode, whether in a breezy and spacious lit tomb, in some cases with a glimpse of something paradisiacal, or in a constricting and oppressive grave in which angels beat the sinful dead until the time of resurrection. On the issue of personal judgment versus final judgment, it is interesting to note that there is a Muslim parallel to the tendency mentioned by Rowell for some Christian thought to see the final judgment as a declaratory enactment of the particular judgment. In his well-known Sufi Qur'ān commentary, 'Abd al-Razzāq al-Kāshānī (d. 1336), a student of the school of Ibn 'Arabī, also mentions that the postmortem judgment is in fact the main event, while the Last Judgment is merely a declaration of that truth on a wider scale.

Historically, one of the lingering questions in the interpretation of the scriptural narratives concerning the Eschaton has been the status of the dead: are they in some sort of extended sleep, or are they experiencing the ontological reality of the postmortem existence—that is to say, experiencing the consequences of their deeds? For if one is to allow for the traditional sequence of the Eschaton, then all of those presently dead would be in a state of interlude awaiting all those remaining on earth to join them before the Last Judgment can take place and individuals are finally and definitively consigned to either Heaven or Hell.

A corollary here, of course, is the question of whether Heaven and Hell have already been created or whether their ontological reality will only unfold at the end of time. This last question was extensively treated in the majority of medieval Muslim theological writings. There was no consensus regarding whether Heaven and Hell had already been created. Some Muslim theologians argued that they had already been created since traditions from the Prophet's life explicitly had him reporting visions of those in Hell. However, others defended the traditional eschatological sequence by arguing that the dead were asleep and that the eternal abodes had not been created yet. These latter could cite numerous Qur'ānic passages in support of this view (for example, 36:52). Indeed, on the Christian side, there were several New Testament passages that said as much (for example, I Thessalonians 4:13). Tertullian (d. ca. 220) argued that souls could not sleep and that something meaningful had to occur in the grave (*De Anima*, 58): here, in fact, was an early form of the idea of Purgatory.

This tension between the dead being asleep (waiting for the end of time) and the dead experiencing a foretaste of their ultimate abode can be explained to a large extent by considering the nature of scriptural narratives. Scripture collapses time as it moves from descriptions of this world to those of the other world. Such a dual context is intrinsic to its message: it addresses people, events, and deeds of this world while describing scenes of the other world. So from one perspective, the Eschaton as it unfolds through the scriptural narrative seems to have already arrived in some dimension and at some level. Perhaps for some theologians, since the dead have in effect passed on from this worldly plane, there must be only one other plane that they have joined, the very same one in which the Eschaton will unfold; this in part helps to explain why the belief has persisted that the dead "know" and experience heaven or hell at some level. On the other hand, because of the interim period presupposed by the traditional apocalyptic sequence of the Eschaton, the dead can only be in a state of inter-mission, waiting for the living to join them so that the final resurrection can take place. Hence the continuous tension between the dead experiencing their final abodes and the dead being asleep, sensing their final abodes but not quite there as they await the final death of all.

My final point concerns the perennial question of whether renewed existence in the afterlife would take on a spiritual, immaterial form, or whether it would in fact constitute a new physical life with a perfected physical form. Philoso-phers, theologians, and mystics, both Muslim and Christian, clearly considered the material descriptions of Heaven (or Paradise) as having been purposely so expressed precisely because they were suitable for the average believer whose limited intellectual capacities could not conceive of, let alone be excited by, an immaterial or spiritual afterlife. However, it is also certain that there were exceptions on both sides and I dare say that many contemporary believers, aware of modern science, might still consider that a perfect physicality that could enjoy a material, physically delightful heaven is not beyond the capabili-ties of God.

Rowell's survey of eschatological beliefs from the second century to the twen-tieth highlights the dynamic nature of what might otherwise seem like a static theological tradition. And while he gauges well the flux over the centuries in Christian beliefs about the Eschaton, I think that there is an equally interesting aspect of stability that we should also note. In fact, underlying all of the eschato-logical themes discussed here, and presupposed by much that the two religious traditions share, there does seem to be a stable stock of eschatological themes that one might call "Abrahamic." What is interesting here is that, notwithstand-ing the continually evolving tradition of eschatological beliefs, there is a sub-stantial stability of a central cluster of ideas or themes, such as resurrection, judgment, possibilities of purgative redemption, and continued existence prede-termined by the nature of the soul as it leaves this world. On the Muslim side, I would say that a classical eschatological scheme has held from about the tenth century to this day. Notwithstanding the somewhat idiosyncratic Sufi concept of a personalized postmortem judgment that naturally deemphasizes the traditional force of the Eschaton, and contemporary modernist musings about the spiritual reality of the afterlife, the vast majority of Muslims continue to cherish the reality of a very physical paradise. This has probably less to do with their exposure, or some might say lack of exposure, to rationalist sensibilities and more with the fact that the anticipation of a perfect life—that is, the reward of Paradise—can generally only be grasped through our current imperfect, physical faculties. For believers, the possibility that these faculties, our senses and physical forms, can be recreated in a perfected state compensates for the deficiencies of one's predicament here on earth while at the same time vindicating the awesome and unknowable extent of God's creative power.

Ultimately, I think, the most spiritually attuned of the Christian and Muslim faithful would agree that even as one, by virtue of one's limitation, is kept guessing about the true form and nature of the Eschaton and its landscape, and whatever eschatological scheme one adheres to, the best hope lies in the anticipation that the divine mercy should suffuse every moment of this world and the next. I think this sobering sense of ultimately not knowing but trusting in the wisdom of the divine scheme is captured by the Prophet's words in the Qur'ān, "Say: I am nothing new when it comes to the matter of Messengers. I do not know what will be done with me or with you. I only follow what is being revealed to me and I am but a warner making things clear" (46:9), and by the words from the Lord's Prayer, "Thy kingdom come; Thy will be done."

Dying Well
Christian Faith and Practice

HARRIET HARRIS

I have been invited to reflect on actual Christian practice today, rather than on what "should" be believed and practiced. My reflections cannot convey the wealth of Christian practices around dying, which vary across the world, across denominations, and even within a single congregation. I take "the West" as my context, in which the wider culture is simultaneously secularized, such that for many people and institutions the church is barely a reference point, and also multifaith, in which health care governs most dying, and in which the term "spirituality" has more currency than "faith."

As if Nobody Died Anymore

"Everything in town goes on as if nobody died anymore," says Philippe Ariès of contemporary Western attitudes: "Except for the death of a statesman, society has banished death . . . the disappearance of an individual no longer affects its continuity."[1] We might say the same of the workplace; somebody dies, an email goes round, and everyone gets on with their day. It is not that we avert our eyes from death. We are intellectually and artistically fascinated by it, producing university courses, book series, conferences, and cultural festivals on the theme. We follow anxiously the shifting thought on the causes of mortality (and thereby learn that dying is something that we should not do), and we debate the rationality of suicide, even beyond the bounds of terminal or life-limiting conditions. Sometimes we are public in our mourning, creating shrines of flowers, for example, where a young person has died, whereas a generation ago we might have visited the family instead. We are more conversant about death than our parents and grandparents and less inclined to shroud it from children, and we have become specialists in bereavement, developing bereavement support tailored, for example, to children, young people, parents, lesbian and gay people, teachers, and others in professional roles.[2] We have a popular phrase, "in denial," which derives from Elisabeth Kübler-Ross's famous model of the stages of dying and grieving.[3] We smile wryly, when, for example, we find ourselves on training courses about "managing change" and are taken through the cycle that Kübler-Ross categorized.

Yet, for all our interest in death, dying, and bereavement, we still behave as though "nobody died anymore." We do our utmost to maintain continuity, hence the popularity at funerals of Henry Scott Holland's words: "Death is nothing at all. I have only slipped away into the next room." (I shall say more about these words shortly.) Sometimes we do not even hold funerals; the deceased have asked not to have one. In Scotland, a practice is developing whereby families hold a private committal at a crematorium first, and follow it not with a funeral, but with a memorial or thanksgiving service. Undertakers encourage this practice because it is straightforward for arranging timings and transport, but they would not encourage it if clients found it insensitive. Mourners opt for short and private committals, which move them quickly on from the finality of death, back to a focus on life. This affects the nature of church provision for them and for the deceased. Funerals help us to receive the dead, send them on their way, and then take our leave; for we must begin the task of adjusting to life without them. Memorials and thanksgivings keep the dead alive, which is of value, but this becomes confused if we almost pretend that they have not died by committing them elsewhere in private.

In the United States, the desire for continuity gives rise to other trends: an increased belief in heaven despite a decrease in most other religious beliefs, and therefore, presumably, a that floats free from the trauma and trials of getting there;[4] and a growing belief in the Rapture among evangelical Christians, which is the hope, based on I Thessalonians 4.17, that Christians who are alive today will not die but will be caught up in the clouds, along with the dead who have been raised, when Jesus returns.

These trends reflect and affect how we are around death. If we do not face death, "death asserts its rule" over us, and we become still less able to face it.[5]

Overcoming Death

In a famous sermon preached in 1907, Albert Schweitzer provokes us to overcome death by becoming familiar with it. He tells us to regard "our lives and those who are part of our lives as though we have already lost them in death, only to receive them back for a little while." He encourages us with insights into the benefits that follow: "true, inward freedom from material things"; feeling "purified and delivered" from our baser selves; a deepened appreciation of the preciousness of life, and of our loved ones so that we "become sacred to the other because of death."[6]

Schweitzer recalls us (as Christians) to our baptism because in our baptism we have already died, and our "lives are hidden with Christ in God" (Col. 3:3). Those "who belong to the Lord in spirit," he says, "have shared with him in spiritual experience his death and resurrection to a new life. They now live in this world as men who are inwardly freed from the world by death."[7]

In context, Holland's message, preached three years later in 1910, is remarkably similar. Holland acknowledges death's reign over us; indeed, he calls it the "King of Terrors," "cruel," "irrational," and "the pit of destruction."[8] And yet death "is nothing at all" because, by our baptism, it is now behind us, not in front. So "let the dead things go, and lay hold on life," Holland exhorts us. "Then the old will drop away from you, and the new wonder will begin. You will find yourself already passed from death to life, and far ahead strange possibilities will open up beyond the power of your heart to conceive."[9]

Schweitzer and Holland believe that we can pass through death to life because Christ conquered death. They do not teach that we can have ongoing life without passing through death, which is the wishful thinking of our own time. But they do suggest that by practicing our passage through death, we can already benefit from some of the fullness of life that death can yield, and we can be somewhat prepared for the losses that our physical death will bring. So they articulate something of the art of dying.

Remembering and Forgetting the Art of Dying

The art of dying teaches detachment from the world. In the centuries following the Reformation, people were instructed to learn this art while they were still in good health and not to leave it to the hour of their death.[10] But since the nineteenth century, we have increasingly medicalized the concept of dying well and have confined it again to a person's last illness, perhaps even to their very final moments.

Today, there is not much awareness that dying was ever considered an art to be learned throughout life. Yet, consciously or otherwise, Christians acquire something of this art through worship and discipleship, where dying and receiving life are central motifs and the essence of our major sacraments or ordinances. In baptism we die and rise in Christ, put off the old and take on the new. At the Eucharist, we remember the death and resurrection of Christ, and we partake of his body so that we are made into his body, our life established by his death.[11] We may also acquire the pattern of dying and rising through regular daily prayers, depending on how regular we are in saying them. At evening and night prayer we pray that God would let us depart in peace. We commend our spirit in to God's hands, our sleep being a kind of death through which we seek God's protection, in which we welcome rest from the changes and chances of this fleeting life, and from which God wakes us with the dawning of a new day. So at Morning Prayer we wake with praise on our lips. Our major annual observances also lead us to reflect upon our own mortality and the life that comes from death, particularly Lent, Holy Week, and Easter, when we remember Christ's passion, death, and resurrection, but also All Saints, All Souls, Remembrance Sunday, and red-letter days, when we remember those who have died before us.

Moreover, Christian spiritual practice, in a positive way, casts most things we do in terms of a process of dying to the old self in order to live our new life in Christ. We die to pride when we ask for forgiveness, we die to grievances when we forgive others, we die to security when we take risks, we die to fear when we love, we die to possessiveness over people we love when we let them go, and so on. "We must all become familiar with the thought of death if we want to grow into really good people," says Schweitzer. "The ambition, greed, and love of power that we keep in our hearts, that shackle us to this life in chains of bondage, cannot in the long run deceive [one] who looks death in the face."[12]

All these mini deaths are echoes of our baptism. If we continually die in prayer, repentance, and service, we approach our physical deaths as people who are continually being transformed. This is why we pray "that we who are baptized into the death of your Son our Saviour Jesus Christ may continually put to death our evil desires and be buried with him; and that through the grave and gate of death we may pass to our joyful resurrection"; or we ask God to "grant us to die daily to sin, that we may evermore live with [Christ] in the joy of his risen life."[13]

Theologically, our hope is not that we can avoid our physical death but that this death is made the passage to our final transformation.[14] "We shall not die,

but we shall be changed," are words (based on I Cor. 15:51–52) said as part of a responsory in the Church of England's provision for prayer at home before a funeral: "The perishable shall be clothed with the imperishable, **and the mortal must be clothed with immortality**."[15]

The process of clothing our mortal bodies with immortality is not seamless, however, and we fear the unknown on this side of death, whatever hope we might attach to the Hereafter. While the central pattern of dying and rising filters through our liturgies and spiritual practices and has some effect on Christian lives, it does not follow that most Christians find a strong connection between spiritually and physically dying, so as to feel prepared for the latter.

Furthermore, Christian worship and teaching are themselves affected by contemporary silences around death and do not say as much on the theme as they might. For example, ministers may conduct several funerals a week, and yet not bring their reflections upon death, dying, and afterlife into their regular Sunday services.[16] I have been struck by how many theologians, clergy, and philosophers disregard the metaphor of dying in our spiritual discipline and prefer other terms such as "letting go" or "unselfing." These gentler terms do not convey the radical way in which our spiritual disciplines can send us back to nothing. We die, and out of that we rise. As a Lutheran minister put it to me: "We do not just 'have a bad day and rise'!"[17] We are sometimes coy about "dying" even in our baptismal liturgies, despite baptism being both our "tomb" and our "womb," as theologians of the early church put it.

In baptism liturgies, the tradition developed, following Hippolytus, of anointing with two oils.[18] Before the baptism, the baptismal candidates are marked with the sign of the cross made with the Oil of Catechumens (which is sometimes called the Oil of Rejection, or the Oil of Exorcism).[19] After their baptism, the candidates are anointed with the Oil of Chrism (which is the oil of gladness). The place of death is the space between the two oils, the space between departing and receiving (or being received). Theologically and spiritually, we make room for the Oil of Chrism by first using the Oil of Catechumens. This remains the practice in Orthodox and Roman Catholic contexts. In the current Church of England rite, only one anointing is specified: either before the baptism, at the point where the candidates reject the devil, renounce evil, repent of their sins and turn to Christ, or after the baptism.[20] In the Anglican Diocese of Edinburgh, the Oil of Catechumens is no longer blessed on Maundy Thursday because the first anointing ritual has so fallen out of use. Not to use that oil, or not to use both oils and thereby not to notice the place between them, suggests that even in church we try to have life without passing through death.

Care for the Dying

When her mother was slowly dying in hospital, it seemed to Karen Armstrong that death was "taboo" even there: "When we go to hospital we are meant to get better and meet government targets," she writes. "We are not supposed to die there anymore." We have "banished death" from modern society, she says, pushing it "off-stage in hospices and nursing homes."[21]

She is right that Western health care too often conveys a sense that death must be resisted, postponed, or avoided.[22] But hospices are not guilty of this offense. Hospice care (which extends to homes, hospitals, and nursing homes) involves an explicit philosophy that death is neither to be postponed nor hastened, and is the area in our culture where we are most attentive to dying. Where churches are developing their understanding of "dying well," they are doing so most extensively in conjunction with hospice and palliative research.

The concept of hospice has been evolving since the eleventh century CE, when, at the time of the Crusades, hospices were founded as places of hospitality for the sick, wounded, or dying as well as for travelers and pilgrims. An emphasis on hospitality remains central to the modern hospice movement, which owes much of its vision and impetus to Dame Cicely Saunders and her founding of St. Christopher's Hospice in London in 1967. Saunders describes the hospice as "a place of meeting. Physical and spiritual, doing and accepting, giving and receiving, all have to be brought together. . . . The dying need the community, its help and fellowship. . . . The community needs the dying to make it think of eternal issues and to make it listen."[23]

Saunders tape-recorded conversations with hundreds of patients at the end of their lives. By listening attentively, she developed the notion of "total pain" to convey pain's physical, emotional, social, and spiritual components. Palliative care treats pain on all of these levels and aims at healing rather than cure (which is the removal of disease). Healing is seen as possible even in death, in a way that is wholly consonant with the Christian hope of transformation. As a writer on palliative care, aging, and spirituality puts it: "Christians believe that even in death there is healing. . . . Healing . . . can occur in the presence of disease, as the person grows into wholeness of body, mind and spirit."[24]

Contemporaries of Saunders who developed similar work in the 1960s and 1970s included Florence Wald and Elisabeth Kübler-Ross, both operating in the United States. There are now more than eight thousand hospices and palliative care units around the world in over one hundred countries.[25]

Saunders's Christian faith was a fundamental motivating factor in her care for the dying. At the same time, she was clear that a hospice is for people of all faiths and none, and that people's spiritual needs are not necessarily to be defined by religion. In hospice settings, "religion" is understood in terms of a set of beliefs or the following of liturgical practice and use of ritual; "spiritual" is understood in terms of an integrated inner life. "Some people are religious and not spiritual," says a Christian hospice chaplain in the United States. "Some are spiritual and not religious: some are both. Intellectual assent to a codified set of doctrines does not provide one with the spiritual resources needed to cope with many of the challenges of life and death." Religion can also be a "double-edged sword": "For those who believe that if they keep praying they will get well and then do not, their faith can be shattered because it was not deeply grounded in the first place."[26] I discussed these observations with a Marie Curie nurse, who agreed but also thought that some patients who are religious have a "better death" because they have more of a sense of where they are going and, in her phrase (to which we will return), they have "more being."[27]

Hospice care is "person-centered": patients define what they mean by a "good death," and the care team helps them achieve it. Religious frameworks are therefore not imposed upon patients who are not religious. Hospice chaplaincy teams are increasingly multifaith, but chaplains recognize that they may not be asked to share the teachings and practices of their own faith. Sometimes a distinction is made between spiritual and pastoral care, where "pastoral" is understood to involve the beliefs and practices of a particular faith tradition.[28] Either way, chaplains are called upon to provide particular expertise, such as conducting a ceremony (for example, a marriage or a naming, blessing, or baptism for a dying baby), listening to a final confession or testimony of faith, or creating a space for family and personal reconciliation.

Spiritual health is highly valued in hospice settings. Palliative care teams recognize that unaddressed spiritual distress can lead to poorly controlled symptoms, an increased need for pain relief, and an unquiet death. One of the many fruits of hospice work is the wealth of research into the nature of spiritual health, which, alongside personal accounts from patients and staff, helps to convey what it is like to be dying, what are the lowest points, and what brings healing.

Spiritual Health and Meaning

Hospice care teams gauge a patient's spiritual health by her ability to find meaning. They take the view that people "can suffer almost anything if there is meaning attached to it."[29] They also observe that when patients are able to tell stories about their lives, or to express themselves creatively, this can reduce the need for pain relief. For this reason, hospices place great value on art and music therapies, ethnography and film, in response to illness.[30]

It is worth exploring the connections and assumptions at work here, for it may be that something less elusive than meaning is at stake. In his seminal work on illness, *The Wounded Storyteller*, Arthur Frank explains that "stories have to repair the damage that illness has done to the ill person's sense of where she is in life, and where she may be going. Stories are a way of redrawing maps and finding new destinations."[31] Stories are also a way of summing up one's life and so of finding it, sometimes for the first time. Marie de Hennezel, a psychologist in a palliative care unit in Paris, describes an encounter with Dominique, who cannot bear being "pinned in bed and waiting to die." Marie asks her if she has "finished living," or if anything is "tethering" her to life. Dominique replies that "there are so many things still unsettled." Marie invites her to tell her about them, and she responds with her life story. She ends by saying "So this is all me. . . . This is my life." "It's your life," Marie reiterates, with the emphasis on *your*. Marie later writes that "the silence that follows holds neither lament nor discomfort. Dominique has fallen asleep, and on her face there is a tiny smile of triumph."[32]

By telling her story, Dominique found her life with sufficient completeness to then be able to let it go. Was "meaning" the crucial quality for her? Palliative researchers often quote Viktor Frankl: "Man is not destroyed by suffering, he is destroyed by suffering without meaning."[33] But the meaning of "meaning" is unclear, even in Frankl's classic study where his prescription for people who are losing hope is to fix their minds on some person or aim for which it is worth staying alive. Frankl promotes a sense of purpose, and sometimes "purpose" is what palliative caregivers also mean by "meaning."[34] But purpose is not what Abigail Rian Evans has in mind when she observes: "When pain is under control, there is more acceptance of the diagnosis, and thus one can find meaning in one's death."[35] Rather, the pattern seems to be that when pain is controlled, people are able to participate in what is happening to them. Feeling engaged and empowered may well be more important than the usually impossible task of establishing meaning. For example, François Mitterrand, when dying from cancer, wrote of Maria de Hennezel's work: "The mystery of existence and death is not solved, but it is fully experienced."[36]

The healing power of stories, then, may have less to do with replotting connections to find new meaning and more to do with shifting the ill person from passivity to activity. To quote Arthur Frank again: "The ill person who turns illness into story transforms fate into experience; the disease that sets the body apart from others becomes, in the story, the common bond of suffering that joins bodies in their shared vulnerability."[37] This insight fits with Cicely Saunders's insight that those who are dying bring gifts, which we receive through listening. It also fits with patients' own accounts of good spiritual care—namely, the practice of being listened to, which engages "their essential 'inner self' rather than their weakening physical 'outer self.'"[38]

Reference to an "inner self" reminds me of the Marie Curie nurse's phrase that religious people seem to have "more being." It echoes Pauline language and returns us to the pattern of baptismal and ongoing transformation. We "do not lose heart," wrote Paul. "Though our outer nature is wasting away, our inner nature is being renewed day by day" (II Cor. 4:16). Paul looked forward to the completion of this transformation on the other side of death. Not everyone, and not all Christians, take a postmortem view of inner growth. Some regard spiritual development when dying as pertinent only for the here and now, and for what can be passed on to others. Either way, an emphasis on the inner person is empowering when one's outer person is fading, and it helps to shift priorities; people come to feel that the most important part of them is growing. In this way, they may feel accomplished in their dying. "Death can cause a human being to become what he or she was called to become," writes Mitterrand; "it can be, in the fullest sense of the word, an *accomplishment*."[39]

Euthanasia and Assisted Dying

The virtues of participation and empowerment become confused in debates over euthanasia and assisted suicide, where loss of physical autonomy and loss of control in relation to our end-of-life care are often the main points of concern.

Euthanasia has been legalized in the Netherlands, Belgium (since 2002), and Luxembourg (since 2009); assisted suicide, in Switzerland (since 1942), and in the states of Washington, Oregon (in the 1990s), and Montana (in 2009).[40] In assisted suicide, the patient is the last causal actor; in euthanasia the doctor or other agent is. An assisted suicide bill was brought before the Scottish Parliament in 2012. The bill is for new legislation to permit assisted suicide for those who voluntarily request it and who have either a "terminal illness" or a "terminal condition" and find their life intolerable.[41] A previous bill, which included provision for voluntary euthanasia, was defeated in 2010, although a poll conducted at the time suggested that 77 percent of adult Scots backed the proposal.[42]

Since compassion is a paramount factor, Christian responses to assisted suicide proposals are divided. There is international research, however, showing that physicians who are religious are less likely than those who are agnostic or atheist to support physician-assisted suicide, and that religious patients are less likely to request it.[43]

Religious people receiving end-of-life care sometimes say that God has a time for them to die, meaning that they will accept death but will not hasten it.[44] For Christians, there may be at least two strains of thought informing this attitude: that it is God who gives and takes life, and that we should not come into God's presence unsummoned.[45] In Christian thinking, we participate in our dying by giving up our spirit. This maps our dying onto the pattern of Jesus's death. Jesus did not befriend death but surrendered to it when his time came, waiting until the conditions were fully ripe for death to yield life.

Correspondingly, chaplains or accompaniers help people to give up their spirit by helping them to resolve any concerns that are "tethering them to life." Chaplains do not, like doctors, have a duty to preserve life, nor are they likely to struggle, as doctors often do, with views of death as a failure. They accept the irretrievable process of dying and, like midwives, help a person through this process when the right time comes.

At least three attitudes toward death are at play in these perspectives, which says much about the complexity of our deliberations. The language of "surrender" is colored by Christian negotiations with death as friend or foe. Death is a friend who can put suffering to an end and can also be our final accomplishment or transformation; death is an enemy, albeit a vanquished enemy, whom we do not embrace until it has come to claim us. We keep these personifications of death out of medical and legal debate, where prolonged illness rather than death is seen as the greater "enemy." More pertinent for public debate is a third attitude to death that is also available to Christians: death as a natural process. This natural attitude sits well with environmental emphases, and is expressed in the wider culture in the growing trend for woodland burials. A natural view is also present in the palliative perspective of letting death run its course, and is apparent in some instances of hospice after-care, as in the case of a toddler being allowed to crawl over the body and coffin of her deceased mother.[46] But a natural view is complex in end-of-life debates because medical science has made new things possible. Our ability to prolong the most limited of lives obscures a sense of a natural end. In the meantime, where people's hopes for euthanasia or assisted suicide are dashed, they are forced to live out prolonged suffering. In this unhappy state of affairs, it is some relief to find statistics showing that where the quality of palliative care increases, the numbers of people opting for euthanasia or assisted suicide (in parts of the world where these are an option) decreases.[47]

The Art of Dying Retrieved

Paradoxically, by "surrendering" to our circumstances, we take part in what is happening to us. There is Christian debate over whether illness is to be resisted or accepted, which parallels the ambiguity over death as enemy or friend.[48] George Sheehan describes his experience of trying each approach when receiving treatment for cancer. Initially he resisted illness, just as Jacob had wrestled with God.[49] Then he surrendered and found himself back in the "Eden" of his childhood: "It is a land where seven and seventy are kin. Where there are no concerns other than playing and learning and loving. The inhabitants of this land are in no hurry. Our days are dense with experiences. We have, as the Spanish say, more time than life."[50] Sheehan is describing what is sometimes called "intensive living," which is a medical, psychological, and social concept that contrasts with hectic living.[51] The concept conveys how life can be transformed in the face and knowledge of death. Alistair Campbell asked his friend Philip Gould, "You can't really be happy you are going to die?" Gould replied, "No," but "these days and weeks have been amazing, maybe the most intense days and feelings of my life. It has made me feel whole. It has made me appreciate my life, my politics, my family, my friendships, more than I would if I had gone on and on and died of old age."[52]

The art of dying is full of the paradoxes of giving things up only to find we get them back in a new way: our loved ones, time, our sense of our own bodies, our dignity, our very lives in terms of the intensity and insight with which we live them.

I do not have room to say much about ministry at the time of death or afterward. The few words I will say in these areas touch on how Christian ministers themselves practice the art of dying as they support and accompany others.

I began this lecture by noting our secular and multifaith context in the West. Throughout I have shown ways in which Christian ministry has needed to adapt, for example, to funerals that are barely funerals, and to spiritual care that is not religious. Health care chaplain Ewan Kelly describes a funeral that he created with a bereaved family and in which there was no mention of God, the afterlife, or any other religious belief or affiliation. (Being approached to facilitate such funerals is increasingly common in Scotland and, I have found, in England.) The funeral director asked Kelly: "Do you find it hard not to mention the Lord?" These are Kelly's reflections: "The Lord was implicitly a large part of . . . the funeral" and of the way it was constructed. This is because Kelly made himself vulnerable as the minister, by being fully alongside the grieving family and responding to their needs in a way that required him to let go of his professional tools. Kelly sees himself as embodying "Christ's life and teaching," serving as Christ would serve.[53] An Australian hospital chaplain puts it this way: "A helping relationship helps by the helper making himself vulnerable— running the risk not just of professional inadequacy but of personal helplessness in order that change may come about. If the helper is not open to change, neither will the patient be open."[54] The proper balance, Kelly explains, is between vulnerability and appropriate use of authority.

I will end with two stories from Christian accompaniers who felt themselves die to their professional knowledge and training and plunge into feelings of helplessness, and in that dying found their Christian ministry returned to them.

A hospital chaplain told me of a time when he was asked to administer the last rites to a man who was greatly distressed but who could not speak. Not being able to hear his confession, the chaplain had to fall back on whatever resources were to hand, which were his hands and those of the nurses present. He asked the man to offer his distress to God, so that God could transform it. The man became calm, and he and the nurses anointed him with oil. This occasion brought peace to the dying man, insight to the chaplain, and also returned something of great value to the nurses. It put them back in touch with what they came to call "the sacramental side of their vocation," as they saw themselves attending to patients bodily in a way that went beyond the basic functions of applying drips and toileting.[55]

The final story is from Jane Millard, a colleague of mine who had a ministry among the many AIDS sufferers in Edinburgh in the 1980s and 1990s. She would clean and shop for them and watch with them when they were dying. As she waited with them, she would jot down thoughts and things they had said that would help her to construct their funerals. She called these jottings "fragments of the Watch." Her bishop at that time, Richard Holloway, has encouraged her to let him publish some of these fragments. One concerns a young woman who was very afraid of dying. "I don't want to die," she said. "Him upstairs will get a big stick and shout at me, tell me to go to hell. I'm frightened. I don't want to be shouted at."

> And I hugged her [Jane Millard wrote], bereft of anything theological to say that sounded real, and she snuggled in.
> "Talk to me," she whimpered.
> "There was a man who had two sons . . ." and I told her the story of the prodigal son and loving father.
> "Will you be with me when I die? Be sure and tell me that story."
> So I did, about an hour ago; now we are waiting for the undertakers.[56]

Notes

1. Philippe Ariès, *The Hour of Our Death: The Classic History of Attitudes Toward Death over the Last One Thousand Years*, trans. Helen Weaver, 2nd ed. (New York: Vintage Books, 2008), 560.

2. Cruse Bereavement Care was founded in 1959 in Richmond upon Thames. www.crusebereavementcare.org.uk/. Specialist bereavement charities include SeeSaw Grief Support, www.seesaw.org.uk/, and www.seesaw.org.uk/files/schoolInfoPack.pdf; Road for you, www.rd4u.org.uk/; and London Friend—Lesbian & Gay Bereavement, www.londonfriend.org.uk.

3. Elisabeth Kübler-Ross, *On Death and Dying* (London: Routledge, 1990); and Elisabeth Kübler-Ross and David Kessler, *On Grief and Grieving: Finding the Meaning of Grief through the Five Stages of Loss* (London: Simon and Schuster, 2005). The five stages discussed are denial, anger, bargaining, depression, and acceptance.

4. John Leland, "Heaven Comes Down to Earth," *New York Times Week in Review*, sec. 4, p. 1, December 21, 2003, quoted in Christopher Morse, *The Difference Heaven Makes: Rehearing the Gospel as News* (London: T&T Clark, 2010), 102. Morse notes that the data has stayed the same at the end of the decade.

5. Albert Schweitzer, "Overcoming Death," in *Reverence for Life*, trans. Reginald H. Fuller (London: SPCK, 1974), 67–76.

6. Ibid., 71, 69, 73–74.

7. Ibid., 75.

8. Henry Scott Holland, "King of Terrors," in *Facts of the Faith: Being a Collection of Sermons Not Hitherto Published in Book Form by Henry Scott Holland*, ed. C. Cheshire, 125–34 (London: Longmans, Green & Co., 1919).

9. Ibid., 134.

10. E.g., Jeremy Taylor, *Rules and Exercises of Holy Dying* (1651), preface. Ariès (*Hour of Our Death*, 196–97) cites a similar work, *Miroir de l'âme du pécheur et du juste: Méthode chrétienne pour finir saintement sa vie*, 2 vols. (1741, 1752).

11. This point can be extended to other rites that are counted as sacraments in parts of the church: confirmation, in which we are strengthened on our baptismal path; reconciliation, in which we die to our sins; anointing of the sick (formerly known as Extreme Unction and performed at the Last Rites); marriage, in which couples make their vows "till death us do part" (formerly "depart"); and the Holy Orders of those who administer the sacraments in their sustaining of the faithful as "a living sacrifice acceptable to God"; *Common Worship*: "The Ordination of Priests, also called Presbyters," from the bishop's introduction to the service. www.churchofengland.org/prayer-worship/worship/texts/ordinal/priests.aspx.

12. Schweitzer, "Overcoming Death," 73.

13. Collects, Evening Prayer on Friday, and Morning Prayer: Easter Season, *Common Worship Daily Prayer* (London: Church House Publishing, 2005), 190, 268.

14. See Henry L. Novello, *Death as Transformation: A Contemporary Theology of Death* (Burlington, VT: Ashgate, 2011).

15. *Common Worship Pastoral Services*, 2nd ed. (London: Church House Publishing, 2011), 236. In the phrases cited, the minister says the first words, and the words in bold are the response.

16. Douglas Davies, *The Theology of Death* (London: T&T Clark, 2008), 10–13.

17. Conversation with Rev. Tom Ravetz, minister of the Christian Community.

18. Hippolytus, *Apostolic Tradition*, 21.9 and 21.19. The tradition of using both oils was developed in the fourth and fifth centuries CE. For an example of contemporary practice, see Adrian Fortescue, J. B. O'Connell, and Alcuin Reid, OSB, *The Ceremonies of the Roman Rite Described*, 14th ed. (Farnborough, Hampshire: Saint Michael's Abbey Press, 2003), 413–14. In Eastern Orthodoxy, the oil of catechumens is used before baptism, and Chrismation is usually performed immediately after baptism as a distinct Sacred Mystery (or Sacrament).

19. Ambrose (e.g., *de Sac.* 1.4) placed greater emphasis on the struggle against the devil rather than on exorcising evil; he likened the oil to that rubbed on athletes, so that the oil came to be seen as strengthening candidates for the struggle (*ascesis*) of the Christian life.

20. *Common Worship: Services and Prayers for the Church of England* (London: Church House Publishing, 2000), 353–57. *Rites on the Way*, published with the new edition of *CW Initiation Services* in 2005, makes provision for anointing at the point of decision (which

might be celebrated at a different time from the baptism). Assurance is given that anointing before baptism "in no way negates the use of the oil of chrism after baptism"; Dana Delap, "Rites on the Way," in *A Companion to Common Worship*, vol. 2, ed. Paul Bradshaw (London: SPCK, 2006), 138.

21. Karen Armstrong, "I Must Hope that Others Will One Day Be Spared My Mother's Fate," *Guardian*, March 25, 2006, 32, quoted in Ewan Kelly, *Meaningful Funerals: Meeting the Theological and Pastoral Challenge in a Postmodern Era* (London: Mowbray, 2008), 20–21.

22. David Clark, "Between Hope and Acceptance: The Medicalisation of Dying," *British Medical Journal* 324: 905–7.

23. Quoted in Sandol Stoddard, *The Hospice Movement: A Better Way of Caring for the Dying* (New York: Vintage Books, 1992), 10–11.

24. Elizabeth MacKinlay, *Palliative Care, Ageing and Spirituality: A Guide for Older People, Carers and Families* (London: Jessica Kingsley, 2012), 68.

25. Scott A. Murray, "Spiritual Wellbeing and Physical Decline: Serial in Depth Interviews in the Last Year of Life," paper presented at Glasgow March 13, 2012.

26. Quoted in Abigail Rian Evans, *Is God Still at the Bedside? The Medical, Ethical, and Pastoral Issues of Death and Dying* (Grand Rapids, MI: Eerdmans, 2011), 279.

27. Wendy Hope, senior health care assistant, Marie Curie, Inverness, in conversation with the author, 2012.

28. Liz Grant, Scott A. Murray, and Aziz Sheikh, "Spiritual Dimensions of Dying in Pluralist Societies," *British Medical Journal*, September 17, 2010, doi:10.1136/bmj.c4859; and Evans, *Is God Still at the Bedside?*, 277–78.

29. Evans, *Is God Still at the Bedside?*, 335; and Neil Pembroke, *Pastoral Care in Worship: Liturgy and Psychology in Dialogue* (London: T&T Clark, 2010), 121.

30. E.g. see the arts projects with schools run by St Christopher's Hospice in London, www.stchristophers.org.uk/public-education/schools-project.

31. Arthur W. Frank, *The Wounded Storyteller: Body, Illness, and Ethics* (Chicago: University of Chicago Press, 1995), 53.

32. Marie de Hennezel, *Intimate Death: How the Dying Teach Us to Live*, trans. Carol Brown Janeway (London: Warner Books, 1997), 34–36.

33. Viktor E. Frankl, *Man's Search for Meaning: The Classic Tribute to Hope from the Holocaust* (New York: Beacon Press, 1959), quoted by many, including Evans, *Is God Still at the Bedside?*, 341.

34. E.g., Grant, Murray, and Sheikh, "Spiritual Dimensions of Dying."

35. Evans, *Is God Still at the Bedside?*, 274.

36. Francois Mitterrand, "Foreword," in de Hennezel, *Intimate Death*, ix.

37. Frank, *Wounded Storyteller*, xi.

38. Grant, Murray, and Sheikh, "Spiritual Dimensions."

39. De Hennezel, *Intimate Death*, ix.

40. Physician-assisted suicide became legal in the Netherlands in 2002, although it is a less popular option there than euthanasia, which has been possible since the 1970s and 1980s through a series of decisions not to prosecute and processes of formalizing criteria.

41. A proposal for consultation was published by Margo MacDonald MSP on January 23, 2012; www.scottish.parliament.uk/parliamentarybusiness/Bills/46127.aspx. Detailed legislation will not be produced unless and until the consultation is concluded and the proposal receives sufficient support from MSPs.

42. Twelve percent opposed it and the remainder were unsure. " 'Support' for MSP Margo MacDonald's Right-to-Die Bill," *BBC*, November 23, 2010, www.bbc.co.uk/news/uk-scot land-11821324.

43. "Religion Is a Factor," *Connection* 1, no. 4 (Summer 2007); and Edmund D. Pellegrino, "Euthanasia and Assisted Suicide," in *Dignity and Dying: A Christian Appraisal*, ed. John F. Kilner, Arlene Miller and Edmund D Pellegrino, 105–99 (Grand Rapids, MI: Eerdmans, 1996), both cited in Evans, *Is God Still at the Bedside?*, 133.

44. Wendy Hope, conversation with author.

45. On this Thomist argument against suicide, see, e.g., Paul Ramsey, *Ethics at the Edge of Life* (New Haven, CT: Yale University Press, 1978), 147.

46. Wendy Hope, conversation with author.

47. Based on findings in the Netherlands, and in Oregon and Washington states. See Evans, *Is God Still at the Bedside?*, 128–30.

48. E.g., Pembroke, *Pastoral Care in Worship*, 122–23, and his discussion of biographies on these themes.

49. He was following the advice of Max Lerner, *Wrestling with the Angel* (New York: W. W. Norton, 1990). This and other narratives are discussed by L. Bregman and S. Thiermann, *First Person Mortal: Personal Narratives of Dying, Death, and Grief* (New York: Paragon House, 1995), which is also discussed by Pembroke, *Pastoral Care in Worship*, 120–23.

50. George Sheehan, *Going the Distance: One Man's Journey to the End of His Life* (New York: Villard, 1996), 87–90, quoted in Pembroke, *Pastoral Care in Worship*, 122–23.

51. Davies, *Theology of Death*, 73–74.

52. Alistair Campbell, *The Happy Depressive: In Pursuit of Personal and Professional Happiness* (Cornerstone Digital [ebook]), January 2012.

53. Kelly, *Meaningful Funerals*, 118–19.

54. Bruce Rumbold, quoted in ibid., 121.

55. Beau Stevenson, pastoral care advisor to the Diocese of Oxford; conversation with the author, 2012.

56. Richard Holloway, *Leaving Alexandria: A Memoir of Faith and Doubt* (Edinburgh: Canongate, 2012), 258.

Response to Harriet Harris

RECEP ŞENTÜRK

D r. Harris's essay has reminded me of my own observations, as an individual and as a sociologist of religion, of practices in the United States and Turkey in the period leading up to the death of my sister, Zeynep. I hope that my response will shed light on the divergent ways in which people in different societies today approach dying and think about what is involved in a good death.

Zeynep was diagnosed with breast cancer at the age of thirty. She was first treated for about a year in New York, where she was living with her family. Eventually, the American doctors advised us to take her to a local nursing home where she would be cared for until her death. But one doctor, a Muslim from Pakistan, advised us to take Zeynep back to Istanbul, so that she could spend the last days of her life in her homeland with her extended family and friends, and we took this advice.

In Istanbul, when Zeynep's situation worsened further, we took her to a hospital. After examining her, the doctors gave conflicting advice. However, one doctor, a pious Muslim, advised us not to check her into the hospital but to take her home. He said: "I can check her in here and wire her up in the intensive care room and charge you for it. You will not be allowed to enter the intensive care room. She will die alone. Why not take her home? Let her die in her home surrounded with her family; read the Holy Qur'ān at her deathbed and comfort her with your presence and good words."

So we took Zeynep home and cared for her during her last hours. The entire family was there, including our parents, sisters, brothers, her husband and children, in-laws, and some friends. They were all reading the Holy Qur'ān, praying and performing *dhikr*. There was no doctor present, and there were no wires on her body. One of us was constantly repeating the words of testimony (*shahāda*): "There is no god but God and Muḥammad is His messenger." Zeynep was herself also repeating these words silently. Then she stopped. She took her last breath in our presence. This was the "good death" (*ḥusn al-khātima*) for which she had prayed her whole life. Muslims pray for a good death and make preparations for it. They believe that a good death is the outcome of a good life. It is commonly repeated that "the way you presently live will be the way you will eventually die."

The experience of Zeynep's death made me aware of the different ways in which death is viewed and approached in the modern world. Both in the United States and in Turkey, we encountered a range of perspectives and of advice from doctors, health care professionals, and clergy. In her essay, Harris also illustrates a variety of opinions and practices regarding the good death and dying well. She describes succinctly how Christians in contemporary Western society, in particular Britain, deal with death and dying in a rapidly changing wider context. She demonstrates that practice is increasingly moving away from traditional Christian forms and attributes this to growing secularization, to the spread of new trends, particularly new forms of spirituality, and to the presence of other religions. Likewise, the role of the doctor, health care professional, and psychologist is increasing at the expense of the role of the theologian and minister.

Harris's essay leaves us with the question: What is the Christian way of dying well in today's world? It seems there is no unanimous and clear answer, partly because of the divergent religious interpretations and practices but mainly because death has become so commercialized and medicalized.

What is death and what causes it? Harris demonstrates that answers to these questions are now provided mostly by medical science rather than by theology. Death is no longer seen as a fate decided by God but rather as the failure of bodily health. Medical science tells us how and why bodily health fails, prior to death, so people turn to the medical doctor and not to the theologian for answers to their questions about death.

Harris shows that Christians are absorbing and internalizing new practices and trends. One could speak of these practices as being Christianized; alternatively, one could say that Christianity, or at least Christian practice, is being changed. Is this good or bad for Christianity? Harris demonstrates the ambivalent feelings of Christians toward recent developments. Christianity continues to bestow meaning upon death and to offer comfort to those who are dying. Yet there are competing efforts, especially on the part of psychologists, to give meaning to death and to comfort those who are dying and those close to them.

I conclude with some brief observations regarding practices around death and dying in Turkey. While most of the issues mentioned by Harris occupy Muslims as well as Christians, since these are common human concerns, there are also some differences. For instance, the practice of cremation, which is so common in the West, is extremely rare in the Muslim world; to my knowledge, there is no crematorium in Turkey or other parts of the Muslim world because this practice is considered a cardinal sin in Islam. In Turkey, municipalities provide free services before the funeral, such as keeping the body in the funeral home or morgue, washing it, and transporting it to the mosque for the funeral prayers and to the cemetery for the burial. The burial site is also provided free by the municipality unless the family wants a lot in a special location. The mosque charges no money for the funeral services. In these and various other ways, we can conclude that in the Muslim world death is less commercialized and medicialized than in the Western world, and that the views of the theologians and traditional religious approaches continue to shape practices around death and dying more strongly than in the West.

A Muslim's Perspective on the Good Death, Resurrection, and Human Destiny

SAJJAD RIZVI

Before we even discuss death and what comes after, let alone attempt to analyze what might be a good death from a Muslim perspective, it's worth raising the difficult question of the horror of death and the consolation and hope that religion provides against it. At least since Plato in the European metaphysical tradition and in the foundational scriptures of what became the Abrahamic faiths of the Near East, one of the central roles of philosophy and religion was to make sense of and overcome death, the corruption and annihilation of the flesh. We see death as an end, a misfortune that strikes us, an evil that deprives us of the liberty of our life and existence, a pain that we feel as we transition away from this world. The horror seems greater if we take death to be a final closure and as a pain and evil that is inflicted not just directly upon us but also on those we leave behind, those who love us and whom we love. The radical idea that the Prophet Muḥammad taught and proclaimed through the early revelations of the Qur'ān was not that death was a certainty (which the pre-Islamic Arabs understood). Rather, he proclaimed that death was an opening to an afterlife and that the sudden shock of death associated in vivid imagery with both natural evils such as earthquakes and moral evils such as witchcraft required that humans understand the message from God to recognize him and to take on a moral obligation to live a good life culminating in a good death so that they may enjoy the fruits of that life and death in everlasting life hereafter.

In the classical philosophical tradition, two central "cures" were suggested for overcoming death. First were the notions that a better understanding of reality would allow one to place death in a wider context, that fleeing evil entails seeking to replicate a rational understanding of the cosmos that is available to God, and that this process involves the apotheosis of the human in which death was merely a short step along the way.[1] A life seeking the truth and dedicated to inquiry was therefore one way of overcoming the horror of death. Seeking the face of God and inculcating within the self the virtues of the divine were the equivalent processes for this practice of philosophy in the Muslim traditions. The second contribution was to posit that true identity and personhood lay with your immortal soul that preexisted and survived the death of the body, which in itself was a material thing that grew and wasted away.[2] A corollary to this was the acknowledgment that true life and death were not defined by the activity of the body; as Imām ʿAlī ibn Abī Ṭālib, the cousin and successor of the Prophet Muḥammad, put it, "people are asleep and when they die, they awake," and "sleep is like death."[3] Being in a state of wakeful awareness was seen as the opposite of death, and life was defined by the presence in the heart of the reality of God and the company of the friends of God.[4] Similarly, the path to God had both an earthly element and a sense in the afterlife; hence, death was only a stage along this path. Death is, therefore, not the worst that can happen to humans, as Plato put it, because it is not an end. Much of the premodern Islamic theological tradition is predicated on developing and disciplining the soul and body with the sense of their radical contingency, dualism, and holism.

Of course, the Epicureans dissented from this discomfort in the face of death and had a different approach, expressed in their famous maxim, "death is nothing to us."[5] If we believe that death is nothingness and nothing comes after it, this forces us to seek the good life (not the good death). One can find similar accounts in nontheistic religions and those that reject the notion of an afterlife. But insofar as death is an evil that we encounter, there is a strong tradition within the monotheisms of pious indignation at it, and of railing at God.[6] Since at least the Enlightenment, the fundamental problem of evil, the existence of both natural disasters such as earthquakes and moral failures such as genocide have provided the primary argument against the existence of God or a singular deity, the so-called argument from evil.[7]

Arguably, polytheisms, whether henotheisms or at least non-monotheisms, have less of a problem here since failings of a human, suprahuman, and natural kind can be explained by the existence of different and even squabbling gods. Even the Qurʾān refers, critically, to this implication of belief in a non-monotheistic order (21:22). Monotheisms tend to see themselves, or so the main narrative seems to suggest, as singular discourses of the power of a God-King whose tyrannical diktat cannot be violated. This idea of the divine could be construed from the divine names themselves: *al-qahhār*, the subduer; *al-ḍārr*, the afflicter; *al-khāfiḍ*, the humiliater; *al-makkār*, the cunning; *al-jabbār*, the compeller; and *al-muqtadir*, the dominator. But he is also the merciful, *al-raḥmān*, and the lover, *al-wadūd*—this contrast between the just and wrathful God and the merciful and loving Lord is a central tension within monotheism.

However, monotheisms also produce the faithful believer who rails against God—a Job, a Kierkegaard, and even a Christ on the cross, figures who, precisely because they believe, cannot stay silent in the midst of trial and tribulation. In Islamic contexts, we tend to prefer the faithful submitter and yet forget, to our spiritual and intellectual peril, the one who will not remain silent. We prefer the pious to be good and to keep their silence, and not to be loud and contrary because of the virtues of thankfulness and patience. In the words of the Qurʾān, "But give glad tidings to the patient, who surely when they are visited by an affliction say, 'surely we belong to God and to him we return,' upon them rest blessings and mercy from their Lord, and they are verily the truly guided" (2:155).[8] Poets such as the twelfth-century liminal poet ʿAṭṭār of Nishapur or Sufis contemporary to ʿAṭṭār such as ʿAyn al-Quẓāt Hamadānī (d. 1131) or Ibn ʿArabī (d. 1240), or even more recently poets such as Muḥammad Iqbāl (d. 1938) are precisely such examples of the believer who must complain to God. Atheism can be just a brief step away from this metaphysical revolt, an expression of a careless neglect, a silence, and an inability to rail against one whom one denies. Ultimately, one only reproaches the object of one's love. But even in the face of horrors such as the misfortune of the death of a child, the ultimate response to human frailty is the Qurʾānic *istirjāʿ*: we are from God and to him we return—or even more strongly, we are God's and we are returning to it (i.e., the state of being God's). Our existence is this world is thus a temporary rupture in our everlasting life as God's; our life in this world is but a transient period of suffering during which we are sustained by the hope of return. In the presence of hope, of a return to an original state of being, of being received back by God, there is always faith.

But the idea of the good death in Islamic traditions is about the culmination of a good earthly life and the transition to the afterlife. It is the success of a believer whose heart, in the words of a famous saying attributed to the successors of the Prophet, the Imāms of the Shīʿī tradition, has been tested for faith: it is this believer who has been tested, *muʾmin mumtaḥan*, whose good death is sought and becomes exemplary. It is such a believer who bears the cause of the friends of God, a cause that is difficult to sustain and is arduous (ṣaʿb mustaṣʿab).[9] Therefore, one cannot fail to locate this trial in narratives and stories of sacrifice and martyrdom; and the preparation for the good death, understanding what that means and how it is sought, is best approached through stories of heroic culmination that speak to our human desire for narrative. I will mention in this context three such stories of sacrifice and martyrdom.

But a quick note before that. In her wonderful trilogy deconstructing the Western metaphysical tradition, Grace Jantzen argued that the obsession with mortality, with violence, and with sacrifice occluded the stress upon natality and life that ought to be central to vibrant and creative religious traditions.[10] In our society, our experience of sacrifice, especially of life, is actually relegated to certain ritual contexts in which we, in a rather impersonal manner, commemorate those who went before, notably in various remembrances that we perform. However, the reality of sacrifice as an infringement upon the self and the altruism of witnessing involved tends to make us uncomfortable—and discomfort is certainly one of the great modern sins. Speaking of martyrdom within an Islamic context further raises all sorts of eyebrows and probably has people reaching for their phones to call the security services. It is indeed one of the great tragedies of our time that the nihilist and thoroughly profane terrorism associated with the al-Qaeda brand has been given the name of a sanctified struggle (jihād) that culminates in martyrdom. Jihād as the existential struggle to become as God wishes us to be has been lost in translation in our public discourse. The difference, of course, between the suicide of such terrorist acts and martyrdom lies precisely in the authenticity of the witness to truth and the desire not only to imitate the good death but also to indicate the good life both on this earth and in the afterlife that the Islamic traditions celebrate. The nihilism of a suicide attack involves an arrogation of power, taking away what was never one's own, instead of the free giving through witness that true martyrdom suggests.

The first sacrifice is that of Abel, an unintentional sacrifice and also arguably the first crime of passion inasmuch as both Cain and Abel are described in the scriptural traditions as vying with each other for the favor of the divine beloved. In the Islamic accounts, Abel's death is, *pace* Jantzen, actually a rejection of violence and an embrace of true life beyond this world. It also bears a key moral, without which it seems we would not know how to transition from this life.

Cain's panic and despondency and sense of guilt at his act of fratricide is par-
tially expiated by the little drama of the two ravens that unfolds before him and
guides him to the means for recognizing the death of his brother and preparing
funerary rites and burial (Qur'ān 5:27–31). That God provides this guidance is
critical—after all, it would be unjust, as the theological traditions have observed,
for God to place upon the shoulders of believers the burden of a moral obligation that they could not bear without also providing guidance and grace to
facilitate their fulfillment of that obligation. In this sense, our every act of burial
of the deceased is an imitation and recollection of this first funeral on the earth.
But this is lost in distant memory.

The next sacrifice is associated with the test of Abraham and his son. It
matters not for me or, indeed, for the argument whether that son was Isaac or
Ishmael. For many a theologian over the ages, it was precisely the most horrific
trial imaginable for a father to be asked to sacrifice his son. The lesson of the
good death implicit in this sacrifice was the central notion of patience and
forbearance: the son says to Abraham in the Qur'ān that he should carry out
the divine command and he will find him to be patient (37:102-3). Such a
sacrifice and embrace of a good death must be based on certainty and trust,
precisely those virtues with respect to the divine and to the afterlife that we find
most difficult to understand because our sense of what we know is often tied
up with what we have experienced in this world. The very idea of accepting the
truth of a vision seems to us absurd. Yet this narrative is for the Muslim reen-
acted in one of the central highlights of the ritual year through the *hajj* pilgrimage and the festival of the sacrifice that coincides with it. Here the believer
makes the sacrifice to connect himself with the tradition and reminds himself
of the certainty of death and the need for patience in the face of it as a transition;
in the cutting of the throat of the animal, the believer symbolically annihilates
the animal self that takes one away from God. The killing of the animal symbol-
izes not the death of the beast but the triumph over the flesh and the spiritual
life that comes from submitting and trusting in God.[11] But the sacrifice of Abraham is also a sacrifice that was intended, not fulfilled but postponed.

The Qur'ān talks about the sacrifice of Abraham being ransomed by a great
sacrifice. and over the centuries exegetes have argued about how the ram could
possibly substitute the son and actually be a "great sacrifice" (*dhibḥ ʿaẓīm*—
37:107). Others, particularly in the Shīʿī tradition, have argued that the substitu-
tion indicated is a postponed sacrifice and martyrdom, again of a son of the

prophet, indeed the grandson of the Prophet Muḥammad, Ḥusayn. This is the third sacrifice and martyrdom that evokes the good death in the Muslim tradition. It is the martyrdom of Ḥusayn at Karbala, alongside his family and small group of companions, and following the example of his father ʿAlī (struck down in the act of prostration by a poisoned sword) and of his brother Ḥasan (poisoned to prevent his speaking truth to power and manifesting the sanctity of his person) that provide those commemorating the events with the ability to see in those acts of sacrifice the culmination of exemplary life that the friends of God present. The association between the good life and the good death is thus memorialized in a famous slogan adorning many a sticker and banner in Shīʿī communities around the world: "Live like ʿAlī and die like Ḥusayn."

The witnessing of Ḥusayn and the pathos of the situation is the passion of many a play and the enactment in which the very narrative of Karbala provides a frame for the understanding of what constitutes good and evil. The suffering of Ḥusayn and his family and companions and the forbearance, patience, and resolution of his sisters, Zaynab and Umm Kulthūm, as well as his son, ʿAlī, are the primarily motifs in an annual commemoration in the month of Muḥarram during which believers, together with others who cannot fail to be moved by the narrative, share in the suffering. As they do so, they understand the primary notion of justice and through their ritual mourning of Ḥusayn grasp the nature of the good life and the good death. Yet there is much about Karbala that goes against the grain. The bodies of the martyrs lie on the sands unburied for days, but once buried, these sacred spaces become locations for shrines, for acts of intercession for believers seeking a better destiny for themselves, and even for burial sites close to the tombs of the saints. The graveyard next to the shrine of ʿAlī, particularly in Najaf, is one of the largest in the world and is called the "valley of peace," linking it to the eschatological space mentioned in ḥadīth where the good reside as they await resurrection. Burying one's beloved in Najaf connects them to that space, but ultimately any godly soul buried anywhere in the world is linked back to that valley.

Mourning for Ḥusayn is much more than just an act of redemptive suffering, more than just a site for understanding Christology in Islam in which Ḥusayn takes on the person and function of Christ.[12] Mourning is a response to the gift of martyrdom and hope carried on to the Eschaton. Whenever someone dies, part of the funerary ceremonies includes the convocation of a mourning session for Ḥusayn in which the story is retold and connected to the death of the deceased. The pain and evil that the family feels at the loss of their beloved pales compared with the loss of the beloved friend of God, the son of Fāṭima, the daughter of the Prophet. The tears shed over Ḥusayn are a cathartic release for the family and the friends. Then, at every level through the funeral prayer, through the ceremonies at the burial, Karbala is evoked and enacted.

The prayer leader testifies on behalf of all those present that we know nothing but good about the deceased, that regardless of the manner of his death, he lived a good life in faith, in remembrance of the friends of God and died in that state. The body is shrouded by cloth that is often acquired from Karbala with talismanic prayers linking the person to the memory of Ḥusayn. As the body is lowered into the grave, usually the son or similar intimate of the dead person addresses him and recites the *talqīn*, a creedal prayer in which the dead person is prepared for the questions in the grave and told to remember that he is a lover of the Prophet and his family and as such can never be harmed by the horror of the grave or by being consumed by the fire. A small clay tablet of earth from Karbala that is normally used ritually in prayer is placed on the chest to symbolize not only the intimacy between the deceased and Karbala but also the location of Karbala in his heart. Often the handkerchief that the deceased may have used to wipe away the tears shed for Ḥusayn is also buried with him. These are all signals to remind those burying the person of the links to the sacred and of death as a transition to the presence of the divine and the company of God's friends, and as a signal for the angels when they come to question the deceased in the grave that here lies a lover of Ḥusayn. Through all these small ritual acts, Karbala defines and determines the good death and the good life for many believers. Through the life of the grave, the lovers of Ḥusayn enjoy a taste of the beatitude that is to come in paradise. When they are raised, the daughter of the Prophet intercedes for them and ushers them into paradise where they enjoy the face of the divine and the company of the friends of God.

One last aspect of the martyrdom of Karbala that should be mentioned here is the messianic element, with its links to eschatology. From an early stage, Muslim beliefs tied redemption through the person of a messianic figure with the Eschaton—the notion of the Mahdī. Messianism was postponed from the person of Muḥammad to one of his descendants. The Shīʿī tradition in particular linked the rising of the Mahdī with the enactment and commemoration of the sacrifice and martyrdom of Ḥusayn. Not only is the Mahdī the descendant and inheritor of Ḥusayn and like him of all the prophets; he is also the avenger of Ḥusayn.[13] The Mahdī calls people to remember the good death of Ḥusayn and to dissociate themselves from the killers of Ḥusayn, not just the historical figures involved in his murder but also the principles of injustice, oppression, lack of mercy, and absence of love that they embody. The vengeance of the Mahdī is about the triumph of love and of life over evil and death. As a figure of the end of days, the Mahdī brings closure, alongside Jesus, to this earthly existence, punctuating it and ushering in the resurrection.[14]

Both the resurrection and final destiny are corollaries to the good life and death of the believer. However, to use the metaphor of the scriptures, the death of the body is not the closing of the book on the worth of the person. Rather, as the famous ḥadīth of the Prophet states, the person continues to flourish in the grave and beyond through her good works performed in the world, through acts of charity and benefit established in the world, and through her children who continue to bear witness to truth and to serve their fellow humans. As mentioned earlier, unlike some other Muslim traditions, the Shīʿī tradition in particular sees the human person as continuing to flourish and grow, constantly being in a state of becoming into the resurrection and beyond. The Safavid religious teacher Mullā Ṣadrā Shīrāzī (d. 1635), for example, held that the very essence of the human was to seek perfection and the good because that was its innate nature embedded in the soul.[15] But that soul could not exist apart from the body. Since the soul was a creative force, linked to the world of the divine command (Qurʾān 17:85), it did not die at the death of the body but merely tasted death and then at the resurrection and again in the afterlife recreated a perfect projection of the book whose memory it retained from this world. In this way, Mullā Ṣadrā attempted to grapple with the philosophical problem of how to demonstrate the scriptural doctrine of bodily resurrection and vindicate belief in a physical heaven and hell.

What sort of ethical implications might this theory of the person have? Most believers would probably be uncomfortable with an entirely metaphorical reading of the scriptural descriptions of the spaces for human destiny while understanding that a literal and physical interpretation is also difficult to defend. At the same time, religious life is not just about ideas and doctrines. The modern notion that we have in liberal, post-Enlightenment societies that restricts faith to matters of belief that are internally held, challenged, and rationally defended seems to be belied not only by the psychology of choices that we make that are not always entirely rational but also by the importance of rituals to symbolize and enact a faith that is not entirely rational. Our desire to reduce the totality of our cognitive agency to a particular form of rationality does not conform to our human experiences. By evoking the narratives and stories of the good death discussed in this essay, I redress such a reading of faith. But I want to finish with a reflection on how Mullā Ṣadrā's account may speak to one of the most challenging ethical dilemmas that we face in our society, the problem of euthanasia.

What can we say about euthanasia or assisted suicide? One's perspective depends on the terminology used. Because suicide is not condoned in most if not all forms of Islamic theological reasoning, the idea of assisted suicide will similarly struggle to find a positive reception. Euthanasia—I refer here to voluntary euthanasia that arises from an individual's choice—is predicated not only on the possibility of the autonomy of an individual's reasoning but also on how we tend to feel about pain and the self in the modern period. If the foundational myth of the modern person is the notion of negative liberty, with its claim that we ought not to be coerced or constrained in what we choose to do, then this raises both the sense of entitlement that we feel toward pleasure and the sense that we have a right not to feel pain, which is seen as an infringement upon our liberty. But such a liberal notion of selfhood and autonomy, which the modified tradition following Kwame Appiah, for example, would not uphold, is at odds with most forms of Islamic theological reasoning, which reject such a form of individual autonomy.[16] Returning to the idea discussed earlier of the believer whose heart is tested in faith, pain is not an end in itself or a state to be considered in isolation; it could be that pain in the short term leads to pleasure in the longer term, taking into consideration both the direct victim of pain as well as the indirect victims such as family and friends affected by a terminally ill person. Pain is recognized as a basic fact of human life; to live with the assumption that it is an infringement on the self or that it can be wholly expunged is rather naïve. Even if we were able to extinguish moral pains and evils (and most religious traditions at the very least seek to overcome them), natural pains and evils will still remain and still allow for the possibility of goodness to flourish in human life.

These are, of course, all points against euthanasia. But if the body of this life decays and is corrupted, and since medical practitioners often make decisions that many of us would recoil from in everyday life, and if the true self resides in the soul with the creative power to act as the instrument of God and recreate the body at resurrection and beyond, then does a momentary act of euthanasia in this life have negative implications for the final destination of the human? Can one decide to terminate the life of the body knowing full well that the soul will revive it in the afterlife? Such a theory may provide one possible way of opening the door for euthanasia, and there is a growing Islamic juridical literature that deals with the ethical problem with levels of ambiguity. The real problem, it seems, relates not to the person who suffers and wishes to end the life of the body but to the wider context—to friends and relatives and to a society that does not wish to see such a choice as a "good death" and indeed sees it as an arrogation of the liberty that humans do not possess.

Dilemmas posed from bioethics require us to think and respond theologically in a manner that is consistent with how we understand, enact, and memorialize the good death. The narratives of sacrifice and martyrdom that I have discussed provide openings through which one may approach the problem, but I do not pretend to offer an answer. I merely raise a few questions and realize that the theological responses that we seek are not primarily about the smaller theological questions of the nature of God, soteriology, and eschatology but about the larger questions of human experience and what we aspire to be in the footsteps of the friends of God.

Notes

1. This is famously discussed by Plato. See Dirk Baltzly, "The Virtues and 'Becoming Like God,'" *Oxford Studies on Ancient Philosophy* 26 (2004): 297–321; John Dürlinger, "Ethics and the Divine Life in Plato's Philosophy," *Journal of Religious Ethics* 13 (1985): 312–31; Pierre Hadot, *Philosophy as a Way of Life: Spiritual Exercises from Socrates to Foucault*, trans. Michael Chase (Oxford: Blackwell's, 1995); and John M. Cooper, *Pursuits of Wisdom: Six Ways of Life in Ancient Philosophy from Socrates to Plotinus* (Princeton, NJ: Princeton University Press, 2012).

2. See Richard Sorabji, *Self: Ancient and Modern Insights about Individuality, Life, and Death* (Oxford: Oxford University Press, 2006).

3. For most of these sayings, I draw upon the Safavid meditation upon the friends of God and their sanctity (*walāya*) articulated in Muḥsin Fayḍ Kāshānī, *Kalimāt-i maknūna*, ed. Ṣādiq Ḥasanzāda (Qum: Intishārāt-i Ishrāq, 1390 Sh/2011), 148, 166.

4. Ibid., 157, 241.

5. See the excellent study of James Warren, *Facing Death: Epicurus and His Critics* (Oxford: Clarendon Press, 2004).

6. Navid Kermani, *The Terror of God: Attar, Job, and the Metaphysical Revolt* (Cambridge: Polity Press, 2011).

7. Peter van Inwagen, *The Problem of Evil* (Oxford: Oxford University Press, 2006); Michael Tooley, "The Problem of Evil," in *Stanford Encyclopaedia of Philosophy*, http://plato.stanford.edu/entries/evil; Eric Ormsby, *Theodicy in Islamic Thought* (Princeton, NJ: Princeton University Press, 1984); Murtażā Muṭahharī, *'Adl-i ilāhī* (rpt., Qum: Intishārāt-i Ṣadrā, 1372 Sh/1993); and Ja'far Subḥānī, *al-Ilāhīyāt 'alā hudā al-kitāb wa-l-sunna wa-l-'aql*, transcribed by Shaykh Muḥammad Ḥasan Makkī al-'Āmilī, 4 vols. (Beirut: al-Dār al-Islāmīya, 1989).

8. Translations from the Qur'ān are my own.

9. Kāshānī, *Kalimāt-i maknūna*, 229.

10. Grace Jantzen, *Death and the Displacement of Beauty I: Foundations of Violence* (London: Routledge, 2004).

11. There is an extensive literature in the Islamic spiritual traditions on the symbolism of such rituals—for one example, see Ja'far al-Ṣādiq, attr., *Miṣbāḥ al-sharī'a [Inner Lanterns of the Path]*, trans. Asadullah Yate (London: Zahra Publications, 1991).

12. Mahmoud Ayoub, *Redemptive Suffering in Islam: A Study of the Devotional Aspects of 'Āshūrā in Twelver Shi'ism* (Berlin: Walter de Gruyter, 1978).

13. Here it is worth mentioning that the commemoration of Ḥusayn includes a salutation known as Ziyārat wārith, which addresses him as the heir of all the prophets whose qualities he bears, including being the heir of the sacrifice to God, Ishmael, and the heir of the Prophet Muḥammad.

14. Perhaps the best account of Shī'ī messianism and eschatology and how it relates to ontotheology is Henry Corbin, *En Islam iranien I* (Paris: Gallimard, 1972).

15. The best account of Mullā Ṣadrā's eschatology and of human becoming is his text *Zād al-musāfir*, embedded within Sayyid Jalāl al-Dīn Āshtiyānī, *Sharḥ bar Zād al-musāfir*, 4th pr. (Qum: Bustān-i kitāb, 1381 Sh/2002).

16. Kwame Anthony Appiah, *The Ethics of Identity* (Princeton, NJ: Princeton University Press, 2007).

Death and the Love of Life
A Response to Sajjad Rizvi

MIROSLAV VOLF

"Your young people love life," said Mullah Omar of the Taliban in Afghanistan about the youth of the West; "our young people love death." In Europe too, less than a century ago, a fascist general during the Spanish civil war exclaimed, "¡Viva la muerte!" ("Long live death!"). Though the terrorist ideologue and the fascist general were good at moving young men to wreak havoc on others and destroy themselves, they were bad interpreters of the religious traditions with which they are associated, Islam and Christianity.

The Christian faith is a religion of life.[1] In the Gospel of John, Jesus says, "The thief comes only to steal and kill and destroy. I came that they [his followers] may have life, and have it abundantly" (10:10). Life, not death, is a friend to love, a gift to celebrate. Since Christians believe in the "resurrection of the dead and the life everlasting" (Apostles' Creed), there is a new beginning even in our earthly end. To put the anthropological import of this eschatological conviction philosophically, our natality (to use the word Hannah Arendt developed into a philosophical category in distinction from her teacher, Martin Heidegger[2]) and the capacity for new beginnings tied to it is more important for the character of our existence than our mortality. We don't live merely toward death (with death being always already part of our existence, as Heidegger noted); we live out of a life always already given and toward the life promised. Death is a moment in a given and promised life, not a shadow cast from life's end over the whole. A proper stance toward life in the face of death is joy over the gift not owed us, not fear over the loss of what is ours by right.

Rizvi's generative essay—a text that invites readers to explore death as the boundary of their own existence, to ponder what the good death might look like, to connect the good death not just to the blissful eternal life that follows it but to the good earthly life that precedes it—makes it plain that Islam, too, is a religion of life, rather than, as Mullah Omar implied, a religion of death.

111

Though all humans are mortal, not all deaths are equal. In one respect, of course, everyone's death is the same: vital functions of the body cease, the heart comes to a halt, breath vanishes, brain activity stops. Yet, depending on the life we lead and how life goes for us, we experience physical death differently. In addition to death as a punishment for a crime, there are at least four significant kinds of death in the Christian sacred text (distinguishable as types but sometimes overlapping in actual experience). Although Rizvi doesn't mention them specifically, all four are implicit in his paper.

First, we experience death as the boundary of a finite life. Like the life of every living being on earth, human life has a beginning, phases of growth and maturation, and an end. Normally, when a life has run its full course, death comes. That's Abraham's death; the father of all the faithful "died in a good old age, an old man and full of years" (Gen. 25:8; see also Gen. 35:29; I Chron. 23:1). Second, sometimes death strikes unexpectedly and interrupts a life in its normal course. A person goes about her life and a mortal illness appears, an accident happens, or a murderer springs out from the shadows, and her life ends prematurely. That's Jairus's daughter's death; at twelve years old, she fell ill and died as her father was looking for help (Mark 5:21–43). Third, a person leads an upright life and receives approval from God and neighbors, but his self-centered competitor, envious and perhaps plagued by unacknowledged guilt, destroys him. That's Abel's death; his older brother, Cain, murdered him because Cain's "own deeds were evil and his brother's righteous" (1 John 3:12). Fourth, sometimes death is the consequence of a life devoted to promoting good in an environment poisoned by evil. A person seeks to change entrenched patterns of untruth, injustice, and violence, but evil, threatened, strikes back with a deadly force. That's Jesus's death; he gave his life to take away "the sin of the world" (John 1:29).

In the biblical traditions, only a death like Abraham's—a death after a life "full of years"—is to be embraced as a positive good, but even this kind of death we are never to seek. Instead, when life has run its full course, we are to welcome it as a gift (though what such welcoming precisely entails in the context of modern medicine will be a matter of debate). The other three kinds of death, however, constitute an enemy. This is obvious in the cases of Jairus's daughter's and Abel's kinds of deaths but perhaps less so in the case of Jesus's kind of death. Consider the following central verse about Jesus's death: "In this is love, not that we loved God but that he loved us and sent his Son to be the atoning sacrifice for our sins" (1 John 4:10). A death like Jesus's is a result of the active pursuit of a course of life—of a mission to which he was sent and which he embraced—and is therefore properly described as self-sacrifice even if others killed him. His death sets a framework for how Christians ought to think about self-sacrificial death and martyrdom.

This is not the place to develop a comprehensive sketch of a Christian theology of martyrdom except to point to three of its pillars. First, in distinction to what is implied in the slogans "¡Viva la muerte!" or "We love death!" the purpose of self-sacrificial death can never be the death of another person. Christ was killed because he refused to kill; he didn't die against anyone but on behalf of all. He died so that all "might live through him" (1 John 4:9). That's why, when he was apprehended, Jesus forbade Peter to defend him with a sword, and while he was hanging on the cross, he entreated God for the forgiveness of his crucifiers.

Second, death on behalf of others is not a good in its own right but, on occasions, a necessary means. True, since God sent Jesus Christ to die on behalf of others, God positively willed his death. But God willed it—and, as the eternal Word become flesh, he embraced it—as a necessary means. Had he seen his death as an unqualified good, Jesus would never have uttered the cry of dereliction on the cross: "My God, my God, why have you forsaken me?" (Mark 15:34).

Third, although Jesus's self-sacrificial death is a manifestation of God's love, his death is not entailed in the reality of God as love. Christ's death is the form God's love takes when faced with the contingent realities of human sin and enmity. Death of the self is not intrinsic to one's love for another; only under certain conditions does one's love for another lead to the death of the self.

As it is with Christ, so it is with his followers (or nearly so, given that none of them actually *are* Christ). Christ's followers must reject all "nihilistic" forms of violence (to use Rizvi's apt description of suicide attacks). When they sacrifice their own lives, they do so not because they love death but because they love life, the lives of others more than their own. Both Jesus and his followers are like a grain of wheat that falls into the earth, dies, and "bears much fruit" (John 12:24). I see analogues to such understanding of death—to Jesus's kind of death—in Rizvi's essay. But there may be also some significant disagreements on this point between Christians and Muslims (beyond the generally accepted, though perhaps not finally settled, difference in opinion among Christians and Muslims about whether Jesus actually died on the cross[3]).

One way to explore the differences between these religions' understandings of self-sacrificial death would be to inquire concerning the implications of the absence of the command to love one's enemies in Islam in contrast to this command's centrality in Christianity. Two and a half years before Islamic extremists killed Fr. Christian Marie de Chergé, prior of the Atlas monastery, along with six other Trappist monks, he composed a testament to be opened in the event of his martyrdom. At the end of the testament, which was read on May 26, 1996, two days after all seven gave their final witness, Father Christian addressed his killer: "And also you, the friend of my final moment, who would not be aware of what you were doing—yes, I also say this THANK YOU and this A-DIEU to you, in whom I see the face of God. And may we find each other, happy 'good thieves' in Paradise, if it pleases God, the Father of us both."[4] These last words of Father Christian's testament echo some of Jesus's last words on the cross (although Father Christian clearly sets himself apart from the innocence of Jesus by recognizing himself as a "thief"). They express love of enemy pushed to the extreme—the enemy is a friend in whom the face of God shines, and the transformed killer and the healed victim are envisioned happy together in paradise. Is a death like Father Christian's possible within Islam? If it is, does it express the highest ideals of Islam as it expresses the purest form of the Christian faith? Or would Muslims, along with many other non-Christians, see in it pitiful weakness masquerading as magnanimity?

The other way to explore the differences regarding self-sacrificial death may be to reflect on the place of forbearance in the face of death in both traditions. Rizvi addresses this issue directly. For Christians, the attitude toward Jesus's kind of death (death embraced in pursuit of the good in an evil world) hovers between the willing embrace of death and a bitter complaint about it, a willing embrace of death on account of the good that the person hopes the death will achieve and a bitter complaint on account of the loss of life that overcoming evil requires. We see this tension in Jesus as he faced death. On the one hand, throughout his ministry, Jesus's face was turned toward Jerusalem, where he knew that he "must undergo great suffering . . . and be killed" (Mark 8:31). On the other hand, in Gethsemane, just before he was arrested, he prayed: "Abba, Father, for you all things are possible; remove this cup from me; yet, not what

I want, but what you want" (Mark 14:36); and on the cross, just before he died, he prayed: "My God, my God, why have you forsaken me?" (Mark 15:34). He both embraced his self-sacrifice and wanted to avoid it; he both acted consistently as God demanded of him (the "must" of his suffering and death to which Mark refers was a "must" of divine decision not of the inexorable push of social and political events or of fate) and complained that God had forsaken him. Might there be a difference on this point between Christianity and Islam? I wish Rizvi had elaborated more on the "tradition of pious indignation" in Islam and explained how it is that the requirement of patience and forbearance doesn't crowd out the complaint and indignation.

The question about these two possible differences between Christianity and Islam leads me to one disagreement with Rizvi. The very last provocative sentence of Rizvi's essay reads: "the theological responses that we seek are not primarily about the smaller theological questions of the nature of God, soteriology, and eschatology but about the larger questions of human experience and what we aspire to be in the footsteps of the friends of God." I am a theologian, and although I can live with the contrast between adjectives "larger" and "smaller" in this sentence, I don't like the conjunction "but." It presumes that questions about "the nature of God, soteriology, and eschatology" aren't in a significant degree about "human experience and [about] what we wish to aspire to be." As I see it, every responsible theological exploration of God, salvation, and the last things *is* also and centrally a reflection on the nature of the self, social relations, and the good. The experience of mortality and the aspiration for a good death to crown a flourishing life are therefore tied up, I think, with our implicit or explicit convictions about God, salvation, and the last things.

Narratives of the lives of the friends of God inform theological convictions, of course. At the same time, these narratives are themselves framed by theological convictions. That's why the differences in theological convictions among religions are always differences—perhaps only slight differences but by no means negligible ones—in their respective accounts of the good life and good death. An adequate Christian engagement with Islam about questions of the good life and good death would need to involve central narratives as well as the central convictions of both religions—on the Christian side the claim of the Christian faith that "God is love" (I John 4:7) and the doctrine of the Trinity; the claim that Christ died for the salvation of the "ungodly" (Rom. 5:6) and the doctrine of justification by faith and judgment of works governed by grace; and the command to love not just one's neighbors but one's "enemies" as well (Matt. 5:44); and on the Muslim side the absence of such claims, doctrines, and commands in Islam.[5] Presumably something analogous would be true of a Muslim engagement with the Christian faith about questions of the good life and good death; Muslims, too, would need to explore how their convictions regarding central theological issues—and the way these differ from Christian convictions—bear on these matters. Only when we have situated our reflection on the good life and good death and their relation to one another within the central narratives and central convictions of each religion will we be able to engage in productive and mutually enriching discussion about these fundamental matters of human existence.

Notes

1. See Jürgen Moltmann, "On a Culture of Life in the Dangers of This Time," in *The Harmony of Civilizations and Prosperity for All: Commitments and Responsibilities for a Better World* (Beijing: Peking University Press, 2010), 20–26.

2. Hannah Arendt, *The Human Condition* (Chicago: University of Chicago Press, 1958), 8–9: "Since action is the political activity par excellence, natality, and not mortality, may be the central category of political, as distinguished from metaphysical, thought." On natality, see Henning Theißen, "Natalität: Eine noch Junge Begriffskarriere in der Anthropologie," *Neue Zeitschrift für Systematische Theologie und Religionsphilosophie* 54, no. 3 (2012): 285–311. See, for example, Martin Heidegger, *Being and Time*, trans. John Macquarrie and Edward Robinson (New York: Harper & Row, 1962), 305: "we must characterize Being-towards-death as a *Being towards a possibility*—indeed, towards a distinctive possibility of Dasein itself."

3. See Joseph Cumming, "Did Jesus Die on the Cross? The History of Reflection on the End of His Earthly Life in Sunnī Tafsīr Literature," available at Yale Center for Faith and Culture, www.yale.edu/faith/rc/rc-rp.htm.

4. Posted on a Facebook page in memoriam to de Chergé: www.facebook.com/pages/Dom-Christian-de-Chergé%C3%A9/183911334986231?v=info. The ideal of love in which an enemy appears as a brother and friend is not to be found only among demanding Christian monastic groups like the Trappists. The father of modern theology, Friedrich Schleiermacher, advocated it, for instance, as evidenced in his sermon on the death of Stephen, the first Christian martyr. See Friedrich Schleiermacher, *Selected Sermons of Schleiermacher*, trans. Mary F. Wilson (Grand Rapids, MI: Christian Classics Ethereal Library, n.d.), 244–46.

5. See Miroslav Volf, *Allah: A Christian Response* (San Francisco: HarperOne, 2011), 127–84.

Reflections

ROWAN WILLIAMS

I n the following reflections, I shall comment on six themes that have emerged during the course of today's discussion, and that I hope may be explored more fully in the course of this seminar.[1]

I shall begin with practical and pastoral questions around death and dying raised by Harriet Harris and Sajjad Rizvi. It struck me very strongly, listening to them both, that there was a question about how and whether we *own* our death. We live in a culture where "ownership" is often seen as the most significant relationship we ever have to anything, and I suspect that some of the passion, anger, and pain around discussion of assisted suicide, for example, has to do with the feeling that religious prohibitions are somehow denying us ownership of our own experience, ownership of our own death. That being said, we have also been introduced to two very different ways of exercising power in approaching death, whether our own or someone else's: either the medical power to prolong life by a kind of flexing of scientific muscle, or the moral power to "end my life when I choose." But both approaches are, in a sense, about taking control.

From both of our traditions we have heard about what it might mean consciously, graciously, to relinquish control—a challenge both to the dying person and to the medical caregiver. It is often assumed that religious attitudes to end-of-life questions are all about prolonging life at all costs, which is an absurdity. But we only get past that particular sterile standoff, I think, if we address this question of whether we are approaching our own death or the death of someone else basically in the spirit of wanting control or in the spirit of creative letting go.

We have also been reminded of that particular cluster of questions represented by the idea of dying before you die—both a Sufi and a Christian commonplace already present in St. Paul's language about dying every day. He speaks of how his ministry to the community involves a kind of "dying" so that life may come into existence in the other, in the neighbor (see, for example, II Cor. 4:7–12).

My second cluster of themes has some connections with the first. There was a question this morning about how our talk of heaven, hell, and the resurrection impacts upon our experience here and now. To talk about dying every day is, of course, one way in which it impacts us. The experience of the community of faith has something about it that encourages us, nurtures us, in the practice of letting go: letting go so that the neighbor may live, not in a self-hating or (in the wrong sense) self-denying way but in a way that acknowledges that part of the providence and purpose of God in the community is achieved by my learning to make room for my neighbor—and therefore saying no to my urge to control and contain my neighbor. That is all part of the daily "dying" that is involved in and enabled by our fundamental relationship to God—the sense in which we relate truthfully and constructively to God only when we learn to make room for God, at the expense of what we feel comfortable with and what we can control.

I think the answer to the question about the impact and relevance of our talk about heaven, hell, and resurrection lies here. Are we now living our way into the kind of relationship that will make heaven a joy? That's what it means to say "Heaven begins here"—to say, with Christian scripture, that our citizenship is in heaven (Phil. 3:20). After all, what are we going to do in heaven (assuming we get there!)? For both the Christian and the Muslim, the answer is: we are going to enjoy God for God's sake. If that is, by the grace of God, how we spend eternity, we had better start getting used to it.

It's as simple as that. The question of the present impact of our talk about the last things is to do with what we do in heaven, with the relationship we begin now—the quality of our looking at God, and looking at our neighbor, which begins here and now. And to speak of hell is, in the broadest possible terms, to speak of a condition where we are no longer able to look at God with joy. And that is a terrible enough thing to say, without going into any science fiction about hell. What would it be to be confronted unambiguously with love and not look at it with joy?

That takes me to my third cluster of themes. One of the areas of possible controversy, possible tension, between our theological traditions that emerged this morning had to do with justice, with whether we are responsible for our own salvation, whether we could rely on the merits or the prayers of others to do something for us. I suspect that in this regard there is enough material here for an entire conference. What we are thinking about in this connection is something to do with acts and consequences. We heard from our Muslim participants a very powerful and lucid statement that there is nothing in the universe that can prevent acts having the consequences that they have. Our acts change us. Our acts make us the kind of people we are. And it is a painful, tempting illusion to suppose that there is something vaguely religious that can stop that being the case.

There is undoubtedly a religious sentimentality that says that God works by magic—that is, God works in disregard for what we have made of ourselves. There is scope for some exploration here. We are who we have made ourselves, but, for the Christian, there is also the question: have we yet made ourselves people incapable of asking for mercy, asking for one another's help, asking for one another's prayers? Because to open oneself to the idea that mercy transforms us, that that transforming mercy can come through the prayers of others, is not to say "Let somebody relieve me of the consequences of my actions," but to say "I'm willing to act, to relate differently—to grow in a new set of relations."

This is a complex area, but it is important for us not to be seduced by the idea that theologies of salvation are only about having all responsibility lifted from our shoulders. I defer to N. T. Wright here, but I think he would agree that justification by faith is not a kind of magic.[2]

That pushes us on to a fourth area to reflect on. Quite often when I am asked questions about the theology of eternal life or the theology of death and resurrection, such questions are couched in terms of surviving death: "Do you believe there is something in you that survives death?" I don't believe that *survival* is the issue at all, for either of our traditions. I frequently find myself saying that, for me, issues around eternal life have to do with *God* before they have to do with humanity. It's because we believe in a God who is faithful to his creation that we believe we are not discarded, rolled up, and tossed away, annihilated. God is faithful to what he has made, and therefore the relation we have with God continues.

What that means theologically, philosophically, and so on is a vastly complicated question. But I think it is important to keep it anchored in what we believe about the character of God's faithfulness rather than tying it down to speculation about some insecure bit of us that somehow manages to survive the annihilating experience of death. This is about God: a faithful God, a God who has a character, who is loyal to what he himself has done and been for us and in the universe.

And the question about "universalism" (is everyone saved?) is one of the questions that comes up here. If this is the character of God, then can we suppose that God abandons any creature? And yet if this is the character of God, can it be the case that God overrides the free decision that he has given to his creatures? Somewhere in between those two questions, we are all stuck. Actually, it's a very good place to be stuck because, were we blandly secure about universal salvation, a great deal of our theology would look and sound very different; were we blandly confident about exactly who was going where in the eyes of God, then that would perhaps be even worse. So I think that particular knife edge is a good place to live for Christians, Muslims, or indeed anybody else.

There are two other questions, neither of them small, both perhaps falling outside the clusters I have already identified, which I shall mention briefly before I finish. One is a question already hinted at: the relation of the individual and the corporate, the question of what it means for a Christian that we die as part of the body of Christ, part of a cosmic community in which our mutual relations make us who we are. What is it for the Muslim to die as a member of the *umma*, as a member of a community again conceived as universal and transformed? What do those relationships with our community actually mean at the point of our dying, at the point of our transition into some different kind of relationship with God? Certainly some Christians (speculating about how our prayers can help the dead grow closer to God) have tried to be extremely precise and exact about what that might or might not mean, and we have sometimes made ourselves look rather foolish with those speculations. And yet, that we do not die alone remains important for both for our traditions. Individual responsibility is clearly a fundamental theme in Islam, and in a different sense, with a different flavor, it is also fundamental in Christianity. Yet, at the same time, I think that Muslims and Christians can agree that "our life and our death are bound up with our neighbor," to borrow the phrase of St. Antony of Egypt.

The last issue, which we have barely begun to touch on, even though it is theologically very interesting indeed, is the *origin* of death. There is a deeply rooted Christian tradition that sees death as bound up with the Fall, with what Cardinal Newman called a "terrible aboriginal calamity" that overwhelmed the human race. In other words, mortality is seen as in some sense not part of God's original purpose. This is, however, a difficult doctrine to maintain, not only in scientific terms but even in theological terms, since embracing our finite character has been so important an aspect of our learning human maturity.

Where, then, does death come from? Is human death part of God's original purpose? Is it the result of a catastrophe? Or is it, as some more modern Christian theologians have suggested, something in between? Is the death that we speak of in these terms a conscious awareness, a *fearful* awareness of our mortality that comes with a particular sense of self and evolves at a particular stage of human or evolutionary history? Is death a problem for the *self-aware* being in a way that it isn't for the animal creation? I don't pretend to have an answer to that, but it's an interesting question. Are we essentially seeing death in terms of punishment and threat, or in terms of something that *becomes* punishment and threat because of a certain quality of human awareness and self-awareness? That is certainly a problem for Christians. How far it's a problem for Muslims, I don't know.

On this last point, and on many others, I am hoping to learn much in the days ahead. But we have had a fine and stimulating beginning to our conversation. Confident in the Living God, we go forward to further reflection and discovery.

Notes

1. This is an edited version of comments made at the end of the first day of the seminar, after hearing the lectures by N. T. Wright, Mona Siddiqui, Geoffrey Rowell, Asma Afsaruddin, Harriet Harris, and Sajjad Rizvi, the edited versions of which are presented in this volume. The responses to these lectures also included in this volume had not been given at this point.

2. N. T. Wright, whose essay appears earlier in this volume.

PART II

Texts and Commentaries

I Corinthians 15

¹Now I should remind you, brothers and sisters, of the good news that I proclaimed to you, which you in turn received, in which also you stand, ²through which also you are being saved, if you hold firmly to the message that I proclaimed to you—unless you have come to believe in vain.

³For I handed on to you as of first importance what I in turn had received: that Christ died for our sins in accordance with the scriptures,⁴and that he was buried, and that he was raised on the third day in accordance with the scriptures, ⁵and that he appeared to Cephas, then to the twelve. ⁶Then he appeared to more than five hundred brothers and sisters at one time, most of whom are still alive, though some have died. ⁷Then he appeared to James, then to all the apostles. ⁸Last of all, as to someone untimely born, he appeared also to me. ⁹For I am the least of the apostles, unfit to be called an apostle, because I persecuted the church of God. ¹⁰But by the grace of God I am what I am, and his grace towards me has not been in vain. On the contrary, I worked harder than any of them—though it was not I, but the grace of God that is with me. ¹¹Whether then it was I or they, so we proclaim and so you have come to believe.

¹²Now if Christ is proclaimed as raised from the dead, how can some of you say there is no resurrection of the dead? ¹³If there is no resurrection of the dead, then Christ has not been raised; ¹⁴and if Christ has not been raised, then our proclamation has been in vain and your faith has been in vain. ¹⁵We are even found to be misrepresenting God, because we testified of God that he raised Christ—whom he did not raise if it is true that the dead are not raised. ¹⁶For if the dead are not raised, then Christ has not been raised. ¹⁷If Christ has not been raised, your faith is futile and you are still in your sins. ¹⁸Then those also who have died in Christ have perished. ¹⁹If for this life only we have hoped in Christ, we are of all people most to be pitied.

²⁰But in fact Christ has been raised from the dead, the first fruits of those who have died. ²¹For since death came through a human being, the resurrection of the dead has also come through a human being; ²²for as all die in Adam, so all will be made alive in Christ. ²³But each in his own order: Christ the first

fruits, then at his coming those who belong to Christ. ²⁴Then comes the end, when he hands over the kingdom to God the Father, after he has destroyed every ruler and every authority and power. ²⁵For he must reign until he has put all his enemies under his feet. ²⁶The last enemy to be destroyed is death. ²⁷For "God has put all things in subjection under his feet." But when it says, "All things are put in subjection," it is plain that this does not include the one who put all things in subjection under him. ²⁸When all things are subjected to him, then the Son himself will also be subjected to the one who put all things in subjection under him, so that God may be all in all.

²⁹Otherwise, what will those people do who receive baptism on behalf of the dead? If the dead are not raised at all, why are people baptized on their behalf?

³⁰And why are we putting ourselves in danger every hour? ³¹I die every day! That is as certain, brothers and sisters, as my boasting of you—a boast that I make in Christ Jesus our Lord. ³²If with merely human hopes I fought with wild animals at Ephesus, what would I have gained by it? If the dead are not raised,

"Let us eat and drink,
   for tomorrow we die."

³³Do not be deceived:

"Bad company ruins good morals."

³⁴Come to a sober and right mind, and sin no more; for some people have no knowledge of God. I say this to your shame.

³⁵But someone will ask, "How are the dead raised? With what kind of body do they come?" ³⁶Fool! What you sow does not come to life unless it dies. ³⁷And as for what you sow, you do not sow the body that is to be, but a bare seed, perhaps of wheat or of some other grain. ³⁸But God gives it a body as he has chosen, and to each kind of seed its own body. ³⁹Not all flesh is alike, but there is one flesh for human beings, another for animals, another for birds, and another for fish. ⁴⁰There are both heavenly bodies and earthly bodies, but the glory of the heavenly is one thing, and that of the earthly is another. ⁴¹There is one glory of the sun, and another glory of the moon, and another glory of the stars; indeed, star differs from star in glory.

⁴²So it is with the resurrection of the dead. What is sown is perishable, what is raised is imperishable. ⁴³It is sown in dishonour, it is raised in glory. It is sown in weakness, it is raised in power. ⁴⁴It is sown a physical body, it is raised a spiritual body. If there is a physical body, there is also a spiritual body. ⁴⁵Thus it is written, "The first man, Adam, became a living being"; the last Adam

became a life-giving spirit. ⁴⁶But it is not the spiritual that is first, but the physical, and then the spiritual. ⁴⁷The first man was from the earth, a man of dust; the second man is from heaven. ⁴⁸As was the man of dust, so are those who are of the dust; and as is the man of heaven, so are those who are of heaven. ⁴⁹Just as we have borne the image of the man of dust, we will also bear the image of the man of heaven.

⁵⁰What I am saying, brothers and sisters, is this: flesh and blood cannot inherit the kingdom of God, nor does the perishable inherit the imperishable. ⁵¹Listen, I will tell you a mystery! We will not all die, but we will all be changed, ⁵²in a moment, in the twinkling of an eye, at the last trumpet. For the trumpet will sound, and the dead will be raised imperishable, and we will be changed. ⁵³For this perishable body must put on imperishability, and this mortal body must put on immortality. ⁵⁴When this perishable body puts on imperishability, and this mortal body puts on immortality, then the saying that is written will be fulfilled:

"Death has been swallowed up in victory."
⁵⁵"Where, O death, is your victory?
Where, O death, is your sting?"
⁵⁶The sting of death is sin, and the power of sin is the law. ⁵⁷But thanks be to God, who gives us the victory through our Lord Jesus Christ.

⁵⁸Therefore, my beloved, be steadfast, immovable, always excelling in the work of the Lord, because you know that in the Lord your labor is not in vain.

St. Paul on the Resurrection
I Corinthians 15

RICHARD A. BURRIDGE

orinth was one of the most important cities in the ancient world. Strad-
dling the narrow isthmus between the southern mass of the Peloponnese
and the famous city of Athens to the north and on to the mountains, connecting
to Europe, Corinth had two harbors: Cenchreae, facing east across the Saronic
Gulf toward the eastern Mediterranean and Asia, and Lechaeum to the west, at
the end of the Corinthian Gulf leading to Italy. Across the four miles of a
narrow land bridge was built the *diolkos* causeway to transport cargo, or even
smaller ships, to avoid the long, dangerous sea voyage around the south. A key
city throughout the classical period of Greece and Hellenism, Corinth was
sacked by the newly emerging Romans in 146 BC, and was refounded by Julius
Caesar in 44 BC. In the first century AD, it was a thriving commercial center—a
gateway between the eastern Mediterranean and the way to Rome, with all the
opportunities for business, culture, sport, games, religion, sex, and power
attracted by the heady mixture of sea and land.

Paul came to Corinth from Athens. He stayed for eighteen months around
AD 50, preaching, teaching, and building a new Christian community among
Jews and Gentiles (Acts 18:1–18) before leaving for Asia and eventually Jerusalem. During the following years, Paul sent various letters with messengers to
the young community he left behind, two of which are preserved in the New
Testament. In I Corinthians, dating from 54–55 AD, Paul refers to at least one
previous letter from himself, and he is replying to a letter from the Corinthians
(see I Cor. 5:9 and 7:1); this correspondence continues in II Corinthians, which
may contain parts of several letters.

In the first six chapters of I Corinthians, Paul expresses concern about things
which have been reported to him (see 1:11; 5:1), such as quarrels between different groups and sexual immorality, before turning to "the matters about which
you wrote" (7:1). In response, he advises the Corinthian Christian community

about marriage, food offered in temples to the gods, and instructions for public worship, before bringing it all to a rhetorical climax with an extended treatment of the resurrection, correcting various views about life after death, which were being debated among the Corinthians (chapter 15, all of which is printed preceding this essay). Personal remarks about individuals, the collection for the relief of the poor, and his travel plans conclude the letter (chapter 16).[1]

Structure of I Corinthians 15

Introduction (vv. 1–2)
The importance of this topic for understanding the gospel and ultimately for our salvation; without this, our faith is in vain.

Section 1
A: The death and resurrection of Jesus Christ (vv. 3–11)
The very early tradition handed on to Paul and from him to his readers (v. 3) of the death, burial, resurrection, and appearances of Jesus, including to Paul.
B: If this is not true, our faith is in vain (vv. 12–19)
The death and resurrection of Jesus is the absolute basis of Christianity.

Section 2
A: The death and resurrection in Christ of all human beings (vv. 20–28)
All human beings die in Adam, and all are made alive in Christ at the end of time when all things are subjected to him and to God the Father.
B: If this is not true, the way we live is in vain (vv. 29–34)
If there is no resurrection, "let us eat and drink for tomorrow we die."

Section 3
- A: The resurrection body and its relationship to the physical body (vv. 35–50)

    The relationship of seeds to their later bodies; earthly and heavenly bodies; the first Adam and the last (Christ); physical/natural and spiritual; dust and heaven.
- B: If this is true, when and how will this happen? (vv. 51–57)

    The last trumpet and the resurrection of the dead to put on immortality; the end of death's sting and the victory of God through our Lord Jesus Christ.

Conclusion (v. 58)
Therefore, be steadfast and labor not in vain.

Commentary

Introduction (vv. 1–2)

The introduction to I Corinthians 15 (vv. 1–2) and the conclusion to the chapter (v. 58) balance each other and make it clear that this topic is essential for understanding the Christian faith in general as well as its beliefs about death, resurrection, and human destiny in particular. Paul is not writing about something new or strange to his readers—but is "reminding" them of the "gospel" (literally "good news" in Greek, *euangelion*) with which he originally "gospelled" or "evangelized" them (*euēngelisamēn*, v. 1). The Corinthians "received" this "gospel" from Paul and held firmly to the message with which Paul evangelized them as essential for their salvation (v. 2). Without this gospel, their faith is all "in vain." Paul uses several different Greek words for this through this chapter to stress its importance: here, without holding fast to his message, they would have believed "in vain" (*eikēi*, "in vain," or "for nothing," v. 2); similarly, without this, God's grace toward Paul himself (including the appearance of the risen Christ to him, v. 8) would have been "in vain" (*kenos*, "empty" or "pointless," v. 10); in verse 14, if Christ has not been raised, both his preaching and their faith have been "in vain" (*kenos* again); equally, if Christ has not been raised, their faith has been "futile" (*mataios*, "worthless," or "useless" v. 17);

finally, if they stand firm and immovable, then their work in the Lord is not "in vain" (using *kenos* again, in v. 58).[2]

Section 1: A. The death and resurrection of Jesus Christ (vv. 3–11)

I Corinthians 15:3–11 is profoundly important for the historical basis of Christianity. Paul uses technical terms for passing on oral tradition from one generation to another; thus, he has "handed on" (*paredōka*) to the Corinthians what he himself had first "received" (*parelabon*)—and it is all "of first importance" (v. 3). Paul himself was probably trained in the rabbinical method (Phil. 3:4–5; Acts 23:6, 26:4–5), where accurate handing on to others of what one had been taught was paramount. This passage, with its list of resurrection appearances and the repetitions of "in accordance with the scriptures," betrays these characteristics of fixed oral tradition. Paul wrote this letter around AD 54 to people he had evangelized in 51, handing on to them what he himself had been taught in the late 30s, following the risen Jesus's appearance to him on the Damascus road (Acts 9:1–30, 22:6–21, 26:12–23; Gal. 1:11–24).[3] Therefore, this historical list goes back to within a few years of the death of Jesus, making it some of the oldest material in the New Testament. Unsurprisingly, it has played a significant role in persuading people across countless generations of the truth of the resurrection of Jesus of Nazareth—myself included, as a young undergraduate studying ancient history at Oxford.

This ancient tradition begins with three clear assertions in verses 3–4—that Jesus died, he was buried, and he was raised on the third day (the passive "raised" stresses that this was a deliberate act of God to raise him, not something that Jesus did of himself). The logic is clear: Jesus cannot be raised from the dead by God without first experiencing death himself and being buried among the dead. Interestingly, Paul does not refer here to Jesus's tomb being found empty, which is important in the gospels' resurrection accounts. (See Matt. 28:1–15; Mark 16:1–8; Luke 24:1–12; John 20:1–18.) This may be because Paul shares the Jewish assumption that if someone who was dead and buried was then raised from the dead, their tomb would necessarily be empty, so it goes without saying; furthermore, here Paul is more interested in the appearances for the purpose of his argument.[4]

The actual list of appearances has produced much scholarly debate, since it does not coincide with those described in the four canonical gospels. Thus, not referring to the empty tomb also means that Paul does not mention any appearances to women, probably reflecting the ancient refusal of women's testimony (see Luke 24:10–11). Some appearances do relate to those in the gospels, to "the twelve" and to "the apostles" (Matt. 28:16–20; Luke 24:36–51; John 20:19–21:23). An individual appearance to Peter (I Cor. 15:5)—here significantly referred to by his earlier Aramaic name, *Cephas* (which, like the Greek, *Petros*, refers to "rock," see Matt. 16:18)—is mentioned in Luke 24:34. However, there is no account of an appearance to James, the Lord's brother, other than I Corinthians 15:7—yet this would explain how James changed from an unbelieving skeptic (see Matt. 13:55; Mark 3:21) to becoming the leader of the Jerusalem church (Acts 12:17, 15:13, 21:18; Gal. 1:18–21, 2:9) and the author of the epistle in his name.

The reference to an appearance to five hundred might relate to the day of Pentecost (Acts 2:1–11; 2:41 says there were at least three thousand there that day) but probably refers to another occasion of which we know nothing; Paul stresses that many of them are "still alive" and can therefore provide eye-witness testimony (I Cor. 15:6). Finally, Paul includes the appearance of the risen Jesus to him on the Damascus road as of the same nature, even if he describes himself as "one untimely born." (The Greek *ektrōma* usually refers to an abortion or miscarried fetus. Here, it either refers to his sudden turnaround, or it reflects his opponents' insulting him as a "monster" or a "freak," as Paul recognizes himself as the "least of the apostles," vv. 8–9). Whatever Paul's disagreements with the other apostles (e.g., see Gal. 2:11–14), the important thing for him here is that both he and they proclaim the same message—that Jesus died on the cross, was buried, and was raised by God—and it is through this preaching that his readers have come to faith (v. 11).

Section 1: B. If this is not true, our faith is in vain (vv. 12–19)

After first proving the resurrection of Jesus from the dead, Paul stresses that Jesus's death and resurrection is the absolute basis of the Christian faith, without which everything is pointless. Furthermore, the link between Christ's resurrection and our human destiny and resurrection is indissoluble, as verse 12 makes clear. Paul's logic is remorseless: he hammers his message home, not once, but twice, repeating the same point, with the same logical sequence, and using similar words in verses 13–17. If there is no resurrection of the dead, then

Christ himself has not been raised (in both verses 13 and 16). This inevitably means that, if Christ has not been raised, then preaching the gospel is in vain, and your faith is in vain (*kenos*, "empty," or "with no substance," v. 14); equally, if Christ has not been raised, your faith is "futile" (*mataios*, "worthless," or "useless") and we are still living the old sinful way of life (v. 17). The consequences for all human beings, dead and alive, are clear: those who have "fallen asleep" in Christ have actually perished, never to be seen again (v. 18), while for those still alive, if the Christian faith is just about this earthly existence, then "we are of all people most to be pitied" (v. 19). Thus, for Paul, the *doctrine* of the resurrection of Jesus Christ from the dead proved by the appearances (vv. 3–11) has enormous implications for the *practice and life* of the church in verses 12–19; without the former, all the latter is pointless and an illusion without substance.

Section 2: A. The death and resurrection in Christ of all human beings (vv. 20–28)

Having established the centrality of the death and resurrection of Jesus for the Christian faith in his first major section, Paul now moves on to the implications of this "fact" (*nuni de* in Greek introduces a logical consequence in verse 20) that "Christ has been raised from the dead" for all human beings in his second section. Christ is the *aparchē*, the "first fruits" or "first installment" of a harvest still to come (vv. 20 and 23). The actual "first fruits" were offered to God in the Old Testament (Ex. 23:19, 34.26; Lev. 23:9–14; Num. 15:18–21; Deut. 18:4), while this word is often used metaphorically in the New Testament for "first installment"; thus, it links this passage to Romans 8,[5] where the Holy Spirit is the "first fruits" of the future "redemption of our bodies" (8:23; see also James 1:18 and Rev. 14:4). Here Jesus's resurrection is seen as the "first fruits" of those who have "fallen asleep" (v. 20).

There follows Paul's first use of the typological parallel between Adam and Christ, to which he will return later (vv. 45–49) and then discuss in more detail in Romans 5:12–21. Thus, as death entered the world through one human being (Adam), so also the resurrection of the dead came through another, Jesus Christ. Since death is a universal experience affecting everyone, Paul's parallelism suggests that "all will be made alive in Christ" (v. 22), while the next verse appears to limit this to "those who belong to Christ" (v. 23). Paul does not resolve this tension because he is concerned instead to explain the proper "sequence" of events: Christ's resurrection comes first as the "first fruits" and everyone else's resurrection comes at the end of the world, when Christ has destroyed all God's enemies, including death, and hands everything over to the Father; this even includes Jesus subjecting himself so that "God may be all in all" (vv. 23–28). Thus our existence today is often termed "between the times," since we do not yet see the universe subject to the gentle, loving rule of God; therefore, we currently exist between the resurrection of Jesus Christ as the "first fruits" and the rest of the harvest. While we wait for all God's enemies to be defeated and destroyed, those who have died already are described as having "fallen asleep," awaiting the final resurrection of everybody at the end of time.

Section 2: B. If this is not true, the way we live is in vain (vv. 29–34)

Just as in the first section Paul works out the practical implications of the doctrine of Jesus's death, burial, and resurrection (vv. 3–11), without which the Christian faith is "in vain" (vv. 12–19), so now he considers the consequences of Christ's resurrection as the first fruits while the rest of the human race awaits the final resurrection (vv. 20–28) for how we live and behave in the present "time between the times" (vv. 29–34). Without Christ's resurrection followed by the end-time resurrection of everyone else, three things make no sense or are "in vain": baptism "on behalf of the dead" (v. 29), risking everything for Christ (vv. 30–32a), and living ethically (vv. 32b–34). The first of these, baptism on behalf of the dead, is usually seen as "a notoriously difficult crux" or the "most hotly disputed" verse in the whole letter.[6] Mormons have built an entire industry of telephone directories and voting registers going back through family genealogies to baptize dead ancestors to gain a better spiritual pedigree; more likely, "baptism *for the sake of* the dead" may refer to people seeking baptism in response to the dying pleas of relatives, who may have suffered for Christ, or to be reunited with loved ones who have died. Whatever explanation is accepted, Paul's logic is clear: if Christ has not been raised as the first fruits of the dead who sleep in him, then baptism into him is worthless (v. 29).

Equally pointless is the dangerous way Paul lives, risking death every day for the sake of the gospel, whether his allusion to "fighting wild animals at Ephesus" is interpreted literally of the Roman arena or figuratively about his opponents (vv. 30–32a); why risk death if there is no hope of resurrection? Finally, there is no value in trying to live a moral life if Christ has not been raised as the "first fruits" who will then judge all those who have fallen asleep at the end of time; instead, why not keep "bad company" and "eat and drink for tomorrow we die" (probably quoting Isa. 22:13, or possibly contemporary Epicurean slogans current in Corinth as a Greek city with many pleasures, vv. 32b–34)? Thus, if the first section of this chapter proves that, without the death and resurrection of Jesus, the *Christian faith* is "in vain," so here in the second section Paul demonstrates that without Christ's resurrection being the "first fruits" for the resurrection of all human beings at the end of time, the *Christian life* is equally pointless.

Section 3: A. The resurrection body and its relationship to the physical body (vv. 35–50)

Having demonstrated the necessity of the death and resurrection for both the Christian faith and the Christian way of life to have any worth or value, Paul now turns to deal with a third objection: how are we actually to understand the resurrection; is it the reanimation of a corpse or a different sort of body all together (v. 35)?[7] As earlier, he uses parallelisms to make his point, first that between seeds and plants, and second, returning to his previous comparison of Adam and Christ. His first, rather dismissive, example to the "fool" of a questioner is to draw a parallel with seeds, which must "die" and be buried under the earth for the plant to produce new life, which then takes a different "body" from its seed (vv. 36–37). Thus, bodies fit their environments: there is one sort of flesh for human beings and different bodies for animals or birds of the air and fish in the sea, not to mention heavenly bodies, the sun, moon, and stars in the sky (vv. 38–41). Such contrasts enable Paul to indicate what the resurrection body will be like: a dead body is buried in the ground like a seed, perishable, dishonored, weak, and on the physical, natural, or human level;[8] however, in the resurrection, it will be raised to all the opposites, imperishable, glorious, powerful, spiritual, and animated by the Spirit of God (vv. 42–44).

For his second point, Paul repeats his earlier parallel of the first and last man (see vv. 21–22): the very name "Adam" comes from the Hebrew for ground or earth, as the Lord God creates the first man from the dust of the earth (which means the physical or natural elements); he becomes a "living being" when God breathes the breath of life into him (v. 45, quoting the Greek version of Gen. 2:7).[9] In contrast, Christ as "the last Adam" became through his resurrection "a life-giving spirit," the man from heaven (vv. 45–47). Human beings, as Adam's descendants, bear all those marks of "the man of dust" in the physical universe; but since Christ is the "first fruits" of the harvest to come (as argued in vv. 20–28 above), when we are raised at the end of time, we will be like him, and will bear his image, since perishable flesh and blood cannot enter heaven (vv. 48–50). So although Paul does not give a definitive answer to his imagined questioner, his two parallels tell us that the resurrection body will be like a plant from a seed, with continuity to what went before, but different and far more glorious; as our human body is made of the physical elements like Adam's, so our resurrection body will be like that of Jesus at his resurrection as the "first fruit" of the harvest at the end of all things.

Section 3: B. If this is true, when and how will this happen? (vv. 51–57)

After the two parallels of plants coming from seeds and Christ as the second or last Adam, Paul returns to the question of verse 35 about how the dead are raised: how do we know that this hope of resurrection is not itself empty and "in vain"? If our perishable bodies of dust must be transformed before we can inherit the kingdom of God (v. 50), when and how will this happen? To answer this, Paul follows through the logic of his previous argument that we live "between the times"—after Christ has been raised as the "first fruits" but before the final resurrection at the End (vv. 20–22). Therefore, he explains the "mystery": while those who die during this interim period have "fallen asleep," the Last Day will finally come when both they and those who are still alive on the earth will all be changed in an instant. At the sound of the last trumpet, the living and the dead alike will change perishable, mortal bodies into glorious imperishable immortality (vv. 51–54). This is when even the last enemy, death itself, will be destroyed and subjected under God's feet (vv. 24–26). As death is swallowed up and the bitter sting of the old sinful life that led to death is finally ended, we can only sing a hymn of thanks to God for his victory, which has come through his experiencing human existence in Jesus Christ, his life, death, burial, and his resurrection, which is now given to us all (vv. 54–57).

Conclusion: Therefore, be steadfast and labor not in vain (v. 58)

Having expressed his concerns (I Cor. 1–6) and dealt with the Corinthians' questions (I Cor. 7–14), in this great concluding treatment of the resurrection in chapter 15, Paul takes great pains to remind his readers of the original gospel which he himself learned and passed on to them, the "good news" of God sharing human life in Jesus of Nazareth, even to the point of experiencing a real death, burial in the earth, and resurrection as the first fruits of the eschatological resurrection of everyone at the End. Without this core belief, Paul has demonstrated that the Christian faith is without substance and "in vain" (vv. 3–19), and also that there is no point or value in living as a Christian (vv. 20–34). But since, in fact, Christ has been raised, then we can look forward with confidence to our resurrection to be with him in eternity (vv. 35–57). Therefore, Paul concludes that his beloved fellow Christians are to be steadfast and immovable, excelling in their work for God because the resurrection guarantees that it cannot be "in vain."[10]

Points for Discussion

The introduction (vv. 1–2) and the conclusion (v. 58) balance each other and make it clear that this topic and chapter are essential for understanding the Christian faith in general, and its particular beliefs about death, resurrection, and human destiny in the resurrected Christ. What would it mean for both Christians and others to recognize that without this stress in the gospel message on the death and resurrection of Jesus Christ, everything is "in vain," empty, worthless, or pointless from a Christian perspective?

Section 1

If the Christian understanding of death, resurrection, and human destiny is so inextricably linked to the historical death and resurrection of Jesus, how do we proceed honestly in dialogue, given the Muslim understanding of Jesus's death? For example, the Qur'ān says, "they did not slay him neither crucified him, only a likeness of that was shown to them" (4:156–59); note also the ḥadīth that suggests that one of his followers volunteered to die in his place and God made him look like Jesus. Further, since verses 12–19 inextricably link our human destiny through death and resurrection to Christ's death and resurrection, rather than the Muslim assumption that resurrection is part of being human for everyone ("He created you the first time, and unto Him you shall be taken back," Qur'ân 41:21), we must be cautious about simply assuming that, in discussing resurrection and human destiny, Christians and Muslims are talking about the same thing.

Section 2

What are the implications (practical and ethical) of this connection between Christ's resurrection on the one hand, and on the other the resurrection of Christian believers or of all human beings?[11] How does this teaching about what happens after death, the intermediate state of "sleeping," and the final resurrection at the End relate to other understandings of life after death throughout the Christian tradition and history, as well as those common among many people in our society today, and to Islamic beliefs about the current state and future destiny of those who have died?

Section 3

How are we to understand Paul's language about seeds and bodies, and the relationship of the old physical, natural, human life in Adam and the new resurrected life animated in the Spirit, or our earthly body of dust in Adam and inheriting the heavenly resurrected body of Christ? How can we interpret today his description of a last trumpet and the end of the world when death is destroyed? As before, how does this teaching relate to other understandings of the resurrection of the dead and life after death throughout the Christian tradition and history as well as those common among many people in our society today, and to Islamic beliefs?

Notes

1. For further background, see C. K. Barrett, *1 Corinthians* (London: A & C Black. 1968); Raymond F. Collins, *1 Corinthians*, Sacra Pagina 7 (Collegeville: Liturgical Press, 1999); Gordon D. Fee, *1 Corinthians*, NICNT (Grand Rapids, MI: Eerdmans, 1987); Joseph A. Fitzmyer,

1 Corinthians, Anchor Bible 32 (New Haven, CT: Yale University Press, 2008); David E. Garland, *1 Corinthians* (Grand Rapids, MI: Baker, 2003); Craig S. Keener, *1–2 Corinthians* (Cambridge: Cambridge University Press, 2005).

2. For discussion of the various nuances of the different Greek words, see Anthony C. Thiselton, *1 Corinthians*, NIGTC (Grand Rapids, MI: Eerdmans, 2000), 1186, 1211–12, 1218–20, 1304; I give page references to Thiselton as perhaps the fullest most recent treatment of I Corinthians, but these issues are also discussed in many other commentaries.

3. See Thiselton, *1 Corinthians*, 29–32, for discussion of the dates of Paul's visit and of writing the letters.

4. See N. T. Wright's essay in this volume; also his *Resurrection of the Son of God* (London: SPCK, 2003) for ancient understanding(s) of the body, death, resurrection, and so on; see also Thiselton, *1 Corinthians*, 1197–1203, on the debates about the empty tomb and whether the appearances are real in "the public domain" or merely internal visions or hallucinations.

5. Romans 8 is also discussed in N. T. Wright's essay in this volume.

6. Thiselton lists dozens of possible explanations held through the centuries; see his *1 Corinthians*, 1240–49.

7. There is great scholarly debate regarding the possible views held by Corinthians about the resurrection and the resurrected body: whether it was about the whole idea of life after physical death or whether some Corinthians thought that they were already living the resurrection life here and now, as well as debates about the nature of both the human body now and the future resurrected body. These issues lie not just behind this chapter but also with regard to other passages such as Paul's discussion of sex and the body (I Cor. 5–7). Probably there were a variety of views held at Corinth, which Paul is attempting to tackle throughout the epistle. See Thiselton, *1 Corinthians*, 1172–77.

8. There is enormous scholarly debate about the translations of the contrasts between *psychikos/psychē* for the human Adamic body and *pneumatikos/pneuma* for resurrected body of and through Christ. Thus some translations have "physical" (NRSV, RSV, REB) or "natural" body (ESV, NJB, NIV, ASV, KJV) for verse 44, and "living being" (NRSV, NIV, RSV, ESV) or "living soul" (NJB, ASV, KJV) for Adam in verse 45; however, they all use "spiritual" body and "life-giving spirit" in the parallel for Christ. The problem is connected with different ancient anthropologies or understandings of human beings. The Greeks held a dualistic view of the dichotomy between the body and the soul (*psychē*); many, particularly those in the Platonic tradition, believed that the *psychē* was immortal, coming from the divine realm, to inhabit (temporarily) a physical body, and returned to the divine after death, often to be reincarnated in another body. However, this is not a Hebrew or biblical view: in Genesis, the Lord God creates Adam from the dust of the ground and breathes the breath of life (*ruach* in Hebrew means both wind and spirit) into him to make him a "living being" (a *nephesh chayya* in Gen. 2:7); when God takes breath away, human beings and animals die (see Psalm 104:29–30). Thus in Hebrew, human beings are *nephesh*, a physical body animated by the breath/wind/spirit as a psychosomatic unity. When this is translated into the Greek version, the Septuagint (LXX), *psychē* is used. Thus, in verse 45, when Paul quotes Genesis 2:7 (LXX), "the first man, Adam, became a living *psychēn*" (for the Hebrew a "living *nephesh*"), he means this Hebraic psychosomatic unity, rather than the Greek idea of a separate soul. While Adam was a "living being," *nephesh*, a creature formed from the dust and physical universe,

he dies when God takes away his breath of life and is buried as a *psychikos* body; the *-ikos* ending for adjectives often denotes "pertaining to" (thus *politikos* is linked to *polis*, as politics are about the affairs of the city), so "a *psychikos* body" here should probably be translated as "a body for the human realm" (Thiselton, *1 Corinthians*), or "the embodiment of ordinary nature" (N. T. Wright, *Resurrection of the Son of God*). Christ, however, the "man from heaven" became a "life-giving spirit" who can give the resurrection life, *to pneumatikon*, animated by the Spirit, "for the realm of the Spirit" (Thiselton again) to others by virtue of his death and resurrection as the first fruits (vv. 44–45). For further discussion, see Thiselton, *1 Corinthians*, 267–70 (on the same issue in I Cor. 2:14) and 1275–85. See also, Garland, *1 Corinthians*, 732–36; Fitzmyer, *1 Corinthians*, 593–98; Fee, *1 Corinthians*, 785–90; Collins, *1 Corinthians*, 569–71; Barrett, *1 Corinthians*, 372–74; and Keener, *1–2 Corinthians*, 132–33.

9. See note 8.

10. In addition to works cited earlier, the following are also useful in understanding this topic: Edward Adams and David G. Horrell, eds., *Christianity at Corinth: The Quest for the Pauline Church* (Louisville, KY: Westminster John Knox, 2004); and Karl Barth, *The Resurrection of the Dead* (London: Hodder & Stoughton, 1933).

11. See also the questions raised by N. T. Wright in his essay regarding this section of I Corinthians 15.

Selected Qur'ānic Texts

67:1–2

[1]Exalted is He who holds all control in His hands; who has power over all things; [2]who created death and life to test you and reveal which of you does best—He is the Mighty, the Forgiving.

21:35

[35]Every soul is certain to taste death: We test you all through the bad and the good, and to Us you will all return.

22:5–7

[5]People, [remember,] if you doubt the Resurrection, that We created you from dust, then a drop of fluid, then a clinging form, then a lump of flesh, both shaped and unshaped: We mean to make [Our power clear] to you. Whatever We choose We cause to remain in the womb for an appointed time, then We bring you forth as infants and then you grow and reach maturity. Some die young and some are left to live on to such an age that they forget all they once knew. You sometimes see the earth lifeless, yet when We send down water it stirs and swells and produces every kind of joyous growth: [6]this is because God is the Truth; He brings the dead back to life; He has power over everything. [7]There is no doubt that the Last Hour is bound to come, nor that God will raise the dead from their graves.

7:37–51

[37]Who is more wrong than the person who invents lies against God or rejects His revelations? Such people will have their preordained share [in this world],

but then, when Our angels arrive to take them back, saying, "Where are those you used to call on beside God?" they will say, "They have deserted us." They will confess that they were disbelievers. [38]God will say, "Join the crowds of jinn and humans who have gone before you into the Fire." Every crowd curses its fellow crowd as it enters, then, when they are all gathered inside, the last of them will say of the first, "Our Lord, it was they who led us astray: give them double punishment in the Fire"—God says, "Every one of you will have double punishment, though you do not know it"—[39]and the first of them will say to the last, "You were no better than us: taste the punishment you have earned."

[40]The gates of Heaven will not be open to those who rejected Our revelations and arrogantly spurned them; even if a thick rope were to pass through the eye of a needle they would not enter the Garden. This is how We punish the guilty—[41]Hell will be their resting place and their covering, layer upon layer—this is how We punish those who do evil. [42]But those who believe and do good deeds—and We do not burden any soul with more than it can bear—are the people of the Garden and there they will remain. [43]We shall have removed all ill feeling from their hearts; streams will flow at their feet. They will say, "Praise be to God, who guided us to this: had God not guided us, We would never have found the way. The messengers of our Lord brought the Truth." A voice will call out to them, "This is the Garden you have been given as your own on account of your deeds." [44]The people of the Garden will cry out to the people of the Fire, "We have found what our Lord promised us to be true. Have you found what your Lord promised you to be true?" and they will answer, "Yes." A voice will proclaim from their midst, "God's rejection [hangs] over the evildoers: [45]those who turned others away from God's path and tried to make it crooked, those who denied the Hereafter."

[46]A barrier divides the two groups with men on its heights recognizing each group by their marks: they will call out to the people of the Garden, "Peace be with you!"—they will not have entered, but they will be hoping, [47]and when their glance falls upon the people of the Fire, they will say, "Our Lord, do not let us join the evildoers!"—[48]and the people of the heights will call out to certain men they recognize by their marks, "What use were your great numbers and your false pride? [49]And are these the people you swore God would never bless? [Now these people are being told], 'Enter the Garden! No fear for you, nor shall you grieve.'"

⁵⁰The people of the Fire will call to the people of Paradise, "Give us some water, or any of the sustenance God has granted you!" and they will reply, "God has forbidden both to the disbelievers—⁵¹those who took their religion for distraction, a mere game, and were deluded by worldly life." Today We shall ignore them, just as they have ignored their meeting with this Day and denied Our Revelations.

75:20–25

²⁰Truly you [people] love this fleeting world ²¹and neglect the life to come. ²²On that Day there will be radiant faces, ²³looking toward their Lord, ²⁴and on that Day there will be the sad and despairing faces ²⁵of those who realize that a great calamity is about to befall them.

Commentary on Selected Qur'ānic Texts

MUHAMMAD ABDEL HALEEM

In the Qur'ān, death, resurrection, and destiny form an inescapable progression for humans. "It is God who created you, then provided for you, then causes you to die and then gives you life again" (30:40). "Then to Him you will return, then He will tell you what you have done" (6:60).

Since nobody seems to deny that humans die, the Qur'ān only reminds people that "every soul shall taste death" (3:185, 21:35) in order to spur them to think of what they should do beforehand and what will happen to them after death. Death is only a landmark between this life and the next.[1] "[God] created death and life to test you and reveal which of you does best" (67:2). Without this test and the resulting destiny in the next life, the creation of human beings merely for life in this world would be in vain, a futile act that does not befit God and would be contrary to divine justice (see, for example, 23:115–16, 95:7–8).

This is the scheme of things in the Qur'ān, but the Meccans, the first recipients of the Qur'ān (like many of those who argue the same way, even now), categorically denied the life to come. They always produced one argument: "What? When we have died and become dust and bones, will we be brought back to life? And our forebears too?" (54:47). Since the resurrection and judgment are so central to Islamic beliefs, the Qur'ān, over and over again during the Meccan period, had to come back to these themes in order to counter the disbelievers' arguments. The biggest hurdle in their minds was that they could not conceive of moving from one stage to another, from being reduced to dust and bones to being raised to life again. The Qur'ān's response was to cite for them situations from their own experience, as can be seen in 22:5–7, one of the selected texts printed earlier.

Seven stages of human development are mentioned in 22:5–7, each of which is new and different, even though we take them for granted and do not reflect on the power that brings about such changes. It is God who makes all this happen, and "He is the one who originates creation, and will produce it again—

147

this is even easier for Him" (30:27). Having shown how God moves his human creation from stage to stage, the Qur'ān then gives an example in the natural world that the disbelievers can see: the dead land that springs to life again (22:5).

We shall now turn to another of the selected Qur'ānic texts, 7:37–51, a lengthy passage displaying a prominent feature of the Qur'ān in that it presents arguments to support its teachings. This passage discusses the destiny of three groups: the disbelievers, the believers, and those in between who are still waiting for judgment, hoping to be admitted to Paradise, and praying not to be sent to join those in Hell. Here, most attention is given to those in Hell; however, it should be noted that, throughout the Qur'ān, the relative space given the three groups of humanity mentioned in 7:37–51 varies according to context.[2]

This passage exhibits other features of the style of the Qur'ān. The first is to involve the readers and listeners, and engage them in the discourse. One way of achieving this is the frequent use of the *jumla inshā'iyya* (affective sentence) in contrast to the *jumla khabariyya* (declarative or informative sentence). An affective sentence asks questions, gives direct commands and prohibitions, calls on people, and so on, rather than simply informing them of one thing or another. In the passage under consideration, five questions are asked: "Who is more wrong than the person who invents lies against God?" (7:37); "Where are those you used to called on beside God?" (7:37); "Have you found what your Lord promised you to be true?" (7:44); "What use were your great numbers and your false pride?" (7:48); and "Are these the people you swore God would never bless?" (7:49). It also speaks of five calls: "A voice will call out to them, 'This is the Garden you have been given'" (7:43). "The people of the Garden will call out to the people of the Fire, 'We have found what our Lord promised us to be true. Have you found what your Lord promised you to be true?'" (7:44). "[The people on the heights of the barrier] will call out to the people of the Garden, 'Peace be with you'" (7:46). "The people of the heights will call out to certain men they recognize by their marks, 'What use were your great numbers . . . ?'" (7:48). "The people of the Fire will call out to the people of Paradise, 'Give us some water, or any of the sustenance God has granted to you!'" (7:50). Thus, people of different groups speak for themselves, causing the passage to be full of life and drama.

Another Qur'ānic feature present here is the practice of rendering the contrast between the people of Paradise and the people of Hell more obvious by making people in each group even more aware of their own situation by seeing the circumstances of the other group. In this passage, those in Paradise are not enjoying their life in isolation, nor are those in the Fire suffering in isolation. They are in sight of each other. Those on the heights recognize each group by their marks, enter into dialogue, and ask questions. The people of the Fire make requests of the people of Paradise, which are refused. This mirrors what happens in the world, where disbelievers often taunt, disparage, or even oppress the believers. The situation, says the Qur'ān, is reversed in the afterlife: they who used to laugh at the believers in the world will be laughed at by the believers after the Judgment (83:29, 34).

In the passage under discussion, the people of the Garden are rejoicing at finding their Lord's promise to be true; the others recognize the truth of the promise in submission (7:44). The people of the Garden will have streams running at their feet (7:43); they will be told, "This is the Garden you have been given as your own" (7:43). The others are told they cannot enter it, "even if a thick rope were to pass through the eye of a needle" (7:40).[3] The people in the Garden are perfectly at peace with each other; all rancor has been removed from their hearts (7:43). The people of Hell blame and curse each other and demand double punishment for each other (7:38). As the Qur'ān says elsewhere, "On that Day, friends will become each other's enemies—not so the righteous" (43:67).

The Qur'ān informs people in this world about their destiny in the next, "giving good news and warning" (41:4). It leaves no excuse for the guilty to say, "Lord, if only you had sent us a messenger, we would have followed your revelations before we suffered humiliation and disgrace!" (20:134). Not only does it give good news and warning, but it also persuades and dissuades (targhīb wa tarhīb), making people desire or fear—which again is a prominent feature in the style of the Qur'ān.[4] This is always the case, even though in some contexts persuasion is given more prominence, and in other suitable contexts dissuasion is more conspicuous.

What are the crimes of the disbelievers in 7:37–51? In the first place, they invented lies about God (7:37), which in the idiom of the Qur'ān refers to ascribing partners to Him.[5] This is the gravest sin: "God does not forgive the joining of partners with Him: anything less than that, he forgives to whoever he will, but anyone who joins partners with God has fabricated a tremendous sin" (4:48). "Whoever does this has gone far, far astray" (4:116). The other grave sin noted in 7:37 is rejecting God's revelations—that is, arrogantly spurning them, turning others away from God's path and trying to make it crooked, disparaging the believers in this world, denying the Hereafter. Those who commit such sins are the ones who are seen here suffering in Hell. No suffering is seen here for ordinary mortals who may regularly commit lesser sins. Perhaps they have been covered by the Qur'ān's proviso that "If you avoid the great sins you have been forbidden, We shall wipe out your minor misdeeds and let you in through an entrance of honor" (4:31).

Moreover, repentance can save even those who commit major sins. In a lengthy aside, amid a description of the servants of God, the Qur'ān states the effects of repentance even after major sins like murder and adultery:

> those who do not invoke any other deity beside God, nor take a life, which God has made sacred, except in the pursuit of justice, nor commit adultery. (Whoever does these things will face the penalty. Their torment will be doubled on the Day of Resurrection and they will remain in torment, disgraced, except those who repent, believe and do good deeds: God will change the evil deeds of such people into good ones. He is most forgiving, most merciful. People who repent and do good deeds truly return to God.) (25:68–71)

Another important observation on 7:37–51 is this: with all the descriptions of the raging fire that would destroy anything instantly, people within Hell are talking and arguing with others. How is this possible? Do they do this during a break? The text is ambiguous about this. This suggests to me that we should reconsider carefully the overall picture of Hell in the entire Qur'ān. Further study is required on the questions of who goes to Hell, the actual extent and nature of the suffering there, and the duration of that suffering.

We turn now to another of the selected texts printed earlier: "On that Day there will be radiant faces, looking toward their Lord, and on that Day there will the sad and despairing faces of those who realize that a great calamity is about to befall them" (75:22–25). This passage gives a glimpse of the conditions of both the blessed and the damned on the Day of Judgment, as shown by the contrasting effects on their faces. It is noteworthy that, in giving the news of the Day of Judgment (in 88:1–13), the Qur'ān again goes straight to its effects on the faces of the damned, then the blessed—as if, between them, they sum up the whole story.[6] In other sūras, the faces of the blessed are described as "shining," "beaming," "laughing," and "rejoicing." The others' faces will be "darkened" (39:60); "humiliation will cover them as though their faces were covered with veils cut from the darkening night" (10:27); and "faces will be dust-stained and covered in darkness" (80:40–1). The radiant faces of the blessed will be "looking toward their Lord" (75:22). "They will be radiant with bliss, well pleased with their labor" (80:38–39). "You will recognize on their faces the radiant bliss" (83:24).

According to the Qur'ān, those guilty of transgression who deny the Day of Judgment in the here and now will be barred in the Hereafter from seeing their Lord (83:15). The vision of God is an issue that occupied a prominent place in theological works. The Muʿtazilites denied *ruʿyat Allah* (seeing God), since seeing something implies that it is a body in a place and a special direction, which then compromises the principle of *tawḥīd*—the oneness of God. Faced with such Qur'ānic references as 75:22–23, the Muʿtazilites set out to interpret them in such a way as to avoid implying that God would be seen. In the case of verses 75:22–23, cited earlier, their strategy was to consider the word *nāẓira-tun*—not as meaning "looking at" or "seeing," as understood by their opponents—but as a different word meaning "expecting" or "looking forward to." They further argued that the expression is elliptical, standing for the reward of their Lord rather than for the Lord Himself. This argument was powerfully refuted by the Ashʿarites and their followers.[7] In fact, the task before the Muʿtazilites was not as easy as they seemed to make it; it is not merely a matter of one or two verses about the face of God and seeing God but also of many verses about the hand of God, His throne and many acts of God, as in 2:245, 2:255, 5:64, 10:3, 39:67, 48:10, and 89:22.

Sayyid Quṭb (d. 1966) points out that arguments were raised about such examples whenever polemics became a favorite occupation—whereas, in fact, the expressions only follow a pattern of presentation common throughout the Qur'ān: *taṣwīr* (representation, use of imagery), which aims at explaining abstract ideas and bringing them nearer to our understanding. It is a consistent pattern that employs concrete imagery and personification. *Tawḥīd* (belief in the oneness of God) may be expected by some to necessitate complete negation of anthropomorphism; the fact that the Qur'ān does not deviate even in this sensitive area from its normal patterns of expression is clear evidence that *taṣwīr* is the basic rule of Qur'ānic expression.[8] Quṭb explains at length how we are filled with joy when we look at the manifestation of God in His Creation, and then goes on to ask: How will it be, then, when we look not at the beauty of God's Creation but at the beauty of God Himself? As for how we will look and with what organs and what means, this is all a discussion that would not occur to a heart that is filled with the joy expressed in the Qur'ānic text. Why should some people deprive their own souls of embracing this light (glowing as it is with joy and happiness) and occupy themselves with polemics (as did the Muʿtazilite theologians and their opponents from Ahl al-Sunna) about the exact nature of looking and seeing in the verse?[9] He concludes: "Let us then look forward to the overflow of happiness and the pure, sacred joy, which radiates from merely visualizing that situation as far as we humans can and let us occupy our souls with seeking this overflow of happiness. This in itself is a blessing, to be excelled only by the blessing of looking at the noble face of God."[10]

Notes

1. Both "life" and "death" are mentioned exactly the same number of times (115) in the Qur'ān. See M. F. ʿAbd al-Baqī, *Al-Muʿjam al mufahras li alfāẓ al-qur'ān al-karīm* (many editions) under *al-dunyā wa al-ākhira*.

2. Al-Shāṭibī, *al-Muwāfaqāt fī uṣūl al-sharīʿa*, part 3 (Beirut: 1975), 360.

3. Note that the Arabic word *jamal* means both "camel" and "thick rope." In 7:40, "camel" does not fit the context. A camel is not needed to demonstrate the impossibility of the situation; a pigeon would have been enough! Therefore, I translate *jamal* as "thick rope" here.

4. Al-Shāṭibī, *al-Muwāfaqāt fī uṣūl al-sharīʿa*, 358–66.

5. The Qur'ān considers this as *ẓulm*; the perpetrators are *ẓālimūn* (see 7:37, 41, 44, and 47). This is a complex term, difficult to translate because it involves *kufr* (disbelief) and injustice against God (see 31:13). Most translators render *ẓulm* and *ẓālimūn* as wrongdoing and wrongdoers, but I argue that this is inadequate. See footnote for 6:82 in M. A. S. Abdel Haleem, *The Qur'ān: a New Translation* (Oxford: Oxford University Press, 2010); see also Jalāl al-Dīn al-Suyūṭī, *Tafsīr al-Jalalayn* (many editions) at 6:82.

6. Muhammad Abdel Haleem *Understanding the Qur'ān: Themes and Style*, (London: I. B. Tauris, 2010), 123.

7. Sayf al-Dīn al-Āmidī, *Ghāyat al marām fī ʿilm al-kalām*, ed. H. M. Abdel Laṭīf (Cairo: Supreme Council of Islamic Affairs, 1971), 174–78.

8. Sayyid Quṭb, *Al-Taṣwīr al-fannī fī l-Qur'ān*, (Cairo: N.p., 1966), 73.

9. Sayyid Quṭb, *Fī ẓilāl al-Qur'ān*, Vol. 6 (Cairo: Dār al-Shorouk, 1985), 3771.

10. Ibid.

Selected Passages from al-Ghazālī's *The Remembrance of Death and the Afterlife*

1. Know that the heart of the man who is engrossed in this world and is given over to its vanities and harbours love for its appetites must certainly be neglectful of the remembrance of death. Thus failing to recall it, when reminded of it he finds it odious and shies away. (7)

2. The Emissary of God (may God bless him and grant him peace) once went out to the mosque and noticed a group of people talking and laughing. "Remember death!" he said. "By Him in Whose hand lies my soul, if you knew what I know you would laugh little and weep much." (10)

3. 'Umar ibn 'Abd al-'Azīz used every night to gather together the doctors of the Law, and they would remind one another of death, the Arising and the Afterlife until they broke out in tears as though at a funeral. (11)

4. Ṣafīya (may God be pleased with her) told of an old woman who once complained to 'Ā'isha (may God be pleased with her) of the hardness of her heart. "Remember death frequently," she told her, "and your heart will be softened." This she did, and her heart was indeed made soft. She went to thank 'Ā'isha (may God be pleased with her). (11)

5. Know that death is a terrible and most perilous thing. The heedlessness with which the people treat it is the consequence only of their insufficient meditation upon it and remembrance thereof. Even the man who does remember it does not do so with an unoccupied heart, but rather with one that is busy with the desires of this world, so that the remembrance of death does not have a salutary effect upon his heart. The way forward here is for the bondsman to void his heart of all things save the recollection of the demise which lies before him, in the way that the man who intends a dangerous journey to a desert place or to set sail upon the ocean does not think of any other matter. When the remembrance of death touches his heart and comes to make some impression upon it his contentment and pleasure in the world will wane and his heart will break. The most productive method

of bringing this about is for him to make frequent remembrance of those of his peers and associates who have passed away before him: he should contemplate their death and dissolution beneath the earth and recall how they appeared in their former positions and circumstances, and meditate upon the way in which the earth has now obliterated the beauty of their forms, and how their parts have been scattered in their tombs, and how they have made widows of their wives and orphans of their children; how they lost their property, and how their mosques and gatherings have become voided of them, and of how their very traces have been wiped away. (12–13)

6. Know that funerals are a lesson to the man possessed of insight, and a reminder and a counsel to all save the people of heedlessness. For these latter are increased only in hardness of heart by witnessing them as they imagine that for all time they will be watching the funerals of others, and never reckon that they themselves must needs be carried in a funeral cortège. Even if they do so reckon, they do not deem this to be something near at hand. They do not consider that those who are carried now in funeral processions thought likewise. Vain, then, are their imaginings, and soon their allotted lifespans will be done.

    Therefore let no bondsman watch a funeral without considering that he himself is the one being borne aloft, for so he will be before long: on the morrow, or on the day that follows: it is as if the event had already occurred. (97)

7. In general, the visitation of graves is a desirable thing, for it instils the remembrance of death and acts as an admonition. To visit the tombs of the righteous in order to obtain blessings and a lesson is desirable likewise . . . the Emissary of God (may God bless him and grant him peace) said "I once forbade you to visit graves, but you should now visit them, for they remind you of the Afterlife. But do not utter defamations." (111–12)

8. It is the preferred practice when visiting a grave to stand with one's back to the Direction of Prayer [qibla] and to orient oneself towards the countenance of the deceased before greeting him. The tomb should not be rubbed, touched or kissed, for such are the practices of the Christians. (113–14)

9. Said Abū Hurayra, "Whenever a man passes by the grave of a man he used to know and greets him, he is recognised and his greeting is returned. And when he passes by the grave of one unknown to him and gives a greeting, his greeting is returned also." (114)

10. The Emissary of God (may God bless him and grant him peace) said, "The dead man in his grave is like a drowning man shouting for help, as he waits for a prayer to come to him from his father, his brother or his friend. When it comes it is more beloved to him than the world and all it contains. Indeed, the gifts of the living to the dead are prayer and the petitioning of God for His forgiveness." (116)

11. Know that men entertain many false and mistaken notions regarding the true nature of death. Some have imagined that death is extinction, and that there is to be neither Resurrection nor Concourse, nor any consequence to good or evil, and that man's death is as the drying up of plants and the death of animals. This is the opinion of the Atheists [al-mulḥidūn] and of all those who have no faith in God and the Last Day.

   Another group has it that man becomes nothingness with death, and that for the duration of his sojourn in the grave he neither suffers chastisement nor feels the delight of any reward until he is restored together at the time of the Concourse. And still others hold that the spirit remains and is not extinguished by death, but that it is the spirits which experience reward or punishment rather than the bodies, which are not restored or resurrected at all.

   These beliefs are all unsound and far removed from the truth. (121–22)

12. The most perfect of delights is that which is the lot of the Martyrs who are slain in the way of God. For when they advance into battle they cut themselves off from any concern with the attachments of the world in their yearning to meet God, happy to be killed for the sake of obtaining His pleasure. Should such a man think upon the world he would know that he has sold it willingly for the Afterlife, and the seller's heart never inclines to that which has been sold. And when he thinks upon the Afterlife, he knows that he had longed for it, and has now purchased it. (128)

13. Know that after the believer dies there is revealed to him of the mightiness and great majesty of God something in comparison to which this world is no more than a narrow gaol [jail]. He is like a prisoner in a gloomy chamber from which a door has been opened onto a spacious garden stretching as far as his eyes can see, containing diverse trees, flowers, birds and fruit, and cannot therefore wish to return to the gloomy gaol. The Emissary of God (may God bless him and grant him peace) provided such a simile when he said, regarding a man who had died, "He has now voyaged from this world and left it to its inhabitants. If he is of the blessed then he will no more

wish to return to it than would any one of you wish to return to his mother's belly." Thus he informs us that the relation between the expanse of the next world and that of this is as the difference between the breadth of this world and the darkness of the womb. (130)

14. In what preceded you came to know how violent are a man's states during the agonies of death and how perilous is his condition as he fearfully awaits his fate, as he endures the grave's darkness and worms, and suffers the Questioning of Munkar and Nakīr, to be followed, should he have incurred God's wrath, by the perils of the Punishment of the Grave.

   More fearsome than all of this, however, are the perils which shall confront him subsequently: the Trumpet-Blast, the Resurrection on the Day of Arising, the Presentation before the Almighty, the Inquisition regarding matters both important and minor, the Erection of the Scales in order that men's destinies might be known, and then the passage over the Traverse despite the fineness and sharpness of its edge. These things shall be followed by the awaiting of the Summons to final judgement, and either bliss or misery.

   You are obliged to know of these circumstances and these terrible events, and to believe in them with a firm and convinced faith; you must ponder them at length so that there might issue from your heart a motivation to make ready for them. For faith in the Last Day has not entered or become firmly established in the hearts of the greater part of mankind, as is demonstrated by the great preparations they make for the summer's heat and the cold of winter, and their making light of the heat of the Inferno and its bitter cold, and the woes and terrors which it contains. Of course, if they are questioned regarding the Last Day their tongues wag in affirmation; however their hearts remain quite heedless of it. (173)

15. So picture yourself, O unfortunate one, with the angels grasping your upper arms as you stand before God (Exalted is He!), as He, speaking with His voice, demands of you, "Did I not bless you with youth? How did you employ it? Did I not grant you long life? How did you spend it? Did I not bestow wealth upon you? Whence did you come by it, and how did you expend it? Did I not ennoble you with knowledge? How did you act by what you knew?" (191)

16. Mankind, after the terrors [mentioned previously], shall be driven to the Traverse, which is a bridge stretched over the gulf of Hell, sharper than a sword and thinner than a hair. Whosoever has in the world kept upright

upon the Straight Path [*al-ṣirāṭ al-mustaqīm*] shall bear lightly upon the Traverse [*ṣirāṭ*] of the Afterlife, and will be saved. But whosoever deviates from uprightness in this world, and weighs down his back with burdens, and disobeys his Lord, shall slip upon taking his first step on the Traverse, and shall go to perdition.

Now meditate upon the terror which shall alight upon your heart at the time when you behold the Traverse and its slenderness, and when your eye then falls upon the core of the Inferno beneath you as your ears are assailed by the moaning and raging of Hell. (206)

17. And he said (may God bless him and grant him peace), "On the Day of Arising I shall lead the Prophets in prayer, and shall preach to them, and shall be the Exerciser of the Intercession; and I do not boast." (211–12)

18. How would you be were you to behold them, when their faces have turned blacker than charcoal, and when their eyes have been put out, their tongues struck dumb, their backs broken and their bones snapped, their ears and noses severed, their skin torn, and their hands shackled to their necks, and their forelocks pressed against their feet as they walk upon the fire on their faces, stepping with their eyeballs upon spikes of iron? The raging fire shall have entered into the depths of their every part, as the snakes and scorpions of the Abyss cling to their extremities. (221)

19. Look now at the serpents and scorpions of the Inferno, their strong venom, their great size, and the hideousness of their appearance. They are let loose against its inhabitants and goaded against them, and do not tire of stinging and biting for a single moment. (226)

20. Such, then, are the varieties of the Inferno's torments described in general terms. The details of the sorrows, laments, trials and sufferings which it shall encompass are without end. Yet despite all the pain that they suffer, their grief over having missed the delight which is in Heaven and the meeting with God (Exalted is He!), and losing His satisfaction, is greater still, for they know that they have sold all of these things *for a paltry price, a few dirhams*, having traded them for nothing more than the base pleasures of the world .... (229)

21. Know that that Abode, the woes and sorrows of which you now have come to know, is complemented by another Abode. (232)

22. The Emissary of God (may God bless him and grant him peace) was once asked about His statement (Exalted is He!), *And goodly dwellings in gardens*

of Eden, and he replied, "They are palaces of pearls, in each of which are seventy ruby mansions, in each of which are seventy emerald rooms, in each of which are seventy beds, on each of which are seventy mattresses of every hue, on each of which is a wife who is one of the Large-eyed Houris. And in every room there are seventy tables, on each of which are seventy varieties of food. In every house are seventy servant-girls. Every morning the believer shall be given strength enough to enjoy all of this." (238)

23. Said Abū Hurayra, "The Emissary of God (may God bless him and grant him peace) said, 'In Heaven there lies a tree in the shade of which a rider could journey for a hundred years without traversing it. Recite, if you wish, *And shade outspread*.'" (239)

24. Abū Hurayra has narrated that the Prophet (may God bless him and grant him peace) once said, "Whoever enters Heaven shall find comfort and no distress; his garments shall not grow threadbare, neither shall his youth ever come to an end. In Heaven there shall be that which no eye has seen, no ear heard, and which has never occurred to mortal mind." (240–41)

25. Muslim relates in his *Ṣaḥīḥ* that Ṣuhayb once said, "The Emissary of God (may God bless him and grant him peace) recited His word (Exalted is He!): *For those that wrought good shall be the greatest good, and even more* [and commented as follows]: 'When the people of Heaven enter Heaven and those of Hell enter Hell, a herald shall call out, saying, "O people of Heaven! There is a tryst for you with your Lord, which He wishes to bring about for you." "What might that tryst be?" they enquire. "Did he not load heavily our scales, and whiten our faces, and bring us into Heaven and deliver us from Hell?" And the veil is lifted, and they gaze upon the countenance of God (Great and Glorious is He!), and never had they been given anything more beloved to them than this.'"

This Tradition of the Vision, which is narrated by a number of the Companions, reveals the supreme height of the *greatest good*, and the very limit of bliss. All that we have detailed regarding the delights [of Heaven] shall at that moment be forgotten, for the rapture felt by Heaven's people at the Meeting shall be without end; neither shall any of the pleasures of Heaven stand any comparison with it at all. (251)

26. And it is related that when the Day of Arising comes, God (Exalted is He!) shall bring forth a book from beneath the Throne, in which it is written: "My Mercy has outstripped My wrath. I am the Most Merciful of all that

show mercy." And from out of Hell shall proceed the number of Heaven's folk twice multiplied.

And God's Emissary has said (may God bless him and grant him peace), "On the Day of Arising, God (Great and Glorious is He!) shall joyfully appear before us, and declare, 'Rejoice, O assembly of Muslims! For there is not one of you that has not had his place in Hell taken by a Jew or a Christian!'" (253–54)

27. It is related that during one of the campaigns a boy was standing and being sold off, this being on an intensely hot summer's day. He was seen by a woman concealed among the people, who made her way forwards vigorously with her companions behind her, until she took up the child and clutched him to her breast. Then she turned her back to the valley to keep the heat away from him, saying "My son! My son!" At this the people wept, and left what they were doing. Then the Emissary of God (may God bless him and grant him peace) came up and stood before them. They told him of what had transpired, and he was delighted to see their compassion. Then he gave them glad news, saying, "Marvel you at this woman's compassion for her son?" and they said that they did. And he declared (may God bless him and grant him peace), "Truly, God (Blessed and Exalted is He!) is even more compassionate towards you all than is this woman towards her son." At this, the Muslims went apart in the greatest rapture and joy.

These traditions . . . give us the glad news of the wide compass of God's Mercy (Exalted is He!). It is our hope that He will not deal with us as we deserve, but will rather grant us that which is appropriate to Him, in His generosity, abundant indulgence, and mercy. (260–61)

Note

From Al-Ghazālī, *The Remembrance of Death and the Afterlife*—Kitāb dhikr al-mawt wa-mā baʿdahu—*Book XL of The Revival of the Religious Sciences*—Iḥyāʾ ʿulūm al-dīn—translated with an introduction and notes by T. J. Winter (Cambridge: Islamic Texts Society, 1989). Numbers in parentheses after each of the passages refer to pages in this volume.

Al-Ghazālī on Death

TIM WINTER

"W ho speaks for Islam?" is, in interfaith discussions as in the general assessment of what is normative in history and Islam's present-day reality, a question that must be variously answered. Traditional Catholicism could title Aquinas the "Angelic Doctor" and set a magisterial seal of approval on his oeuvre; but for Islam, the decentered nature of religious authority into a madrassa-based establishment in some respects resembling the rabbinate, has always militated against the emergence of a unanimous Muslim vote. Still, to judge by the number and geographical extent of manuscript copies of his work, and the very widespread acknowledgment of his own claim to have been the Renewer (*mujaddid*) of his century, it is conventional and quite justifiable for Islamic Studies to consider al-Ghazālī "the greatest Muslim after Muḥammad"—as normative a figure as the religion can produce.

Abū Ḥāmid al-Ghazālī (d. 1111) was born in the city of Ṭūs in Central Asia. He studied under some of the greatest legal and theological minds of his time before being appointed, at the age of only thirty, to a prestigious theology chair by the Seljuk grand vizier Niẓām al-Mulk. Some five years later, he experienced a shattering crisis of personal faith that forced him to resign his chair and adopt the lifestyle of a wandering seeker after truth. Some ten years later, he returned to teaching, having apparently found answers to his questions—the "light of certainty" having been cast by God into his heart.

Al-Ghazālī wrote dozens of significant and often lengthy works, including major compendia of Islamic law and a monument of sophisticated philosophical polemic, *The Incoherence of the Philosophers*, in which he showed the internal contradictions in some of Avicenna's positions on cosmology. This and some other metaphysical works by him were translated into Latin, and he was known to Scholastics as "Algazel."

His work on metaphysics, however, needs to be seen in the context of his nuanced juxtaposition of formal philosophical theology with Sufism. The latter discipline had furnished him with the answers he sought, not through ratiocination but by what he calls "tasting"—direct religious experience. In a number of his later works, he seeks to resolve the evident tension between the two paths to knowing God—including in his *Restraining the Commonalty from the Science of Philosophical Theology*, finished only a few days before his death. These works proved hugely influential in the Sunni Islamic world, demonstrating that although reason had its uses, and that the exposition of truth and the refutation of heresy needed to make masterful use of logic, it could not reliably bring human beings to a knowledge of God. That task was the responsibility of the Sufi sages, who taught a program of self-abnegation and service rooted in what al-Ghazālī sees as the most fundamental of Islamic virtues: the principle of love (*maḥabba*).

Despite the wide influence of many of his other works, which continue to be central to the Islamic intellectual curriculum today, al-Ghazālī's most original and widely read text was almost certainly his *Revival of the Religious Sciences* (*Iḥyāʾ ʿUlūm al-Dīn*). This lengthy encyclopedia of religious knowing, composed in forty books, was written in a particularly powerful hortatory spirit, in a lucid and compelling Arabic that throughout appeals to the emotions of the God-conscious believer who "hopes for God's mercy and fears his own sin." The meaning of the title of the *Revival* is disputed, but it seems likely that al-Ghazālī intended to galvanize what he saw as the worldly and complacent religious classes of his time with a summons to action "on the path of the Afterlife."

The *Revival* follows a complex structure, but al-Ghazālī's usual pattern is to open each section by deploying relevant scriptural passages from Qurʾān and Ḥadīth, followed by sayings of the Sufi masters, and then—where he judges it necessary—his own disquisition. Part of the power of his text lies in its display of the remarkable comprehensiveness of Qurʾānic teaching: on each of his literally hundreds of legal, spiritual, ethical, and dogmatic subjects, he is able to produce Qurʾānic citations; indeed, the *Revival* has sometimes been treated as a complex meditation on the revealed text itself.

Central to al-Ghazālī's strategy of warning his contemporaries—and the complexity of some of the theological issues discussed in parts of the *Revival* suggests that he hoped that very senior scholars would be moved to read it—was his proclamation of the need to ready oneself for death. In this, commentators have often seen a characteristically Ghazālian ability to energize his work with the spirit of the Qurʾānic revelation, many of whose earliest passages warned of the end of time and the inexorability of judgment. The inner traumas through which he had passed in his own life also allowed him to preach powerfully on the topic of death and the gravity of human transgression, since his own crisis and subsequent repentance were clearly triggered or at least intensified by a consciousness of his own mortality.

The Remembrance of Death and the Afterlife is the fortieth and last "book" of the *Revival.*[1] The forty books begin with a *Book of Knowledge,* followed by a *Book of Foundational Doctrines,* after which al-Ghazālī progresses through a treatment of the inner significance of worship, the ways of sacralizing daily life (marriage, travel, business, etc.), a list of vices, and then a list of "Saving Virtues," of which remembering death is the last. But throughout the *Revival,* the reality of death is a leitmotif, energizing his writing about the urgency of repentance and rededication to God. Death is the reason why we should take life seriously: all we have will pass away, and to emulate the Prophet fully is to "be in this world as a stranger or a wayfarer."[2] His life of holy poverty is constantly invoked, as is his unremitting recollection of God. Here, as throughout the *Revival,* the spiritual path is identical to the process of conforming to the Prophetic excellence, the *imitatio Muhammadi.* As the Qur'ān says: "Say: if you love God, then follow me" (3:31).

The *Remembrance of Death* is the longest book in the *Revival*—almost three hundred pages in the English translation—partly because it is so wide-ranging. Early chapters deal with the need to remember death, the virtue of harboring "short hopes" in this world, the exemplary deaths of the Prophet and the Four Caliphs, and the agonies of death together with information on visiting graves and what may be expected when experiencing a dream of someone who has died. There is also an extensive treatment of the *barzakh*—the intermediate state in the grave between death and resurrection—which serves as a kind of anticipation of one's final destiny.

This is followed by a second part that covers the usual doctrines developed by al-Ghazālī's Ashʿarī tradition about the sequence of events at the Resurrection and subsequently: the angel Isrāfīl will blow the Last Trump in Jerusalem, and the quick and the dead will rise in terror to confront the divine wrath under a burning sun. A "balance made of light" will be set up, in which one's deeds are weighed; there is also a bridge "sharper than a sword" stretched across Hell, over which all must pass—the ill-fortuned will fall to destruction. A long section details the Prophet's intercession (*shafāʿa*) for mortal sinners, explaining that at this time the Prophet's unique name of "God's Beloved" will be manifest for all the nations to see: everyone else is thinking only of themselves, but the Prophet is pleading for sinners, the "Banner of Praise" in his hand.

Al-Ghazālī recounts, essentially in the words of scripture, the joys of Paradise and the torments of Hell and includes a section on the creedally important doctrine that the believers will experience a beatific vision of God in Paradise—a doctrine affirmed by Sunnism but denied by many early sects. Finally, he ends with "Chapter on the Wide Compass of God's Mercy," in which he lists a number of well-known ḥadīths indicating the primacy of the principle of divine mercy, which, as a ḥadīth says, "overcomes God's wrath."[3]

Although al-Ghazālī was inspired by earlier devotional works such as the *Food of Hearts* of Abū Ṭālib al-Makkī (d. 996) and the *Book of the Mind's Depiction* of al-Ḥārith al-Muḥāsibī (d. 857), and he generally locates himself in the "sober" and devotional Baghdad school of Sufism, the *Remembrance* is very original in its form. It is not only written as a dazzling and terrifying cadenza to the long meditations of the *Revival* but also as a means of demonstrating how formal doctrines are useful as tokens of orthodox adherence and are all spiritual tools that help to melt our hearts. That is his final purpose in his *Revival*: to show that "spirituality" is not an addendum to Islam but is synonymous with it. All the complex doctrines and liturgical and legal rites are part of a single project whereby the Muslim overcomes passion and selfhood and reconfigures himself in the image of the Prophet, whose balance between fear and hope yielded such a passionate love for God and His creatures. As recent studies by Eric Ormsby and Frank Griffel have shown, love is the key religious driver for al-Ghazālī.[4] Even in this terrifying book about God's wrath and judgment, we are regularly and discreetly reassured that mercy will have the last word.

The power of the book ensures that it has a life outside the formal processes of studying al-Ghazālī's *Revival*. It is very often used as the basis for Friday sermons and television and radio broadcasts, and is found published separately in Arabic bookshops and across the Muslim world. Meditation on death and firm belief in the events of the next world are still normal in Islamic piety. The great majority of Muslims continue to believe strongly in the doctrines and attitudes presented in this book.[5]

Notes

1. See Abū Ḥāmid al-Ghazālī, *The Remembrance of God and the Afterlife*, 7th ed., trans. T. J. Winter (Cambridge: Islamic Texts Society, 2008).

2. Bukhārī, *Riqāq*, 4.

3. Bukhārī, *Tawba*, 15.

4. See Eric Ormsby, *Ghazali: the Revival of Islam* (Oxford: Oneworld, 2007); and Frank Griffel, *Al-Ghazālī's Philosophical Theology* (Oxford: Oxford University Press, 2009). See also, Abū Ḥāmid al-Ghazālī, *Love, Longing, Intimacy and Contentment*, trans. Eric Ormsby (Cambridge: Islamic Texts Society, 2011).

5. For further reading, in addition to works already cited, see Timothy J. Gianotti, *Al-Ghazālī's Unspeakable Doctrine of the Soul: Unveiling the Esoteric Psychology and Eschatology of the Iḥyā'* (Leiden: E. J. Brill, 2001); Jane Idleman Smith and Yvonne Haddad, *The Islamic Understanding of Death and Resurrection*, 2nd ed. (New York: Oxford University Press, 2002).

Selected Passages from Dante's
The Divine Comedy

Inferno 3, 1–9 *Words inscribed in the portal above the wide-open entrance to Hell*

"THROUGH me you pass into the city of woe:
Through me you pass into eternal pain:
Through me among the people lost for aye.
Justice the founder of my fabric mov'd:
To rear me was the task of power divine,
Supremest wisdom, and primeval love.
Before me things create were none, save things
Eternal, and eternal I endure.
All hope abandon ye who enter here."

Inferno 5, 109–23 *Dante relates his encounter with Paolo and Francesca in the Circle of the sinners of Lust*

At hearing which downward I bent my looks,
And held them there so long, that the bard cried:
"What art thou pond'ring?" I in answer thus:
"Alas! by what sweet thoughts, what fond desire
Must they at length to that ill pass have reach'd!"
    Then turning, I to them my speech address'd.
And thus began: "Francesca! your sad fate
Even to tears my grief and pity moves.
But tell me; in the time of your sweet sighs,
By what, and how love granted, that ye knew
Your yet uncertain wishes?" She replied:
"No greater grief than to remember days
Of joy, when mis'ry is at hand! That kens
Thy learn'd instructor."

Inferno 7, 106–26   *Entry into the Circle of Anger whose inhabitants are indistinguishable one from another because of the nature of their sin*

Far murkier was the wave
Than sablest grain: and we in company
Of th' inky waters, journeying by their side,
Enter'd, though by a different track, beneath.
Into a lake, the Stygian nam'd, expands
The dismal stream, when it hath reach'd the foot
Of the grey wither'd cliffs. Intent I stood
To gaze, and in the marish sunk descried
A miry tribe, all naked, and with looks
Betok'ning rage. They with their hands alone
Struck not, but with the head, the breast, the feet,
Cutting each other piecemeal with their fangs.

      The good instructor spake; "Now seest thou, son!
The souls of those, whom anger overcame.
This too for certain know, that underneath
The water dwells a multitude, whose sighs
Into these bubbles make the surface heave,
As thine eye tells thee wheresoe'er it turn.
Fix'd in the slime they say: "Sad once were we
In the sweet air made gladsome by the sun,
Carrying a foul and lazy mist within:
Now in these murky settlings are we sad."
Such dolorous strain they gurgle in their throats.
But word distinct can utter none."

Inferno 28, 118–42   *Encounter with one of the sowers of Discord in the ninth pocket of Fraud (Eighth Circle)*

I saw, and yet it seems to pass before me,
A headless trunk, that even as the rest
Of the sad flock pac'd onward. By the hair
It bore the sever'd member, lantern-wise

Pendent in hand, which look'd at us and said,
"Woe's me!" The spirit lighted thus himself,
And two there were in one, and one in two.
How that may be he knows who ordereth so.

When at the bridge's foot direct he stood,
His arm aloft he rear'd, thrusting the head
Full in our view, that nearer we might hear
The words, which thus it utter'd: "Now behold
This grievous torment, thou, who breathing go'st
To spy the dead; behold if any else
Be terrible as this. And that on earth
Thou mayst bear tidings of me, know that I
Am Bertrand, he of Born, who gave King John
The counsel mischievous. Father and son
I set at mutual war. For Absalom
And David more did not Ahitophel,
Spurring them on maliciously to strife.
For parting those so closely knit, my brain
Parted, alas! I carry from its source,
That in this trunk inhabits. Thus the law
Of retribution fiercely works in me."

Inferno 34, 10–69 *At the frozen core of Hell Dante sees Satan; those being devoured by him—Judas, Brutus and Cassius—are examples of treachery*

Now came I (and with fear I bid my strain
Record the marvel) where the souls were all
Whelm'd underneath, transparent, as through glass
Pellucid the frail stem. Some prone were laid,
Others stood upright, this upon the soles,
That on his head, a third with face to feet
Arch'd like a bow. When to the point we came,
Whereat my guide was pleas'd that I should see
The creature eminent in beauty once,

He from before me stepp'd and made me pause.
    "Lo!" he exclaim'd, "lo Dis! and lo the place,
Where thou hast need to arm thy heart with strength."
    How frozen and how faint I then became,
Ask me not, reader! for I write it not,
Since words would fail to tell thee of my state.
I was not dead nor living. Think thyself
If quick conception work in thee at all,
How I did feel. That emperor, who sways
The realm of sorrow, at mid breast from th' ice
Stood forth; and I in stature am more like
A giant, than the giants are in his arms.
Mark now how great that whole must be, which suits
With such a part. If he were beautiful
As he is hideous now, and yet did dare
To scowl upon his Maker, well from him
May all our mis'ry flow. Oh what a sight!
How passing strange it seem'd, when I did spy
Upon his head three faces: one in front
Of hue vermilion, th' other two with this
Midway each shoulder join'd and at the crest;
The right 'twixt wan and yellow seem'd: the left
To look on, such as come from whence old Nile
Stoops to the lowlands. Under each shot forth
Two mighty wings, enormous as became
A bird so vast. Sails never such I saw
Outstretch'd on the wide sea. No plumes had they,
But were in texture like a bat, and these
He flapp'd I' th' air, that from him issued still
Three winds, wherewith Cocytus to its depth
Was frozen. At six eyes he wept: the tears
Adown three chins distill'd with bloody foam.
At every mouth his teeth a sinner champ'd
Bruis'd as with pond'rous engine, so that three
Were in this guise tormented. But far more
Than from that gnawing, was the foremost pang'd

By the fierce rending, whence ofttimes the back
Was stript of all its skin. "That upper spirit,
Who hath worse punishment," so spake my guide,
"Is Judas, he that hath his head within
And plies the feet without. Of th' other two,
Whose heads are under, from the murky jaw
Who hangs, is Brutus: lo! how he doth writhe
And speaks not! Th' other Cassius, that appears
So large of limb. But night now re-ascends,
And it is time for parting. All is seen."

Purgatorio 1, 1–6   *Dante, poet and pilgrim, enters Purgatorio*

O'er better waves to speed her rapid course
The light bark of my genius lifts the sail,
Well pleas'd to leave so cruel sea behind;
And of that second region will I sing,
In which the human spirit from sinful blot
Is purg'd, and for ascent to Heaven prepares.

Purgatorio 3, 121–23   *Manfred, natural son and grandson of emperors, explains how even a sinner and excommunicate like he is redeemed*

My sins were horrible; but so wide arms
Hath goodness infinite, that it receives
All who turn to it.

Purgatorio 4, 88–96   *Virgil, symbol of correct human reason, reveals the plan of Purgatorio to Dante*

He thus to me: "Such is this steep ascent,
That it is ever difficult at first,
But, more a man proceeds, less evil grows.
When pleasant it shall seem to thee, so much

That upward going shall be easy to thee.
As in a vessel to go down the tide,
Then of this path thou wilt have reach'd the end.
There hope to rest thee from thy toil. No more
I answer, and thus far for certain know."

Purgatorio 16, 1–24   *Dante, himself not immune to this sin in his former life, enters the terrace where the elect are purged of all stain of anger*

Hell's dunnest gloom, or night unlustrous, dark,
Of every planes 'reft, and pall'd in clouds,
Did never spread before the sight a veil
In thickness like that fog, nor to the sense
So palpable and gross. Ent'ring its shade,
Mine eye endured not with unclosed lids;
Which marking, near me drew the faithful guide,
Offering me his shoulder for a stay.
     As the blind man behind his leader walks,
Lest he should err, or stumble unawares
On what might harm him, or perhaps destroy,
I journey'd through that bitter air and foul,
Still list'ning to my escort's warning voice,
"Look that from me thou part not." Straight I heard
Voices, and each one seem'd to pray for peace,
And for compassion, to the Lamb of God
That taketh sins away. Their prelude still
Was "Agnus Dei," and through all the choir,
One voice, one measure ran, that perfect seem'd
The concord of their song. "Are these I hear
Spirits, O master?" I exclaim'd; and he:
"Thou aim'st aright: these loose the bonds of wrath."

Purgatorio 18, 89–105   *Dante experiences the zeal expressed in the prayer of the penitents of the sin of sloth*

       for suddenly a multitude,
The steep already turning, from behind,
Rush'd on. With fury and like random rout,
As echoing on their shores at midnight heard
Ismenus and Asopus, for his Thebes
If Bacchus' help were needed; so came these
Tumultuous, curving each his rapid step,
By eagerness impell'd of holy love.
       Soon they o'ertook us; with such swiftness mov'd
The mighty crowd. Two spirits at their head
Cried weeping; "Blessed Mary sought with haste
The hilly region. Caesar to subdue
Ilerda, darted in Marseilles his sting,
And flew to Spain."—"Oh tarry not: away;"
The others shouted; "let not time be lost
Through slackness of affection. Hearty zeal
To serve reanimates celestial grace."

Purgatorio 27, 19–57   *Dante is urged by Virgil to overcome the final trial of Purgatorio before he can be with Beatrice*

Th' escorting spirits turn'd with gentle looks
Toward me, and the Mantuan spake: "My son,
Here torment thou mayst feel, but canst not death.
Remember thee, remember thee, if I
Safe e'en on Geryon brought thee: now I come
More near to God, wilt thou not trust me now?
Of this be sure: though in its womb that flame
A thousand years contain'd thee, from thy head
No hair should perish. If thou doubt my truth,
Approach, and with thy hands thy vesture's hem
Stretch forth, and for thyself confirm belief.
Lay now all fear, O lay all fear aside.

Turn hither, and come onward undismay'd."
I still, though conscience urg'd no step advanc'd.
     When still he saw me fix'd and obstinate,
Somewhat disturb'd he cried: "Mark now, my son,
From Beatrice thou art by this wall
Divided." As at Thisbe's name the eye
Of Pyramus was open'd (when life ebb'd
Fast from his veins), and took one parting glance,
While vermeil dyed the mulberry; thus I turn'd
To my sage guide, relenting, when I heard
The name, that springs forever in my breast.
He shook his forehead; and, "How long," he said,
"Linger we now?" then smil'd, as one would smile
Upon a child, that eyes the fruit and yields.
Into the fire before me then he walk'd;
And Statius, who erewhile no little space
Had parted us, he pray'd to come behind.
     I would have cast me into molten glass
To cool me, when I enter'd; so intense
Rag'd the conflagrant mass. The sire belov'd,
To comfort me, as he proceeded, still
Of Beatrice talk'd. "Her eyes," saith he,
"E'en now I seem to view." From the other side
A voice, that sang, did guide us, and the voice
Following, with heedful ear, we issued forth,
There where the path led upward.

Paradiso 3, 70–87   *The response of Piccarda, whom Dante
had known as a nun in Florence, when asked by him whether
she regrets the relatively low place in Paradise assigned to her
by God.*

    "Brother! our will
Is in composure settled by the power
Of charity, who makes us will alone

What we possess, and nought beyond desire;
If we should wish to be exalted more,
Then must our wishes jar with the high will
Of him, who sets us here, which in these orbs
Thou wilt confess not possible, if here
To be in charity must needs befall,
And if her nature well thou contemplate.
Rather it is inherent in this state
Of blessedness, to keep ourselves within
The divine will, by which our wills with his
Are one. So that as we from step to step
Are plac'd throughout this kingdom, pleases all,
E'en as our King, who in us plants his will;
And in his will is our tranquillity;
It is the mighty ocean, whither tends
Whatever it creates and nature makes."

Paradiso 5, 100–108   *As Beatrice and Dante enter a further realm of Paradise, heavenly beings draw near to them in joy, welcoming Dante as one of their own*

As in a quiet and clear lake the fish,
If aught approach them from without, do draw
Towards it, deeming it their food; so drew
Full more than thousand splendours towards us,
And in each one was heard: "Lo! one arriv'd
To multiply our loves!" and as each came
The shadow, streaming forth effulgence new,
Witness'd augmented joy.

Paradiso 20, 67–72   *The eagle of justice concludes his survey of just rulers in Paradise with this note of surprise at the presence of Riphaeus, a pagan dead long before Christ's birth*

"Who in the erring world beneath would deem,
That Trojan Ripheus in this round was set

Fifth of the saintly splendours? now he knows
Enough of that, which the world cannot see,
The grace divine, albeit e'en his sight
Reach not its utmost depth."

Paradiso 31, 1–3; 25–27; 49–51 *Dante describes how the souls of all the blessed gathered together to appear to him in the Empyrean where they all dwell with God*

In fashion, as a snow-white rose, lay then
Before my view the saintly multitude,
Which in his own blood Christ espous'd.
. . .
All there, who reign in safety and in bliss,
Ages long past or new, on one sole mark
Their love and vision fix'd.
. . .
Looks I beheld,
Where charity in soft persuasion sat,
Smiles from within and radiance from above,
And in each gesture grace and honour high.

Paradiso 33, 22–27; 82–145 *Bernard, Dante's final guide in Paradiso, prays that Dante be granted entry into God's presence. Dante then attempts to put the ineffable experience of the beatific vision into words: he speaks first of all things cohering together in God; then of the Triune God and the Incarnation.*

"Here kneeleth one,
Who of all spirits hath review'd the state,
From the world's lowest gap unto this height.
Suppliant to thee he kneels, imploring grace
For virtue, yet more high to lift his ken
Toward the bliss supreme.'

. . .

O grace! unenvying of thy boon! that gav'st
Boldness to fix so earnestly my ken
On th' everlasting splendour, that I look'd,
While sight was unconsum'd, and, in that depth,
Saw in one volume clasp'd of love, whatever
The universe unfolds; all properties
Of substance and of accident, beheld,
Compounded, yet one individual light
The whole. And of such bond methinks I saw
The universal form: for that whenever
I do but speak of it, my soul dilates
Beyond her proper self; and, till I speak,
One moment seems a longer lethargy,
Than five-and-twenty ages had appear'd
To that emprize, that first made Neptune wonder
At Argo's shadow darkening on his flood.
        With fixed heed, suspense and motionless,
Wond'ring I gaz'd; and admiration still
Was kindled, as I gaz'd. It may not be,
That one, who looks upon that light, can turn
To other object, willingly, his view.
For all the good, that will may covet, there
Is summ'd; and all, elsewhere defective found,
Complete. My tongue shall utter now, no more
E'en what remembrance keeps, than could the babe's
That yet is moisten'd at his mother's breast.
Not that the semblance of the living light
Was chang'd (that ever as at first remain'd)
But that my vision quickening, in that sole
Appearance, still new miracles descry'd,
And toil'd me with the change. In that abyss
Of radiance, clear and lofty, seem'd methought,
Three orbs of triple hue clipt in one bound:
And, from another, one reflected seem'd,
As rainbow is from rainbow: and the third

Seem'd fire, breath'd equally from both. Oh speech
How feeble and how faint art thou, to give
Conception birth! Yet this to what I saw
Is less than little. Oh eternal light!
Sole in thyself that dwellst; and of thyself
Sole understood, past, present, or to come!
Thou smiledst; on that circling, which in thee
Seem'd as reflected splendour, while I mus'd;
For I therein, methought, in its own hue
Beheld our image painted: steadfastly
I therefore por'd upon the view. As one
Who vers'd in geometric lore, would fain
Measure the circle; and, though pondering long
And deeply, that beginning, which he needs,
Finds not; e'en such was I, intent to scan
The novel wonder, and trace out the form,
How to the circle fitted, and therein
How plac'd: but the flight was not for my wing;
Had not a flash darted athwart my mind,
And in the spleen unfolded what it sought.

     Here vigour fail'd the tow'ring fantasy:
But yet the will roll'd onward, like a wheel
In even motion, by the Love impell'd,
That moves the sun in heav'n and all the stars.

Note

The passages included here are from the translation by Henry Francis Cary (1772–1844), *The Vision: or, Hell, Purgatory and Paradise of Dante Alighieri* (New York: Lovell, 1881). At the seminar, these passages were studied in the more recent version by Robert Hollander and Jean Hollander. For copyright reasons, the Hollander version cannot be reproduced here, but it can be accessed at http://etcweb.princeton.edu/dante/pdp/.

The Afterlife as Presented by Dante Alighieri in *The Divine Comedy*

DENNIS McAULIFFE

Dante Alighieri, born in Florence in 1265, was not only a poet but also a political leader in his native city, from which he was exiled by opposing political factions in 1301. His great poem *The Divine Comedy* narrates his journey through life as an exile longing to return home, mirroring humankind's own journey from exile.[1] Expelled from earthly Paradise, the Garden of Eden, after the original sin of the first human parents, Adam and Eve, this exiled humanity longs to return home to God. Dante situates his vision of the journey from this life on earth to life after death in Holy Week, the period from Holy Thursday to Easter Wednesday, of the year 1300. He portrays the afterlife in three parts: Hell (*Inferno*), Purgatory (*Purgatorio*), and Paradise (*Paradiso*). Each is a condition of the soul after death and Dante describes the three states as they were understood by fourteenth-century Christians, drawing from the earlier writings of the Greco-Roman and Judeo-Christian philosophers and theologians. Dante spent almost fifteen years composing the *Comedy*, working on it from around 1307 to the time of his death in exile in 1321. In this essay I explain some of the principles on which he based his description of Hell, Purgatory, and Paradise and give some context in which to understand the lines of the poem that have been selected for reading and discussion.

Basic Principles

For Dante, the numbers 3 and 1 are key. They are fundamental to understanding both the nature of God and God's Creation. The entire poem is divided into three parts or canticles (like the canticles of the Hebrew Bible and the New Testament), and each part consists of thirty-three cantos. These ninety-nine cantos, when added to the introductory canto at the beginning of the *Inferno*, form the perfect number one, followed by two zeros. The lines of the poem are gathered into "threes," or tercets, composed in the metrical scheme called "terza rima," in which every third line rhymes. There are three women in Heaven who help Dante initiate his journey, and three guides who help him reach his destination. Dante's triadic repetition in the structure, rhyme scheme, and figures of the poem reflect the Christian doctrine of the Trinity, God with one nature and three persons.

Dante begins the first line of the *Inferno* with the words, "In the middle of the journey of our lives" (Nel mezzo del cammin di nostra vita), signaling that he expects this to be the reader's journey, not just his own. Dante continually brings the reader into the story, referring to what the reader must notice and understand, and often speaking directly to the reader about the extended meaning of the literal story.

The poem's first canto takes us to Hell. Hell is constructed on the principle of justice, called *contrapasso*, meaning that every crime must be matched by suitable punishment. Hell is the condition in which people dwell who rejected Christ and his gift of redemption from sin. Dante organizes Hell according to the three Aristotelian categories of vice: incontinence, mad bestiality, and malice. Twenty-four examples of vice populate the nine circles of Hell, starting with those to which humans most easily succumb—the sins of the flesh, and ending with the worst humans commit against each other—sins of treachery.

The second canticle, *Purgatorio*, builds on the concept of redemption: that Christ suffered and died to atone for Original Sin. Every human who is not consigned to suffer eternal punishment for rejecting salvation is destined for eternal life with God. Justice requires, however, that the stains of all sins that human beings commit during their lifetime must be purged from their souls so they can present themselves to God's sight in the pure state of grace. Dante depicts Purgatory as a mountain where this purgation is accomplished. The souls of the saved arrive on the mountain having repented of their sins and eager to undertake the last step of giving due satisfaction for them. The purgatorial mountain consists of seven terraces where, according to the Christian concept, reparation is made for each of the seven capital sins by practicing the opposing virtue. The only way that the souls in Purgatory can move more quickly toward the reward of Heaven is if prayers are offered for them by people on earth or by the Blessed in Heaven.

In the final canticle, *Paradiso*, the whole of Creation is seen from the Creator's perspective. Dante's understanding of the heavens reflects a Ptolemaic cosmology. Earth is the farthest from God and the center of material creation. On the top of the mountain of Purgatory stands the earthly Paradise, where Adam and Eve dwelt in peace with God before Original Sin. Beyond that are seven planetary spheres circumscribed by the heaven of the fixed stars and the First Mover (*Primum Mobile*). Outside of time and space is the Empyrean, where all the Blessed live together with God in the Beatific Vision. The Empyrean is the center and the circumference of all things. In the course of Dante's travels through the nine heavens to the Empyrean, he meets Blessed Souls who manifest themselves to him in the various spheres along the way. The first three spheres are within the shadow cast by the earth and represent differing dispositions that are not free from defect. The Blessed in the Moon are defective in fortitude; those in Mercury, in justice; those in Venus, in temperance. But they all assure Dante that they are completely happy in the acceptance of the reward that God has given them.

Starting with the Sun, the Blessed show themselves as perfect in the four cardinal virtues (Sun, prudence; Mars, fortitude; Jupiter, justice; Saturn, temperance), complemented by the three theological virtues (faith, hope, and charity), on which Dante is examined by Saints Peter, James, and John in the Heaven of the Fixed Stars. The principle of differentiation undergirds the discourses on the structure of Creation: that God's gifts are distributed in various degrees throughout Creation explains the individuality that characterizes it. But above all, Paradise is founded on love, the unconditional love that God gives to all his creatures in infinite amounts and that creatures give back to God through one another in ever-increasing quantities. Love and the praise that goes with it are the singular condition of the Blessed in Paradise.

Comments on the Chosen Passages

The passages excerpted from the poem are chosen as examples of the different conditions to which the souls are assigned after death. As the two poets Dante and Virgil begin their travels together, they learn from an inscription over the open gates of Hell that it was made by God's wisdom, power, and love, motivated by justice (*Inferno* 3, 1–9).

In the first of the three circles of the vices of incontinence (lust, gluttony, and avarice), Dante recounts one of the poem's most moving dialogues. Dante is overcome with pity, as is the reader, in realizing how easy it is to succumb to sexual temptation. We listen to Francesca sorrowfully tell the story of her courtly relationship with her husband's brother, Paolo. Their punishment is to be caught up in the whirlwind of their adulterous embrace for all eternity in the despairing knowledge that they will never reach true happiness with God (*Inferno* 5, 109–23).

In the first circle of the second Aristotelian category of vices, mad bestiality (sins of violence against man, God, and nature), Dante encounters those who refuse to live life in joy, appreciation, and gratitude for the gifts with which the Creator graces Creation. For example, those who live their lives in this world in a state of anger are forever submerged in the muddy Stygian swamp where they strive to punish each other as they themselves are punished in inarticulate agony (*Inferno* 7, 106–26).

The third and final Aristotelian category of malice is divided into ten pockets (*bowges*) that house the vices related to fraud and the three most evil degradations related to treachery. In the ninth pocket of fraud is Bertran de Born, whose evil counsel divides king and crown prince from each other, thus disrupting God's plan for peaceful temporal governance. Dante depicts Bertran's *contrapasso* with graphic horror: his body is forever divided into two, with his lower body carrying his severed head (*Inferno* 28, 118–42).

Finally, with Dante and Virgil we reach the center of the underworld where Satan dwells. Satan, God's most beautiful angelic creation, eternally attempts to elevate himself to his Creator's exalted status by flapping his six bat-like wings. His frantic efforts only keep him frozen at the furthest point of Creation from God's presence. In his three horrific faces, Satan cannot speak because his multiple mouths constantly chew on the worst traitors of history, the two murderers of Caesar, founder of the Roman Empire and, worst of all, Judas, who betrayed Christ (*Inferno* 34, 10–69).

After spending twenty-four hours traveling through Hell and learning to despise the vices that lead to damnation, the reader follows Dante and Virgil up and out through a narrow, difficult, torturous passage onto the shores of Purgatory. It is Easter morning, and the first sight is the four stars of the southern hemisphere, which symbolize the four cardinal virtues. These stars are reflected in the face of Cato, a suicide of Roman antiquity who, in the Stoic tradition, chose death rather than a life deprived of freedom. Thus we enter the realm of the afterlife of the saved. Those who reach the shores of the

Mountain of Purgatory will eventually reach Heaven, but first they must strive to remove the stain of the sins that they committed before death (*Purgatorio* 1, 1–6).

Prior to entering Purgatory proper, Dante speaks with three fraternities of penitents who must spend time in the Ante-Purgatory. Here they must wait until enough time has passed to make up for the time that they lost during life before converting to the true way of repentance. One group comprises those who died in the state of ecclesial excommunication. Manfred, the natural son of the Emperor Frederick II, is an example. A Ghibelline, he fought against the Guelfs and the temporal authority of the Church and was therefore excommunicated. Now he must wait thirty times the period he spent outside the Church before he can begin climbing the mountain and doing reparation for his many sins. Unlike in Hell, however, in Purgatory the infinite goodness of God has redeemed even the horrible sins of one such as Manfred (*Purgatorio* 3, 121–23).

When Dante enters Purgatory proper, he encounters the penitents who have begun their process of purgation so they can remove all stain of sin and present themselves to the Beatific Vision of God in Heaven. In contrast to Hell, organized according to the non-Christian scheme of Aristotelian vices, Purgatory is structured according to the conception of seven capital sins: pride, envy, wrath, sloth, cupidity, gluttony, lust. In order to make reparation for these sins, the penitent must spend time on the seven ascending terraces of the mountain doing penance, following a pattern similar to that of the *contrapasso* in Hell. Simultaneously, penitents are reminded of the vice to which they were addicted during life as well as the opposing virtue, which they did not practice sufficiently. This activity, however, can only be performed during the twelve hours of daytime. At night the penitents contemplate the three theological virtues—faith, hope, and charity—symbolized by the three stars that rule the night sky.

When Dante meets the Guardian of Purgatory and is admitted through the narrow entryway (unlike the wide-open gate of Hell), seven "P"s are etched on his forehead. They represent the seven *peccata*, or sins, of which pride is the first and the foundation of the others. As Dante moves from one circle to the next, a "P" is removed by the angel of that particular pass of pardon and a rejoicing liturgical hymn is sung. Dante then climbs more easily and swiftly to the next terrace, having been freed from the weight of the purged sin.

On the second terrace, the penance that purges the wrathful is a dense blinding smoke. In life, their anger would not permit these penitents to see and enjoy the goodness of God's Creation, and it made them see others as their enemies. In Purgatory, the blinding smoke forces them to band together in mutual fraternal dependence. Dante, the pilgrim, suffers the same blindness and must hold onto Virgil for protection (*Purgatorio* 16, 1–24). On the third terrace, those who did not pursue the good with sufficient zeal, the slothful, do penance by racing around the mountain. They are constantly reminded of the zeal with which Mary, pregnant with Christ, raced to be with her cousin Elizabeth who was about to give birth to John the Baptist (*Purgatorio* 18, 88–105).

On the final terrace, where the penitents are purged of the sin of lust and urged to chastity, Dante must walk through a wall of fire before he can climb the rest of the way to earthly Paradise. Faced with the flames, Dante needs Virgil's urging. Virgil repeats his promise of protection and reminds Dante that he kept him from harm when the monster Geryon, representing fraud, carried Dante and Virgil down to the lower reaches of Hell. Even more persuasively, Virgil repeats the promise that Dante will finally meet his beloved Beatrice on the other side of the blaze (*Paradiso* 27, 19–57).

It should be mentioned that Dante and Virgil are accompanied on these last terraces of Purgatory by the poet Statius who, by his own admission, was converted to Christianity by the poetry of Virgil. After spending over a thousand years in Purgatory, he has been released and is now on his way to Heaven. On the other side of the wall of fire, Dante is crowned and mitered by Virgil in recognition that he has mastered all that Virgil could teach him. Now Dante moves on to meet Beatrice, his guide through the heavenly spheres where he will meet the souls of the Blessed and acquire knowledge of spiritual things in preparation for his encounter with God, the Beatific Vision.

Dante has spent three days climbing the mountain of Purgatory. On the Wednesday after Easter, at the perfect hour of Noon, he ascends with Beatrice to the heavenly spheres. The first heavenly sphere where Dante finds himself is the Moon. Here the Blessed manifest themselves to Dante in recognition of the universal love shared in common by all. In conversation with one of these Blessed, Piccarda, Dante discovers that not all the Blessed share the Beatific Vision to the same degree. There is a hierarchy in which Piccarda and others like her who were insufficiently steadfast in keeping their vows occupy the lowest place. Despite this condition, they are completely happy and at peace in the knowledge that their place was assigned to them by the Divine Will. No one in Heaven, says Piccarda, wills anything other than what God wills, since the acceptance of their just place in Heaven reflects the unity of love that God has for them and they have for God (*Paradiso* 3, 70–87).

From the Moon, Dante travels through six other heavenly spheres, Mercury, Venus, the Sun, Mars, Jupiter and Saturn, where he meets outstanding examples of rulers, lovers, theologians, martyrs, the just, and mystics. In each, he learns something about the infinite divine goodness that God desires to share with humanity. Dante experiences the love that all the Blessed share with each other, a love that ultimately reflects God's unconditional love. Love and its manifestation are the sole occupation of the Blessed in Heaven, and the more love is shared, the more there is to share and the greater is their joy (*Paradiso* 5, 100–108).

In the sixth heaven, Jupiter, where the just dwell, Dante discovers two souls who were not from the Judeo-Christian tradition but were pagans: the Roman emperor Trajan and the Trojan Riphaeus. This is one of several indications in *The Divine Comedy* that Dante believed in the inclusivity of salvific grace (*Paradiso* 20, 67–72). A critical realization of Dante's heavenly journey is that the Blessed he meets do not actually dwell in the heavenly spheres where they manifest themselves to him for his edification. Rather, they all dwell in the Empyrean, beyond time and space, with God. There are two realms that Dante travels through beyond the seven heavenly spheres before reaching the Empyrean, the eighth heaven of the Fixed Stars where the individual characteristics of God's Creation are determined, and the ninth heaven of the *Primum Mobile* where God's angelic ministers guide creation according to God's laws.

Finally emerging miraculously into the Empyrean, Dante sees all the Blessed, including Beatrice, who now leaves Dante's final guidance to the great contemplative monk, Bernard of Clairvaux. They are all in their proper places of the Beatific Vision, imaged in the petals of a white rose, resplendent in the light of God's love (selections from *Paradiso* 31). The final canto of the poem opens with Bernard's prayer to Christ's mother, Mary, to whom Bernard was greatly devoted, asking her, the great mediatrix between Christ and mankind, to intercede with her son and grant Dante the object of his desire, the Beatific Vision. The rest of the last canto is Dante's attempt to put this ineffable vision into words (selections from *Paradiso* 33, with references to the Trinity at verses 115–26 and the Incarnation at verses 127–38).

Conclusion

Readers of Dante's *Divine Comedy* have been inspired throughout the ages, and continue to be inspired both by the depth and breadth of his poetic vision and by his illuminating explanations and representations of philosophical and theological concepts. Three of the most important doctrines of the Christian faith that underlie Dante's vision are the Trinity, the Incarnation, and the Resurrection of the Body. Dante's attempt to express an understanding of the Triune God in the *Paradiso* is based on his extensive knowledge of the history of orthodox Christian theological doctrine as established and passed down in the writings of theologians, such as Augustine of Hippo and Thomas Aquinas. Dante recognized the ineffable character of the Trinitarian nature of God but attempted, nevertheless, to articulate it in passages of the *Paradiso*, such as its concluding section where his vision of God as Trinity moves into a vision of the Incarnation of the Son of God, God's assumption of human nature in the enfleshing of Godself in Jesus Christ (33, 115–38). Jesus is, according to Dante's understanding of orthodox Christian theology, one person in two natures. Dante illustrates this doctrine in his persistent attempt to reconcile duality and nonduality. In the *Paradiso*, this is evident in his depiction of Heaven as both the nonphysical Empyrean where the Blessed are in the presence of God and the seven physical heavens where Dante encounters them. He relates this universal concept of nonduality to all humankind in his description of the Blessed who await the resurrection of the body in imitation of Jesus's resurrected body, the visible sign of the unity of God and also of humankind's unity with God, of which Dante catches a glimpse in Heaven.

Note

1. This commentary has in mind the translation of *The Divine Comedy* by Robert Hollander and Jean Hollander, which was studied at the seminar. For copyright reasons, it cannot be reproduced here, but it can be accessed at http://etcweb.princeton.edu/dante/pdp/.

Selected Passages from *Journey to the Afterlife*

Preparations for the Funeral and Burial

THE time lapse between death and burial should be short; after the death the deceased should be buried as soon as possible. The body should not be kept for too long unnecessarily. Postmortem should not be allowed; the Prophet (PBUH[1]) said "Breaking a bone of a dead person is like breaking a bone of a living person" (Tirmidhi). It is against the dignity of a Muslim.

Immediately after the death, preparations are made for washing the body, shrouding, the funeral prayer and the burial.

Washing the Body

To wash (*ghusl*) the dead body is a communal obligation (*fardun kifayah*). Someone from the community must do it.

The method of washing the body is as follows:

1. The body is laid on a platform, which is fumigated with scent and sweet fragrance.
2. The body will be covered between the navel and the knees with a cloth.
3. The washing starts by cleaning the private parts by pouring water over them three times. The washer of the body should wear plastic gloves and must not even look at, let alone touch, the private parts. This is followed by *wudu* (ablutions); the mouth and nose wiped with cotton swabs, the face and the arms to the elbow washed three times. The head is wiped and feet washed.
4. Wash the head using shampoo then turn the body to the left hand side and pour water from head to feet, soap can be used. Repeat this method for the right hand side.

5. Gently rinse the head and the upper part of the body, gently massage the abdomen. If there is excretion wash it away. There is no need to wash the whole body again.
6. Finally pour camphor scented water over the whole body and dry with a towel.

Miscellaneous Points

1. It is compulsory to pour water once over the whole body and Sunnah to do so three times. When washing the body it is recommended that the body should be placed in such a way that the face is towards *Ka'bah*.
2. The person doing the washing should be in a state of *wudu*.
3. The husband cannot wash the body of his wife, nor can he touch her.
4. If the deceased died in a state of major impurity (*junub*) or state of menses or post-natal bleeding, the above described washing sequence is enough.
5. If the body is swollen and cannot be touched, it is sufficient to just pour water over it.
6. Both hands should be placed on the sides, not on the chest.
7. The hair should not be cut or combed; nails should not be cut either.

The Shroud

To shroud the body after washing is a communal obligation.

The shroud for men is:

1. A large sheet used as an envelope and wraps the whole body. It should be longer than the length of the body.
2. An inner envelope.
3. A *qamees* (long shirt or tunic)—from the neck to below the knees.

The shroud for women has the following two extra items:

1. An apron to cover the head this should be 1 metre by 0.5 metre.
2. A cloth tied around the chest down to the abdomen.

How to Put on the Shroud

After the body has been washed and dried it is shrouded in the following way.

1. Put perfume on the shroud and the body as well, and then spread the large envelope of the shroud on a dry platform.
2. Lay the inner envelope of the shroud on top of this then lay the *qamees* on top of this. Now put the body on top of this.
3. After putting on the *qamees*, wrap the inner sheet around the body, then wrap the outer sheet and tie it at the bottom of the feet and at the other end on the top of the head.
4. For women tie chest band last of all, also split hair in two halves and put one half on top of the left hand side of the chest and the other on the right.

It is permissible to lay an embroidered and colourful sheet on top of the shroud. Similarly to lay wreaths of flowers on the shroud or the grave is permissible. This is a mark of respect and honour for the deceased.

The Funeral Prayer

This is a communal obligation (*fardun kifayah*). If only a few people perform it, everyone else from the locality is relieved of the burden.

The conditions for the funeral prayer are exactly as that for a normal prayer; however, the conditions for the dead body are as follows:

1. The body must be of a Muslim, there is no *salah* (prayer) for a *kafir* (unbeliever). Allah says "And do not say *salah* on any of them." (*Surah Tawbah*: 82)
2. The body must be present whole, half, or at least its head. The *salah* on the absent body is not permissible. The Prophet's (PBUH) *salah* for the people of Ethiopia was his special privilege.
3. The body must be clean; i.e., it must be washed or given *tayammum* (alternative to *wudu* when no water is available).
4. The body must be in front of the Imam. It is not permissible to have it at the back.

5. The body should not be carried by people or an animal at the time of prayer.

The Compulsory Acts

1. The four *takbirs*. Each *takbir* (saying *"Allahu akbar,"* God is greater) is equivalent to one *rakat* (sequence of prescribed movements and words during *salah*) and therefore the prayer is invalid even if one *takbir* is missed.
2. Stand up straight. It is not permissible to sit and pray.
3. There is no *ruku* (bowing) or *sajdah* (prostration).

The Sunnah

1. Raise your hands and say *"Allahu akbar,"* and fold below the navel. Then recite the *thana*:
   > Glory be to Allah and all praise, your name is blessed and mighty and great is your hymn and there is no God besides You.
2. After the second *takbir* to read the *darood sharif* upon the blessed Prophet (PBUH):
   > O God, bless our lord Muhammad and the progeny of our lord Muhammad
   > as Thou hast blessed our lord Abraham and the progeny of our lord Abraham.
   > Truly Thou art Praised, Glorious.
   > O God, grace our lord Muhammad and the progeny of our lord Muhammad
   > as Thou hast graced our lord Abraham and the progeny of our lord Abraham in all the worlds.
   > Truly Thou art Praised, Glorious.
3. To read the *dua* (supplication) for the deceased after the third *takbir*.
   a. The following *dua* is for male and female adults:
      > O my Lord! Forgive our living, our dead, those who are present and then are absent and our young ones and our grown ups, our men and our women. O Lord whosoever you keep alive amongst

us keep him alive on Islam. And whosoever you cause to die let him die with faith. (Tirmidhi)

b. The *dua* for a male child is:

O Lord! Make him provision, reward, and a treasure for us in the hereafter.

Make him as our intercessor whose intercession is acceptable.

c. The *dua* for a female child is:

O Lord! Make her provision, reward and a treasure for us in the hereafter. Make her as our intercessor whose intercession is acceptable.

If those *duas* are not known, then any other *masnoon dua* can be read.

4. It is recommended that the Imam stands in line with the chest of the dead or in line with his head or middle.

5. It is recommended to have three rows. The blessed Prophet (PBUH) said "If three rows have prayed on him then he has been forgiven" (Tirmidhi). However, if the number of people is very large then seven rows should be formed.

The Procedure for the Funeral Prayer

Funeral prayer is offered standing only; there is no bowing or prostration. It is comprised of four *takbirs*. After the intention, state the first *takbir* and raise the hands to the ears and fold them. Read *thana* and then say the second *takbir*, do not raise the hands. Now read the *dua* and then say the fourth and the last *takbir*. Then turning right say the *salam* and then to the left.

1. Do not raise the hands when saying the *takbir*.
2. If the Imam by mistake says five *takbirs* then the *muqtadi* (person following the imam in prayer) should not follow him but wait for him to do the *salam*.
3. The Glorious Quran should not be read on this occasion for *dua*. However it is permissible to read *Surah Fatihah* as a *dua*.
4. If the funeral is presented at *Maghrib* (evening) prayer then the funeral should precede the *Maghrib* Sunnah prayers.

5. If someone joins the funeral prayer late and has missed one or more *takbirs* then he should make up for his missed *takbirs* after the Imam has done the *salam* and thus make up for the missed *takbirs*.

6. If a child is born and dies without making a movement or a sound, then he will be buried without the funeral prayer. However if he makes any kind of noise or shows signs of life before death, he will be washed and the funeral prayer performed.

7. If he is buried without the funeral prayer, then prayer should be said on his grave.

8. If someone dies at sea and the land is far, then he will be washed and the funeral prayer offered and he will be cast into the sea.

9. Funeral prayer in the mosque is *makruh* (permissible but discouraged) but permissible in case of rain or for any other excuse.

Offering Condolences

It is Sunnah to express sympathy and to comfort the relatives of the deceased. One can simply offer the condolence in his own words by saying "May God forgive him/her and bless him/her with His mercy and may God give you patience and forbearance."

Ibn Majah reports in his book that the blessed Messenger (PBUH) said "When a Muslim expresses condolences to his bereaved brother, God will honour him with an abode on the day of Judgement." According to another hadith he said "whoever comforts the distressed he will be rewarded like the afflicted" (Tirmidhi).

It is permissible to give condolences before the burial, but it is better to delay until afterwards. It is not permissible to wear black dress for mourning since it is imitating the non-Muslims.

Mourning is only permissible for three days; however, a widow can mourn for her husband for four months and ten days. Wailing and lamenting in high pitched voice is strictly forbidden, however weeping, crying, and sobbing are natural emotions which express grief and are allowed. When the Prophet's (PBUH) infant son Ibrahim died, he cried. The Prophet (PBUH) has strictly forbidden wailing accompanied by tearing clothes or physical injury like beating the forehead or the chest (Bukhari).

Bereavement is a sorrowful event, but a Muslim only utters "To God we belong and to Him we shall return."

Esale Thawab and khatam sharif

This literally means to transmit reward or to bestow reward. This term is used for the devotional activities of a living person which have been performed with the intention of benefiting a dead person. For example, a son reads *Surah Ya Sin* and afterwards asks God to bless his dead father with the reward to his father as well. *Esale Thawab* is an established practise of the *Ahl-e-Sunnah*; there is evidence from the Quran and Sunnah for this ritual.

The Glorious Quran tells the believers to "Co-operate in matters of goodness and piety" (*Surah Maidah*: 2).

Muslims are urged over and over again to help one another and to relieve one another's problems. It is easy to understand how we can help a living person, but how do we help a dead person? Is there any way that we can help a deceased relative or a friend? Yes, a dead person can be helped, gifts can be given to him, they will not reach him in physical form but in spiritual form, the reward of our good actions can be transmitted to our loved ones. Saad's (RA[2]) mother died and he came to the Prophet (PBUH) and asked him "O Messenger of God my mother has died. Which is the best charity?" The Prophet (PBUH) replied "water." Saad dug a well and announced this was for the mother of Saad (Abu Dawud).

This is clear evidence for *Esale Thawab*; the good action of digging the well by Saad earned him reward, but he wished to transmit that reward to his dead mother! Saad would also reap the reward too!

The Prophet (PBUH) used to sacrifice two rams every year on the occasion of *Eid ul Adha*. And he used to say "O God this one is from me and the other from my people" (Abu Dawud).

Here the blessed Mustafa (PBUH) is transmitting the reward to the whole of his *ummah*. The only Muslim sect which denies the validity of *Esale Thawab* has been the Muʿtazilites (the rationalists). Sadly, some modern sects have also borrowed their ideas today. A popular way of *Esale Thawab* is as follows:

1. Read *Darood Shareef* three times.
2. Read *Surah Fatihah*.

3. Read *Ayat ul Kursi* (verse 254 of *Surah Baqarah*)
4. Read *Surah Ikhlas* three times.
5. Read *Darood Shareef* three times.

Then raise both hands in front of the chest and pray by saying "O my Lord whatever reward you have bestowed upon me for these readings please bestow the same upon the beloved Prophet and all the other prophets and their successors, and all your friends and O God bestow this reward upon my parents."

In some parts of the Muslim world, people do *Esale Thawab* only on certain days particularly on the third day following the death, or the seventh or the fortieth. There is nothing *haram* in this custom; this is not a ruling of Shariah, and no one claims that there are only certain days for *Esale Thawab*. *Esale Thawab* can be done at any time anywhere and with any good action.

Notes

This material is reproduced, with some minor alterations and additions, from Musharraf Hussain al-Azhari, *Journey to the Afterlife* (Nottingham, UK: Invitation Publications, 2010), 18–29, with permission. The approach here to transliteration of Islamic names and terms differs from that in the rest of this volume.

1. PBUH means "Peace be upon him."
2. "RA" abbreviates a traditional Arabic expression meaning "May God be pleased with him/her."

Muslim Funerals

MUSHARRAF HUSSAIN

Islamic funeral rituals are performed in a set order prescribed and demonstrated by the Prophet Muḥammad (PBUH[1]), from whom they have been passed down from generation to generation, remaining unchanged over the past fourteen centuries. As well as connecting Muslims to their glorious past, Islamic funeral rituals, which are performed in the same way throughout the world, are an enactment of Islam's doctrinal, moral, and social teachings concerning death, ultimate human destiny, the dignity of the deceased, and the need to care for the bereaved and unite Muslims everywhere in a profound sense of solidarity. These rituals give the faithful a sense of shared identity in fundamental Islamic beliefs concerning the One God, revelation, and resurrection and life in the Hereafter, teaching important truths and connecting people to their deepest selves.

Death is defined as a permanent ending of the bodily functions that are needed to keep a person alive. In Islamic terms, death is the departing of the soul from its bodily abode. The Qur'ān tells us, "Every person will taste death" (3:185) and "There is a time set for every person: they cannot hasten it, nor, when it comes, will they be able to delay it for a single moment" (7:34). Death is never "untimely" since it only comes at the time fixed by God. In his *Sharḥ al-Ṣudūr*, Imām Jalāl al-Dīn al-Suyūṭī, a fifteen-century theologian, said: "Death is not annihilation and mere extinction but the separation of the soul from the body, a change of state, and transportation from one house to another."[2]

For Muslims, death does not signify the "end of life." It is merely a transition from one realm of existence to another. Muslims believe that God created our souls when He created Adam and Eve. One hundred and twenty days after conception, the soul enters the fetus and human life begins. The period from birth to death is referred to as the worldly life. This is a probationary period, a time of preparation for the life hereafter by carrying out the divine will. Death, therefore, marks a return once more to the realm of souls; and it is interesting that Muslim scholars often use this term "return," signifying that our souls are conveyed to a place where they have already been. The Qur'ān says, "it was He who created you the first time and to Him you have been returned" (41:21).

Approaching Death

Muslims are taught to be ever ready for death. An important expression of this readiness is to prepare a will giving clear advice to one's heirs to adhere to the oneness of God, to believe in the beloved Prophet (PBUH), to be steadfast in following the Sharīʿa, in creating peace among people, in striving for nearness to God, and in fleeing from hatred, sins, and evil. The will should give clear instructions to prevent conflict among one's heirs. The will should also give instructions for following the Sunna in preparation for one's shrouding and burial. One should practice what one has written in one's will by repenting and turning toward God and his Messenger and being prepared to meet death, showing no distress or anxiety—as this may lead to loss of faith. The Prophet of God (PBUH) said, "Whoever loves to meet God, God loves to meet him; and whoever dislikes meeting God, God will dislike meeting him." When asked by his Companions, "O Messenger of God! Who amongst us would not dislike death?" the Prophet (PBUH) answered, "When somebody is about to die, at that point he should love to be meeting his Lord" (Bukhārī).

If a Muslim approaching death has not fulfilled the devotional obligations of giving zakāt or fasting during the month of Ramaḍān or praying the five daily prayers, or has not performed the pilgrimage, then he should be quick about it and ensure that he atones for these failings. If he is unable to perform the pilgrimage, then he should appoint someone to carry it out for him at his expense. He must also repay other people what he owes them and ask for forgiveness if he has wronged them—since these wrongs will not be forgiven by God until the victim forgives. To ask for forgiveness is not humiliation; true humiliation will be to stand in the court of the Lord unable to repay those we have slandered or to whom we have been malicious or whom we have harmed in any way. They will deserve to take our merits and credits on the Day of Judgment; we will have to carry the burden of their sins.

When a person is about to die, those sitting around him should encourage him to say the shahāda (declaration of faith)—"There is no God but Allah, and Muḥammad is the Messenger of God"—because at that critical moment, Satan comes to dissuade the believer and rob him of his faith. So this encouragement is really to counter Satan's attack. The dying person should make the declaration of faith once and then not repeat it unless he has subsequently spoken of something else. This is because the *shahāda* should be the last words he utters.[3] Those with the dying person are also encouraged to recite Sūra *Yā Sīn*.

Preparations for the Funeral and Burial

Upon hearing the news of someone's death, the immediate response of a Muslim is to say "We belong to God and to Him we shall return" (Qur'ān 2:156); or, very simply, this is the divine will. Immediately, the family and friends begin the preparations for the funeral and burial. As mentioned in the passage from *Journey to the Afterlife*, printed earlier, the time lapse between death and burial should always be short. Muslims speak of death as the bridge that unites the lover with the beloved; thus, they feel that there should be no delay at this point. The haste in burying the dead is for the dignity of the deceased, as deterioration and disintegration of the body is rapid, particularly in hot climates. More generally, the way in which the body is treated before burial (particularly the washing and shrouding described in *Journey to the Afterlife*) reflects the respect Muslims have for the human body that God has created. Postmortems are discouraged because for Muslims such procedures are an offense against the dignity of the deceased; the Prophet (PBUH) said, "Breaking a bone of a dead person is like breaking a bone of a living person" (Tirmidhī). However, if the coroner orders an autopsy, then it must be carried out, but use of noninvasive techniques such as a body scanner or an MRI will be preferred.

The Funeral Prayer

The Prophet (PBUH) said: "When a group of people pray the funeral of someone, God accepts their intercession" (Tirmidhī). The funeral prayer can be likened to presenting the deceased one to the King, the Lord of the universe, and pleading on his behalf for his forgiveness. The larger the congregation, the more likely it is that their intercession will be accepted. As mentioned in *Journey to the Afterlife*, this is a communal obligation; if only a few people perform it, everyone else from the locality is relieved of the burden. It is customary for the imām of the locality to give a sermon just before the funeral prayer is offered.

The purpose of the sermon is to remind the congregation about the purpose and meaning of life and death. This is a poignant moment to encourage people to reflect on their own lives. The themes that I often talk about on this occasion are the ephemeral nature of worldly life, the fear of God, the beauty and joy of Paradise, and the frugal and austere life. The funeral, the mourning, and the somber mood of the congregation are sufficient to remind us of our own fate, as "death is an exhortation itself."

The given passage from *Journey to the Afterlife* explains the main regulations concerning the funeral prayer and the compulsory acts and words that are involved. There is much that could be said about these, but here I will make just a few comments.

The funeral prayer does not involve the usual bowing or prostration required in the five daily prayers. It simply consists of four *takbīrs* for Sunnīs and five *takbīrs* for Shī'ites. An interesting feature of the funeral prayer is the place it gives to the invocation of blessings upon the Prophet, known as the Darood Sharif.[4] This particular blessing mentions the Prophet Muḥammad (PBUH), the Prophet Ibrāhīm (PBUH), and their progeny. Ibrāhīm has a special place in Islam; in fact, the Qur'ān calls Muslims the nation of Abraham, and Muslims are proud of this appellation.

Also to be noted here is the special provision made for children in the funeral prayer. Muslims believe that when children die, they go straight to Paradise because they are born pure and sinless. As mentioned in *Journey to the Afterlife,* when the funeral is for a child, the parents say, "O Lord, make him/her provision, reward and a treasure for us in the Hereafter. Make him/her as our intercessor whose intercession is acceptable." This prayer explains the Muslim attitude of being the trustees and caretakers of children, not their owners; for God is the absolute owner. The Arabic word *faraṭa* is translated here as "provision" but also implies one who has escaped (possibly an illness), one who has preceded, and one who will be replaced. This expression of submission to the divine will helps the Muslim not to fight the natural process of death but to accept it. The funeral prayer for children vividly expresses these sentiments.

The Burial

Some comments should be made about Islamic burial practice because this is not covered in the passage from *Journey to the Afterlife* printed earlier. It should first be noted that burial is the invariable norm for Muslims; cremation, now so widespread in the Western world, is not acceptable to Muslims as an alternative to burial. Cremation is regarded as a punishment that has been reserved for the people of hell and offends the dignity of the human body. The Qur'ān teaches that human beings were created from the earth and should be returned to the earth from where again they will be resurrected. God says: "From the earth We created you, into it We shall return you, and from it We shall raise you a second time" (20:55).

The grave should be dug as a large rectangle, with a further rectangle in the middle which should be longer than the height of the deceased person; the width should be half of the height, and the depth should be four or five feet. This is where the body is placed, laid flat on the bed of the grave with the head turned toward the *qibla*. The grave is closed by placing wooden planks across it and filling the hole with soil. The shape of the grave should be raised by at least one foot above the surrounding ground, thus creating a hump.

Much is said in the traditions about the state of those in the grave. For example, the Prophet (PBUH) describes the grave as "either a pit of hellfire or a garden of heaven" (Tirmidhī). When one of the Companions died, the Prophet (PBUH) prayed for him with these words: "O Lord! Make his grave spacious for him and brighten it" (Muslim). Ibn Abi Adunya, a tenth-century Muslim scholar, says, "When a righteous person dies, a bed from paradise is brought for him and he is told to sleep cheerfully and comfortably, for the Lord is happy with him, and then his grave is opened for him and he enjoys its beauty and smells its fragrance. His prayers, devotions and good deeds are his companions until the Day of Judgment."[5]

Offering Condolences

Journey to the Afterlife mentions some of the traditions concerning the offering of condolences and mourning after a death. Other recommended practices include providing food for the bereaved and looking after their needs for three days. The death of loved ones is always painful, so Muslims are encouraged to console those who mourn. However, as can be discerned in the passage from *Journey to the Afterlife*, although Islam allows for a proper expression of grief, it also prohibits certain excessive forms of mourning. The underlying concern is that excessive mourning implies a lack of faith in God the Almighty and Merciful and thus is inappropriate for Muslims.

Esale Thawab and Khatam Sharīf

Journey to the Afterlife also refers to Esale Thawab, a theological concept that explains the traditional Islamic practices of reciting the Qur'ān and then blessing the soul of the deceased person.[6] It is also known as Khatam Sharīf, referring to the complete reading of the Qur'ān followed by blessing of the deceased. As mentioned, these practices have been questioned by some Muslims, but they remain accepted and important within the mainstream of traditional Islam. *Journey to the Afterlife* comments on the assumption underlying these practices—that it is possible for us to bring spiritual help to the deceased.

Final Thoughts

Various aspects of Muslim practice before and after death have been described in the excerpts printed earlier from *Journey to the Afterlife*, and some further comments have been added in this essay. These practices all arise from the fundamental Islamic belief in the afterlife and the hope of a blessed eternal home for the righteous. However, this does not guarantee a blissful outcome for all in the world to come. The idea of an eternal, blissful life for the righteous after the Day of Judgment and divine proximity in Paradise—or, alternatively, separation and punishment in Hell—are basic articles of Islamic faith. These beliefs offer a clear meaning and purpose for human life. A key feature of this perspective is the conviction that every individual has both the dignity and the responsibility of being the *khalīfat Allāh*—the vicegerent or representative of God on earth.

These beliefs are deeply ingrained in the minds of Muslims and help to shape a particular attitude to life and death that underlies the practices of Muslims around the time of death. Death is not viewed as a macabre, gruesome, and draconian punishment marking the end of life. It is not the end but a new beginning. Some even regard it as a divine gift. This kind of attitude makes death easier to face. Death is not a bizarre event but as natural as other laws of nature such as gravity. Muslims are, therefore, constantly advised to remember death and to be ready to meet it—vigilant in holding to their faith and trusting in the mercy of God.

Notes

1. PBUH means "Peace be upon him."
2. Imām Jalāl al-Dīn al-Suyūṭī, *Sharḥ al-Ṣudūr* (Beirut, Lebanon: Dar al-Kutub Alilmiyya, 1997).
3. Maulana Ahmed Raza, *Fatawa Rizwiya*, vol. 9 (Gujarat: Markaz Ahl usunnah Barkat Raza, 2003).
4. Darood Sharif may also be transliterated *durūd sharīf.*
5. Hafiz ibn abi Adunya, *Qisar al Amal* (Beirut, Lebanon: Dar ibn Hazm, 1997).
6. Esale Thawab may also be transliterated *iṣāl al-thawāb.*

Contemporary Funeral Liturgy in the Church of England

The following material is from the Church of England's website, from the section on baptisms, weddings, and funerals.[1] It is reproduced here with minor presentational adaptations and has been arranged in four sections:

- Funerals: Some introductory remarks.
- The Funeral Service: An explanatory outline of the funeral service.
- The Funeral Service: The funeral liturgy from *Common Worship*, including a range of options at various points in the service. This constitutes most of the material presented here.
- Notes on the Funeral Service.

There is much else on the website that can be explored—including, for example, the rather different funeral liturgy in the *Book of Common Prayer* (1662), which remains part of the Church of England's liturgy, although *Common Worship* (2000) is much more widely used.

Here we have restricted ourselves to material from the Church of England. The liturgical resources of other Christian traditions can also readily be explored on the internet.

Funerals

A funeral is used to mark the end of a person's life here on earth. Family and friends come together to express grief, give thanks for the life lived, and commend the person into God's keeping. These can be a small, quiet ceremony or a large occasion in a packed church.

Everyone is entitled to either a burial service (funeral) or to have their ashes buried in their local parish churchyard by their local parish priest regardless of whether they attended church. Speak to your local vicar for more information, or, if you do not know who your local vicar is, use the website to search for your local Church of England church.

If the churchyard has been closed, then the Local Authority will provide alternative places of burial and the minister can carry out the service there instead of the church or crematorium.

The Funeral Service

[The following is an explanatory outline of the funeral service.]

The service will follow a clear plan. The focus moves from earth to heaven as the service moves from greeting the mourners, to remembering the one who has died, all the while asking for God's comfort and then committing your loved one into God's care.

Entry of the Coffin

Traditionally, the minister meets the coffin at the door and leads it and the mourners in. The minister will say some reassuring words from the Bible, for example:

"I am the resurrection and the life. He who believes in me will live, even though he dies," says the Lord. (John 11:25)

"For I am convinced that neither death nor life, neither angels nor demons, neither the present nor the future, nor any powers, neither height nor depth, nor anything else in all creation, will be able to separate us from the love of God that is in Christ Jesus our Lord." (Rom. 8:38, 39)

"Blessed are those who mourn, for they will be comforted." (Matt. 5:4)

Welcome and Introduction

After the welcome and first prayer, there may be a hymn or a tribute to the person who has passed away. This can be done by family and friends or the minister. Sometimes symbols of the person's life are placed on or near the coffin as a part of this.

Sometimes there is a prayer for forgiveness. It's common to feel we have let a loved one down after they die, that there were things we could have done or should not have done. The prayer for forgiveness can help with these feelings.

Readings and Sermon

A Psalm comes next. "The Lord is my shepherd" is comforting because it speaks of God being with us in death and grief. The Bible readings focus on God's care and the hope of eternal life. The sermon speaks of the Christian hope of life beyond death and relates it to your loved one.

Prayers

The funeral prayers recall the promise of the resurrection. They ask for God's presence with those who mourn and give thanks for your loved one's life. The prayers normally end with the Lord's Prayer.

Commendation, Farewell, and Committal

The minister says a prayer to commend the person to God's love and mercy. Then the body is "committed" for burial or cremation.

> We now commit his/her body to the ground;
> earth to earth, ashes to ashes, dust to dust:
> in the sure and certain hope of the resurrection to eternal life . . .

The Committal prayer might be said in church, or at the graveside, or in a crematorium as the curtains close around the coffin. It will be a very emotional time, a clear "good-bye" to your loved one for this life.

The Burial

In Christian tradition the funeral ends with a burial of either the coffin or ashes. If you have chosen a cremation, you may bury the ashes in the churchyard or use the crematorium's Garden of Remembrance. The ashes may be buried a few days after the funeral with a very brief service.

The Funeral Service

The Gathering

The coffin may be received by the minister.[2] One or more sentences of Scripture may be used.

"I am the resurrection and the life," says the Lord. "Those who believe in me, even though they die, will live, and everyone who lives and believes in me will never die." (John 11:25, 26)

I am convinced that neither death, nor life, nor angels, nor rulers, nor things present, nor things to come, nor powers, nor height, nor depth, nor anything else in all creation, will be able to separate us from the love of God in Christ Jesus our Lord. (Rom. 8:38, 39)

Since we believe that Jesus died and rose again, even so, through Jesus, God will bring with him those who have died. So we will be with the Lord for ever. Therefore encourage one another with these words. (I Thess. 4:14, 17b, 18)

We brought nothing into the world, and we take nothing out. The Lord gave, and the Lord has taken away; blessed be the name of the Lord. (I Tim. 6.7; Job 1.21b)

The steadfast love of the Lord never ceases, his mercies never come to an end; they are new every morning; great is his faithfulness. (Lam. 3:22, 23)

Blessed are those who mourn, for they will be comforted. (Matt. 5:4)

God so loved the world that he gave his only Son, so that everyone who believes in him may not perish but may have eternal life. (John 3:16)

Introduction

The minister says

We meet in the name of Jesus Christ,
who died and was raised to the glory of God the Father.
Grace and mercy be with you.

The minister introduces the service in these or other suitable words

We have come here today
to remember before God our *brother/sister N;*
to give thanks for *his/her* life;
to commend *him/her* to God our merciful redeemer and judge;
to commit *his/her* body to be *buried/cremated,*
and to comfort one another in our grief.

The minister may say one of these prayers

God of all consolation,
your Son Jesus Christ was moved to tears
at the grave of Lazarus his friend.
Look with compassion on your children in their loss;

give to troubled hearts the light of hope
and strengthen in us the gift of faith,
in Jesus Christ our Lord.
[All] Amen.

(or)

Almighty God,
you judge us with infinite mercy and justice
and love everything you have made.
In your mercy
turn the darkness of death into the dawn of new life,
and the sorrow of parting into the joy of heaven;
through our Saviour, Jesus Christ.
[All] Amen.

A hymn may be sung.
A brief tribute may be made[3]

Prayers of Penitence

These or similar words may be used to introduce the confession
As children of a loving heavenly Father,
let us ask his forgiveness,
for he is gentle and full of compassion.

Silence may be kept.
These words may be used
God of mercy,
we acknowledge that we are all sinners.
We turn from the wrong that we have thought and said and done,
and are mindful of all that we have failed to do.
For the sake of Jesus, who died for us,
forgive us for all that is past,
and help us to live each day
in the light of Christ our Lord.
[All] Amen.

(or)

> Lord, have mercy.
> [All] Lord, have mercy.
> Christ, have mercy.
> [All] Christ, have mercy.
> Lord, have mercy.
> [All] Lord, have mercy.

The minister may say

> May God our Father forgive us our sins
> and bring us to the eternal joy of his kingdom,
> where dust and ashes have no dominion._
> [All] Amen.

The Collect

The minister invites the people to pray, silence is kept and the minister says this or another suitable Collect.

> Merciful Father,
> hear our prayers and comfort us;
> renew our trust in your Son,
> whom you raised from the dead;
> strengthen our faith
> that all who have died in the love of Christ
> will share in his resurrection;
> who lives and reigns with you,
> in the unity of the Holy Spirit,
> one God, now and for ever.
> [All] Amen.

Readings and Sermon

A reading from the Old or New Testament may be read.[4]
This or another psalm or hymn is used.[5]

> [1]The Lord is my shepherd; •
> therefore can I lack nothing.

²He makes me lie down in green pastures •
   and leads me beside still waters.
³He shall refresh my soul •
   and guide me in the paths of righteousness for his name's sake.
⁴Though I walk through the valley of the shadow of death,
   I will fear no evil; •
for you are with me;
   your rod and your staff, they comfort me.
⁵You spread a table before me
   in the presence of those who trouble me; •
you have anointed my head with oil
   and my cup shall be full.
⁶Surely goodness and loving mercy shall follow me
   all the days of my life, •
and I will dwell in the house of the Lord for ever. (Psalm 23:1–6).

A reading from the New Testament (which may be a Gospel reading) is used.
A sermon is preached.

Prayers

A minister leads the prayers of the people.
The prayers usually follow this sequence:
   Thanksgiving for the life of the departed
   Prayer for those who mourn
   Prayers of Penitence (if not already used)
   Prayer for readiness to live in the light of eternity

This form may be used. If occasion demands, the responses may be omitted and the
concluding prayer said by the minister alone.[6]
   God of mercy, Lord of life,
   you have made us in your image
   to reflect your truth and light:
   we give you thanks for *N*,
   for the grace and mercy *he/she* received from you,
   for all that was good in *his/her* life,
   for the memories we treasure today.

[*Especially we thank you . . .*]
Silence
Lord, in your mercy
[All] hear our prayer.
You promised eternal life to those who believe.
Remember for good this your servant *N*
as we also remember *him/her.*
Bring all who rest in Christ
into the fullness of your kingdom
where sins have been forgiven
and death is no more.
Silence
Lord, in your mercy
[All] hear our prayer.
Your mighty power brings joy out of grief
and life out of death.
Look in mercy on [. . . *and*] all who mourn.
Give them patient faith in times of darkness.
Strengthen them with the knowledge of your love.
Silence
Lord, in your mercy
[All] hear our prayer.
You are tender toward your children
and your mercy is over all your works.
Heal the memories of hurt and failure.
Give us the wisdom and grace to use aright
the time that is left to us here on earth,
to turn to Christ and follow in his steps
in the way that leads to everlasting life.
Silence
Lord, in your mercy
[All] hear our prayer.
[All] God of mercy,
entrusting into your hands all that you have made
and rejoicing in our communion with all your faithful people,
we make our prayers through Jesus Christ our Savior. Amen.

The Lord's Prayer may be said.

As our Savior taught us, so we pray
[All] Our Father in heaven,
hallowed be your name,
your kingdom come,
your will be done,
on earth as in heaven.
Give us today our daily bread.
Forgive us our sins
as we forgive those who sin against us.
Lead us not into temptation
but deliver us from evil.
For the kingdom, the power,
and the glory are yours
now and for ever.
Amen.

(or)

Let us pray with confidence as our Savior has taught us
[All] Our Father in heaven,
hallowed be thy name;
thy kingdom come;
thy will be done;
on earth as it is in heaven.
Give us this day our daily bread.
And forgive us our trespasses,
as we forgive those who trespass against us.
And lead us not into temptation;
but deliver us from evil.
For thine is the kingdom,
the power and the glory,
for ever and ever.
Amen.

A hymn may be sung.

Commendation and Farewell

The minister stands by the coffin and may invite others to gather around it.
The minister says

Let us commend N to the mercy of God,
our maker and redeemer.

Silence is kept.
The minister uses this or another prayer of entrusting and commending[7]

God our creator and redeemer,
by your power Christ conquered death
and entered into glory.
Confident of his victory
and claiming his promises,
we entrust N to your mercy
in the name of Jesus our Lord,
who died and is alive
and reigns with you,
now and for ever.
[All] Amen.

If the Committal does not follow as part of the same service in the same place, some sections of the Dismissal may be used here.[8]

The Committal

Sentences of Scripture may be used.[9]
The minister says

The Lord is full of compassion and mercy,
slow to anger and of great goodness.
As a father is tender towards his children,
so is the Lord tender to those that fear him.
For he knows of what we are made;
he remembers that we are but dust.
Our days are like the grass;

we flourish like a flower of the field;
when the wind goes over it, it is gone
and its place will know it no more.
But the merciful goodness of the Lord endures for ever and ever toward
   those that fear him
and his righteousness upon their children's children.

(or)

We have but a short time to live.
Like a flower we blossom and then wither;
like a shadow we flee and never stay.
In the midst of life we are in death;
to whom can we turn for help,
but to you, Lord, who are justly angered by our sins?
Yet, Lord God most holy, Lord most mighty,
O holy and most merciful Savior,
deliver us from the bitter pain of eternal death.
Lord, you know the secrets of our hearts;
hear our prayer, O God most mighty;
spare us, most worthy judge eternal;
at our last hour let us not fall from you,
O holy and merciful Savior.

The minister uses one of the following forms of Committal.
At the burial of a body
We have entrusted our *brother/sister N* to God's mercy,
and we now commit *his/her* body to the ground:
earth to earth, ashes to ashes, dust to dust:
in sure and certain hope of the resurrection to eternal life
through our Lord Jesus Christ,
who will transform our frail bodies
that they may be conformed to his glorious body,
who died, was buried, and rose again for us.
To him be glory for ever.
[All] Amen.

(or, in a crematorium, if the Committal is to follow at the burial of the ashes)

We have entrusted our *brother/sister* N to God's mercy,
and now, in preparation for burial,
we give *his/her* body to be cremated.
We look for the fullness of the resurrection
when Christ shall gather all his saints
to reign with him in glory for ever.
[All] Amen.

(or, in a crematorium, if the Committal is to take place then)

We have entrusted our *brother/sister* N to God's mercy,
and we now commit *his/her* body to be cremated:
earth to earth, ashes to ashes, dust to dust:
in sure and certain hope of the resurrection to eternal life
through our Lord Jesus Christ,
who will transform our frail bodies
that they may be conformed to his glorious body,
who died, was buried, and rose again for us.
To him be glory for ever.
[All] Amen.

The Dismissal

This may include
- The Lord's Prayer (if not used earlier)
- The Nunc dimittis
- One or more suitable prayers
- An Ending

THE LORD'S PRAYER

As our Saviour taught us, so we pray
  All: Our Father in heaven,
  hallowed be your name,
  your kingdom come,
  your will be done,

on earth as in heaven.
Give us today our daily bread.
Forgive us our sins
as we forgive those who sin against us.
Lead us not into temptation
but deliver us from evil.
For the kingdom, the power,
and the glory are yours
now and for ever.
Amen.

(or)

Let us pray with confidence as our Saviour has taught us
[All] Our Father in heaven,
hallowed be thy name;
thy kingdom come;
thy will be done;
on earth as it is in heaven.
Give us this day our daily bread.
And forgive us our trespasses,
as we forgive those who trespass against us.
And lead us not into temptation;
but deliver us from evil.
For thine is the kingdom,
the power and the glory,
for ever and ever.
Amen.

Nunc dimittis (The Song of Simeon)
Now, Lord, you let your servant go in peace: •
your word has been fulfilled.
My own eyes have seen the salvation •
which you have prepared in the sight of every people;
A light to reveal you to the nations •
and the glory of your people Israel. (Luke 2:29–32)

Glory to the Father and to the Son
and to the Holy Spirit;
as it was in the beginning is now
and shall be for ever. Amen.

Prayers

One or more of these prayers, or other suitable prayers, may be used
[All] Heavenly Father,
in your Son Jesus Christ
you have given us a true faith and a sure hope.
Strengthen this faith and hope in us all our days,
that we may live as those who believe in
the communion of saints,
the forgiveness of sins
and the resurrection to eternal life;
through Jesus Christ our Lord.
Amen.

[All]God be in my head,
and in my understanding;
God be in my eyes,
and in my looking;
God be in my mouth,
and in my speaking;
God be in my heart,
and in my thinking;
God be at my end,
and at my departing.
Amen.

Support us, O Lord,
all the day long of this troublous life,
until the shadows lengthen and the evening comes,
the busy world is hushed,
the fever of life is over

and our work is done.
Then, Lord, in your mercy grant us a safe lodging,
a holy rest, and peace at the last;
through Christ our Lord.
[All] Amen.

Ending

One of these, or another suitable ending, may be used
    May God in his infinite love and mercy
    bring the whole Church,
    living and departed in the Lord Jesus,
    to a joyful resurrection
    and the fulfilment of his eternal kingdom.
    All   Amen.

    May God give *you*
    his comfort and his peace,
    his light and his joy,
    in this world and the next;
    and the blessing of God almighty,
    the Father, the Son, and the Holy Spirit,
    be among *you* and remain with *you* always.
    [All] Amen.

    God will show us the path of life;
    in his presence is the fullness of joy:
    and at his right hand
    there is pleasure for evermore. (see Psalm 16:11)

    Unto him that is able to keep us from falling,
    and to present us faultless before the presence of his glory
    with exceeding joy,
    to the only wise God our Saviour,
    be glory and majesty,
    dominion and power,

both now and ever. (Jude 24, 25)
[All] Amen.

Notes to the Funeral Service

1. Sentences
Sentences of Scripture may be used at the entry, after the Introduction, or at other suitable points.

2. Psalms and Readings
Psalms and Readings should normally be drawn from those set out. A psalm should normally be used. It may be in a metrical or hymn version, or be replaced by a scriptural song [i.e., one of the Canticles]. There must always be one reading from the Bible.

3. Hymns
Points are suggested for these, but they may be sung at any suitable point.

4. Tribute
Remembering and honouring the life of the person who has died, and the evidence of God's grace and work in them, should be done in the earlier part of the service, after the opening prayer, though if occasion demands it may be woven into the sermon or come immediately before the Commendation. It may be done in conjunction with the placing of symbols, and may be spoken by a family member or friend or by the minister using information provided by the family. It is preferable not to interrupt the flow of the Reading(s) and sermon with a tribute of this kind.

5. Sermon
The purpose of the sermon is to proclaim the gospel in the context of the death of this particular person.

6. Creed
An authorized Creed or an authorized Affirmation of Faith may be said after the sermon.

7. Receiving the coffin

- The coffin may be received into the church at the beginning of the service, or earlier in the day, or on the day before the funeral.
- A candle may stand beside the coffin and may be carried in front of the coffin when it is brought into the church.
- The coffin may be sprinkled with water on entry. This may occur at the Commendation, or at the Committal.
- A pall may be placed over the coffin in church by family, friends or other members of the congregation.
- Before or at the start of the service or after the opening prayer and hymn, and with the minister's agreement, suitable symbols of the life and faith of the departed person may be placed on or near the coffin.
- At the sprinkling, the placing of the pall or symbols, [various texts] may be used.[10]

8. The Committal

The Committal is used at the point at which it is needed, for example:
- at the burial of the body in a cemetery or churchyard,
- at the interment of ashes when this follows on the same day or the day following cremation, in which case the second 'preparation for burial' prayer [see Funeral Service, above] is used at the crematorium, or
- at a crematorium when the interment of ashes is not to follow immediately.

Forms of Commendation and Committal are provided, but when occasion demands, other authorized forms may be used.

When the body or the ashes are to be deposited in a vault, mausoleum or brick grave, these words may be used at the Committal:

We have entrusted our *brother/sister* N to God's mercy, and now we commit *his/her* body to its resting place.

9. The Funeral Service within Holy Communion

The Notes to the Order for the Celebration of Holy Communion, as well as the Notes to the Funeral Service, apply equally to this service. Texts are suggested at different points, but other suitable texts may be used. In the Liturgy of the Word, there should be a Gospel reading, preceded by either one or two other readings from the Bible.

Notes

1. See www.churchofengland.org/weddings-baptisms-funerals/funerals.aspx. Last accessed November 28, 2012.

2. For details, see section "Notes to the Funeral Service," note 7.

3. The reader is directed here to "Notes to the Funeral Service," note 4.

4. For appropriate readings from which to choose, the reader is directed elsewhere on the website. Recommended texts include John 6:35–40; John 11:17–27; John 14:1–6; Romans 8:1–end; 1 Corinthians 15:1–26, 35–38, 42–44a, 53–end (or 1 Cor. 15:20–end); 1 Thessalonians 4:13–end; Revelation 21:1–7. See: www.churchofengland.org/prayer-worship/worship/texts/pastoral/funeral/readingspsalms.aspx.

5. For details, see "Notes to the Funeral Service," note 2. For examples of Canticles, see www.churchofengland.org/prayer-worship/worship/texts/pastoral/funeral/canticles.aspx.

6. For other prayers from which to choose, the reader is directed elsewhere on the website. See www.churchofengland.org/prayer-worship/worship/texts/pastoral/funeral/prayers.aspx#thanksgiving, particularly, "Thanksgiving for the Life of the Departed."

7. "Prayers for Commending and Entrusting" are found elsewhere on the website. See www.churchofengland.org/prayer-worship/worship/texts/pastoral/funeral/prayers2.aspx#entrusting.

8. For Dismissal texts, see www.churchofengland.org/prayer-worship/worship/texts/pastoral/funeral/funeral.aspx#dismissal.

9. Many text choices are provided at www.churchofengland.org/prayer-worship/worship/texts/pastoral/funeral/supplementarytexts.aspx#sentences. Among them are Psalm 46:1; Job 19:25–27; and Matthew 5:4.

10. See "Some Texts which May Be Used by the Minister" at www.churchofengland.org/prayer-worship/worship/texts/pastoral/funeral/supplementarytexts.aspx#sprinkling.

Christian Funerals

MICHAEL IPGRAVE

The several purposes of a Christian funeral are succinctly set out in the introduction that the minister gives to the *Common Worship* service of the Church of England (printed earlier): "to remember before God our sister *N*; to give thanks for her life; to commend her to God . . . ; to commit her body . . . ; and to comfort one another in our grief." Remembrance, thanksgiving, commendation, committal, and consolation are distinguishable activities, and at least some of the verbs associated with them have different objects—most obviously, it is the dead who are commended and the living who are consoled—but their subject is the same—namely, the community who participate in the funeral service. The intention is that the liturgy will enable all these purposes to be delivered together; in practice, one or other aspect of the funeral service may come to dominate over others in different situations.

The context within which the liturgy is conducted is of course that of Christian faith, and in *Common Worship* three key affirmations of that faith are clearly expressed. First is the expectation of resurrection, articulated in the clarion call of the opening sentence taken from the Gospel of John (11:25–26) and repeated elsewhere. This is the hope in which the dead are handed over, and it injects a note of joy into even the saddest of farewells. Second, while God is acknowledged as judge, there is an emphasis on divine love and mercy. There is a balancing of these two aspects in the double provision for the committal—either psalm verses, "The Lord is full of compassion and mercy, slow to anger and of great goodness," (Ps. 103:8, 13–17) or the alternative, a composite of scripture (Job 14:1–2) and the traditional antiphon *Media vita*. In general, though, the two are not separated but unified ("Almighty God, you judge us with infinite mercy and justice and love everything you have made . . ."), and for the mourners in particular the consoling kindness of God is stressed. Third, the assurance of mercy and the hope of resurrection are both grounded in the history of Jesus "who died and rose again." It is in his name that the dead are entrusted to God, and this marks the distinctiveness of a Christian funeral.

221

These five purposes (remembrance, thanksgiving, commendation, committal, and consolation) and three affirmations (hope of resurrection, judgment in mercy, and centrality of Jesus) that can be identified in the *Common Worship* liturgy could be taken as characteristic of virtually any Christian funeral rite. Within this overall framework, however, Christian funeral practices are marked by great variety; in the remainder of this presentation, I wish to mention briefly seven different types of that variety.

Liturgical Choice

Most obviously, in the printed version of the *Common Worship* service there are various points at which alternative texts or alternative versions of texts are supplied. Some of these are of no apparent religious significance—for example, the two different translations of the Lord's Prayer. Others, however, are capable of conveying slightly different emphases—for example, the alternative verses mentioned earlier at the time of committal, or the freedom to choose from a menu of suggested Old and New Testament readings.

The provision of alternatives is a common feature of Anglican liturgy. In the case of the pastoral offices, it is designed both to allow the minister to design a service most closely meeting the needs and opportunities of a given situation and to allow those to whom ministry is being offered to feel a stronger sense of participation in the worship through exercising some choice in its design. In the case of a wedding, the minister will often use a discussion of these alternatives as a way of entering into a conversation with the couple about the meaning of Christian marriage. In the case of a funeral, a conversation of this kind with the deceased will obviously not be possible, but a similar discussion may take place with the bereaved family, and sometimes the minister may have had the opportunity to talk these issues through with the deceased before death.

Personal Adaptation

Beyond a choice between different liturgical or scriptural texts, contemporary Anglican practice allows for a much wider variety in funeral design in several ways. One is indicated in note 4 attached to the service, which refers to the possibility of somebody giving a spoken tribute to the deceased. This is a custom that has grown rapidly in recent years as a way of allowing family or friends to recall their memories and impressions of the person they have lost. Other ways of remembering the particular character of the deceased include choice of music (usually recorded), placing personal mementoes or idiosyncratic floral designs around the coffin, dressing the corpse in the colors of a favored football club, and so on.

What seems to be sought here is some sense of personalization of the liturgy. There is a certain paradox here: as the experience of dying has become more remote from everyday life, so also there has been an increased concern to make what seem like impersonal rites more familiar to mourners and more intimately referenced to the individual details of the deceased. As an archdeacon, when I received complaints about clergy conduct of funerals, they were almost always couched in such terms as: "He didn't make it feel at all personal for Dad," or whoever. The most serious complaints, of course, concerned those unfortunate instances where the priest had mistaken the name of the deceased. Distress in such a situation is understandable, but it is a relatively modern phenomenon: it is noteworthy that in the 1662 *Book of Common Prayer* the Burial Office includes no mention of the name of the deceased, who is referred to as "this our brother." The personal tailoring of funerals to reference the earthly particularities of the deceased can be carried to such an extent that the eschatological horizon of death, judgment, and new life is obscured; it is for this reason that *Common Worship* insists—for the first time in the Church of England—that "a sermon is preached," and explains (in note 5) that "the purpose of the sermon is to proclaim the gospel in the context of the death of this particular person."[1]

Cultural Diversity

When people die, they die not only as individuals and members of families but also as members of wider communities. Customs relating to death can vary tremendously from one community to another, and much of that variety has been taken into the practice of the Christian church, where funerals are adapted to very different cultural norms. In the remarkably diverse world of South London, for example, some funerals will take twenty minutes and some two days; some will be attended by hundreds or thousands of people, others by a mere handful; some will involve the consumption of prodigious quantities of food and drink, others will be much more abstemious; in some the immediate family will play a key part, in others they will be absent; and so on.

This huge variety can pose real challenges for a multicultural community of faith such as the Church of England. Christians of different backgrounds want to respect and support their fellow church members in their death as they did in their life, but expectations around funerals can be so different that they can sometimes become occasions of separation rather than of solidarity. "We do not live to ourselves, and we do not die to ourselves," Paul wrote (Rom. 14:7). He was reminding the Roman Christians that their living and dying were to the Lord, but he was writing in the context of different practices within the community. It is a lesson at which we still need to work in unexpected ways.

Theological Difference: Prayers for the Dead

The forms of variety I have mentioned can all be seen within one Anglican funeral rite. However, there are also of course wide varieties between the different Christian traditions; indeed, not only variations but disagreements too. In the past, funeral practices in the broad sense—that is, liturgical expressions of how Christians thought they should or should not relate to their departed brothers and sisters—formed one of the subsidiary theological battlegrounds over which Christians fought one another. Attitudes of mutual hostility have in large measure ameliorated now, but there remain deep disagreements over some questions, notably that of prayer for the dead. In Orthodox and Roman Catholic practice, prayer offered for the departed is seen as a natural and appropriate Christian activity, and it plays a major part in the funeral liturgy. The General Introduction to the Roman Catholic *Order of Christian Funerals*, for example, states: "At the death of a Christian, whose life of faith was begun in the waters of baptism and strengthened at the eucharistic table, the Church intercedes on behalf of the deceased because of its confident belief that death is not the end nor does it break the bonds forged in life." In the sixteenth century, the Protestant Reformers—repulsed by what they saw as an elaborate, unjustified, and corrupt system of belief in Purgatory, and noting the absence of any unambiguous scriptural warrant for the practice, largely rejected or strongly discouraged any offering of prayer for the dead. This continues to be the position taken by many Protestant churches today.

As is the case with many disputed theological issues, there has been a variety of opinion and practice within Anglicanism, although the overall tendency has undoubtedly been toward a gradual reinstatement of prayer for the dead. In 1928, attempts to revise the *Book of Common Prayer* were aborted as a result of opposition in Parliament. One of the contested points was the inclusion (for optional use) in the revised prayer book of the traditional antiphon for the departed, "Grant unto him eternal rest // And let perpetual light shine upon him," and prayers expressing the same sentiment. Those who emphasized the Reformed and Protestant nature of the Church of England felt that this, like other features of the revision, was an intolerable reintroduction of pre-Reformation errors and opposed it accordingly.

In contemporary Church of England practice, prayer for the departed is widespread though not universal. In many churches, such prayer occurs on a regular commemorative basis throughout the year as well as on particular occasions like All Souls Day or Remembrance Sunday. In the setting of the funeral rite, its permissibility is clearly if modestly affirmed in at least two places. One is in the "Prayers," where the second petition asks: "Remember for good this your servant *N* as we also remember *him/her*. Bring all who rest in Christ into the fullness of your kingdom." The other is one of the "suitable endings" to the rite, which prays: "May God in his infinite love and mercy bring the whole Church, living and departed in the Lord Jesus, to a joyful resurrection." Some would also argue that the very idea of "commending" to God somebody who has already died is in fact a form of prayer for the departed—and indeed some would oppose it on those grounds.

Historical Development: Commendation and Committal

The history of the "commendation" in the Anglican burial office is in fact a striking illustration of the variety across time that Christian funerals have demonstrated, even within the same tradition. The first Reformed English liturgy, Cranmer's Prayer Book of 1549, recognized two distinct acts, commendation and committal, even though it coordinated them in time, as the minister said: "We commend unto thy hands of mercy, most merciful Father, the soul of this our departed *brother/sister*. And *his/her* body we commit to the earth." We can note here that commendation and committal are distinguished by their objects—it is the soul which is commended, while the body, from which it is separable, is committed.

Three years later, in 1552, Cranmer produced a second, more radically reformed Prayer Book—which was to be reaffirmed, with a few minor changes, as the 1662 *Book of Common Prayer*. Here the commendation disappears altogether, leaving only a committal of the body, which is introduced with these words: "Forasmuch as it hath pleased Almighty God of his great mercy to take unto himself the soul of our dear *brother* here departed, we therefore commit *his* body to the ground; earth to earth, ashes to ashes, dust to dust." The anthropology of a soul separable from the body has not changed here; what is different is the abolition of the idea of commendation since this is seen as human presumption in praying for the departed—rather than it being commended to him, God has *taken* the soul for himself.

In *Common Worship*, the commendation has been reintroduced, and it is now clearly something different from the committal, as the typography demonstrates. Now, however, it is the soul–body distinction that has disappeared; whereas it is still the body that is committed to the ground, the object of the commendation (for which the verb "entrust" is also used) is not "the soul of *N*" but, quite simply, "*N*," or "our *brother/sister N*." In other words, it is the person herself who is commended to God. If "soul" language is to be used in this context (*Common Worship* in fact avoids the word "soul," but there are good traditional reasons why it should be retained), then it must indeed refer "not to the disembodied entity hidden within the outer shell of the disposable body, but rather to what we would call the whole person or personality as being confronted by God."[2] Commendation and committal are distinguished not through operating on different components of the human being but through being oriented toward different recipients—respectively, God and either the earth or the flames.

Social Adaptation: Inhumation and Cremation

This brings me to another, and perhaps the most obviously startling, variable within contemporary Christian funeral practice—namely, that two major methods of disposal of the corpse are used: inhumation (burial) and cremation. Such at least as is the pattern in most Western churches today, though it has a history of only a little over a hundred years. Despite the evident and dramatic differences involved in this change, I believe that the acceptance of cremation is in fact a development of little theological significance.

This may seem a surprising claim to make since for most of Christian history inhumation has been unquestionably accepted as the normative way of disposing of the remains of the departed. There is a seamless continuity in practice between Christianity and Judaism in this respect; on the other hand, in the archaeological record, the transition from pagan to Christian societies is often indicated by the shift from cremation to inhumation cemeteries.[3] The reasoning is not hard to see: while pagan cremation involved the destruction of the body, thus enabling the soul to be set free, inhumation delivered the corpse to the ground in a proclamation of the expectation that it would be raised up again. Apart from the deliberate infliction of burning alive as a punishment and a few rare exceptions of cremation made in the interest of health (after some battles, for example), the only alternative allowed to inhumation was the necessary rite of burial at sea, where the words used still spoke of the expectation of rising again: "We therefore commit his body to the deep, to be turned into corruption, looking for the resurrection of the body, when the Sea shall give up her dead."[4]

However, those words "to be turned into corruption" are very significant, for they express the recognition that inhumation was not only a pledge of resurrection but also a means of dissolution of the body. In the late nineteenth century, concern was acute in the crowded cities of Western Europe over both the availability of burial space and the hygiene implications of overcrowded cemeteries. Attempts were made to address these issues through promoting so-called earth-to-earth burials, that is, inhumations that avoided sealed vaults and airtight coffins, and thereby speeded up the natural decay of the corpse. Soon after, however, this movement was eclipsed by the growing promotion of cremation, presented with the same pragmatic justification as a method that would hasten the process of corporeal dissolution.[5] In England, there were indeed objections to this from those who saw it as an attack on belief in resurrection, but these objections were never expressed as fiercely as in Mediterranean countries, where cremation was seen as (and largely was) a campaign linked to anticlerical rationalism.

Cremation therefore became accepted as a legitimate Christian practice in the West precisely insofar as it was not seen as involving a change in theology.[6] This is indeed the explicit position of the Roman Catholic Church, which has accepted cremation since 1963, subject to this canonical restriction: "provided that it does not demonstrate a denial of faith in the resurrection of the body."[7] In fact, the *Common Worship* rite, in common with other funeral liturgies, accepts cremation within what is still a liturgy primarily oriented to inhumation: changes are made to the words of committal, but the funeral ends at the point at which the body is passed into the cremation chamber, where normally the flames cannot be seen; there is no suggestion that participants should witness, as in a pagan cremation, the actual destruction of the body by fire. Whichever means of disposal of the body is used, then, the belief is that natural dissolution will follow, but there is hope of resurrection.

Christian Identity: The Place of the Eucharist

Finally, the last "note" appended to the *Common Worship* funeral briefly mentions the possibility of holding the service within a celebration of Holy Communion.[8] Although this may feel rather like an afterthought, the Eucharist has played a very significant part in Christian funerals. Perhaps originating with masses commemorating the sacrificial death of the martyrs, its celebration is well attested by the fifth century and became central to the Catholic liturgy in the specific form of the Requiem Mass. Within contemporary Anglicanism, celebration of the Eucharist has become increasingly common at funerals of active church members and is now one of the ways in which those are distinguished from the funerals of people with a more tenuous connection to the life of the worshipping community.[9]

In part, this is for pragmatic reasons: at the funeral of someone unconnected with the church, there will probably be few or no people to receive communion. At a deeper level, though, a Eucharist at the funeral of a faithful Christian proclaims in the strongest terms the identity of the departed and their union with those who remain on earth, members together of Christ's Body.[10] It is a joyful affirmation of the fulfillment of the Christian's baptismal vocation and a foreshadowing of the heavenly feast to which Christians believe we are all journeying. This is powerfully expressed in the words used at the end of the mass over the coffin:[11] "*N* has fallen asleep in the peace of Christ. . . . In baptism *he* was made by adoption a child of God. At the Lord's table, *he* was sustained and fed. May *he* now be welcomed at the table of God's children in heaven and share in eternal life with all the saints."[12]

Notes

1. *Common Worship,* "Notes to the Funeral Service," no. 5.
2. N. T. Wright, *Surprised by Hope* (London: SPCK, 2007), 28.
3. Other distinctive Christian characteristics include an absence of grave goods buried with human remains and an orientation of bodies to the east. On the difficulties of applying these criteria strictly, and of interpreting the evidence clearly, see, e.g., Charles Thomas, *Christianity in Roman Britain to AD 500* (London: Batsford, 1981), 228–39.
4. *Book of Common Prayer,* "Forms of Prayer to be Used at Sea." The rubric introduces this statement as follows: "The Office in the Common Prayer-Book may be used; only instead of these words [We therefore commit . . .] say. . . ."
5. Christopher Hamlin describes the conflict between proponents of earth-to-earth burial and of cremation as "a largely literary conflict between two groups of body-disposal reformers, both of them objecting—on grounds of health, decency, harmony with nature, and wise land use—to an antiseptic embalming mentality of the sort that led to the burial of the Duke of Wellington within three layers of lead." Hamlin, "Good and Intimate Filth," in *Filth: Dirt, Disgust and Modern Life,* ed. William A Cohen (Minneapolis: University of Minnesota Press, 2005), 15. He also points out that there were Anglicans in both camps.
6. "Scientific argument was used to demonstrate that dissolution by fire posed no more insuperable task for the Almighty than decay in the earth." James Stevens Curl, *Death and Architecture* (Stroud, UK: Sutton, 2002), 303.
7. *Catechism of the Catholic Church,* §2301.
8. *Common Worship,* "Notes to the Funeral Service," no. 9.
9. The Roman Catholic Church now also makes available the funeral liturgy in two forms, within and without a Requiem Mass. A *Guide to Catholic Funerals* posted on the Catholic Liturgy Office website states: "The Church encourages a Mass since the eucharist remembers and celebrates Christ's own death and resurrection. However, while the eucharist is our central liturgy, it is not always the best option for every funeral." www.liturgyoffice .org.uk/Resources/OCF/FuneralsGuide.pdf.
10. Elizabeth Stuart points to the symbolism of the *Order of Christian Funerals* as a sign of the secondary nature of any nonbaptismal constructions of human identity (including those based on sexuality): "The Church teaches that in the end all other identities other than that conveyed through baptism are eclipsed . . . there is only one identity stable enough to hope in." Stuart, *Gay and Lesbian Theologies: Repetitions with Critical Difference* (Aldershot, UK: Ashgate, 2004), 2.
11. Traditionally, the coffin is at this point sprinkled with holy water as a reminder of the baptism in which the deceased was regenerated, and it is censed as an anticipation of the heavenly life to which she is summoned.
12. Taken from the Roman Catholic *Order of Christian Funerals,* this form is often used also in the context of an Anglican funeral mass and is authorized as part of the *Common Worship* provision, "Prayers of Entrusting and Commending," §69.

Conversations in Canterbury

DAVID MARSHALL

This volume consists mainly of edited versions of the various papers and responses to papers that were prepared before the seminar and delivered in either public or private sessions in the course of its three days. However, a great deal of the seminar was naturally given over to unscripted discussion and conversation. On the first day of the seminar, lectures were delivered at King's College London in sessions open to the public, with opportunity for questions to the speakers from a large audience. Video recordings of these sessions are available on the Building Bridges website.[1] For its second and third days, the seminar moved into its private phase in the precincts of Canterbury Cathedral, where participants met in plenary sessions and in small groups for further discussion, which now focused on the selected Christian and Islamic texts included in this volume. It has been the experience of many Building Bridges participants that the most valuable dialogue occurs in these private sessions, especially in the time spent in small groups of seven or eight in which it is possible to develop conversation marked by theological depth, personal openness, and a willingness to engage in frank questioning. The intention here is to offer a brief account of some of the main topics that emerged in these conversations in Canterbury. Differences between Christian and Islamic perspectives will be evident in what follows, but so will some similarities. Differences between coreligionists will also be apparent. Indeed, some participants made observations or assertions that may strike some readers as marginal to the mainstream of their respective traditions.

As at many other Building Bridges seminars, it was impossible to go far into the discussion of this year's theme of death, resurrection, and human destiny without raising the fundamental question of how Christians and Muslims understand what scripture is and what expectations we have of our different scriptures.[2] A Muslim participant admitted to being puzzled by N. T. Wright's comment (included in his chapter in this volume) that "belief in resurrection

hardly features in the Old Testament at all." In contrast, the reality of the resurrection is affirmed on nearly every page of the Qur'ān. Why, then, had God not
clearly revealed such a vital doctrine in the Old Testament?

Various points were made in response. For Christians, the Old Testament is
understood as providing not "a list of true doctrines" but rather a narrative of
the people of God, a narrative "within which you live and within which you
learn as you go along." Furthermore, another Christian pointed out, the Bible
is not "a book." Rather, it is a collection of books, as the Greek plural *ta biblia*
indicates. The plurality of the books of the Bible is often ignored by Christians.
Here we should note the considerable influence of the King James Version,
which gives a strong impression of the Bible as one book within which all its
characters speak the same Jacobean English. The richness and diversity of the
human authorship of the biblical books should be affirmed by Christians and
does not contradict their divine inspiration. There is thus an unfolding revelation within the Bible, which explains why a doctrine as important to the Christian faith as the resurrection is not present in its earlier books. A Christian also
made the point, now very familiar in Christian–Muslim dialogue, that whereas
for Muslims the Qur'ān is the Word of God, for Christian it is ultimately Jesus
who is the living Word of God, to whom the words of scripture bear witness;
another Christian, however, warned against pressing the Qur'ān–Jesus analogy
too far and thus underplaying the proper sense in which the Bible remains the
Word of God for Christians. A Muslim pointed out that there is some parallel
to the idea of Jesus as the living Word in the description in Shī'ī Islam of the
imām as *al-qur'ān al-nāṭiq* ("the speaking Qur'ān") and of the text of the
Qur'ān as *al-qur'ān al-ṣāmit* ("the silent Qur'ān").

There was further exploration of the question of what scripture is as well as
its relationship to tradition. An interesting intra-Muslim exchange concerned
how to understand the Arabic word "*kitāb*." Although this has often been translated "book," one Muslim preferred "scripture"; others raised the question of
whether "*kitāb*" must indicate something that has been written, or whether the
reference can be to that which has been confirmed. It was noted that whereas
in the modern Western world a "book" is usually understood as an object that
we can own, for Christianity and Islam the word denotes an event or act that
impinges upon us, "not just an object on a shelf." Another recurrent topic was
the relationship, in both Islam and Christianity, between scripture and tradition. For both faiths, there is much in the realm of beliefs about the Hereafter

that is not found explicitly in the Bible or the Qur'ān but rather derives from tradition. The same applies to many devotional practices concerned with the dead in both traditions. Purgatory was mentioned as an example of an area over which Christians disagree; underlying the disagreements are different views on how to relate scripture to tradition. The inclusion among the texts for study of passages from classical texts by al-Ghazālī and Dante also raised the question of the theological status of such works. One group had a particularly interesting discussion of the sense in which *The Divine Comedy* could, or could not, be described as an authoritative religious text; this led into thoughts about the status of canonical books and the idea of a (loosely defined) canon that inspires as distinct from a (precisely defined) canon that is inspired.

Discussion of I Corinthians 15 generated a number of questions. What kind of arguments is Paul using here, and what are they intended to achieve? One Muslim wondered whether their primary purpose was to persuade believers of the internal coherence of their faith rather than to convince unbelievers. Another Muslim asked what evidence Christians would point to that Jesus is already ruling over all creation. In similar vein, another Muslim asked what impact on the world the alleged resurrection of the Messiah has had. This prompted Christian comment on the unfinished nature of God's work of salvation in Christ. It has become a theological commonplace for Christians to speak of the tension between the "already" and the "not yet"; the full outworking of what God has done in Christ is yet to be accomplished. Belief in the Second Coming of Christ relates to this Christian sense of a story of salvation yet to be completed. Meanwhile, a Christian acknowledged, the high claims of the Christian faith can appear vulnerable in the midst of a world still acutely in need of redemption. Discussion also touched on the Christian hope for the making new of all things—not just human beings. This is an important part of Paul's eschatological vision, especially in Romans 8:18–25, where he speaks of a "groaning" creation being "set free from its bondage to decay." This passage has acquired new resonance in the growing environmental crisis. It was asked what, if any, parallels there are in Islam to this already/not yet tension that marks Christian eschatology.

Much discussion clustered around the theme of salvation. A Muslim mentioned the frequent need to explain to Christian friends that Islam is not fundamentally about acquiring "credits" with God through meritorious practices in order to enter Paradise. Yes, Islam does refer to the rewards associated with various practices, but a ḥadīth speaks of none entering Paradise on account of good deeds; entry into Paradise ultimately depends on God's grace. It was acknowledged that we should avoid simplistic comparisons between a Christianity focused on grace and an Islam focused on good works; the reality is that within both Islam and Christianity there is a range of understandings of the relationship between faith and good works in the process of salvation. Words from the great Christian poem *Dies Irae* were cited: "cum vix iustus sit securus." If, on the Day of Judgment, "hardly even the righteous person will be safe," this challenges any facile contrasts between Christian assurance and Muslim fear of judgment. However, another Christian reflected that although both faiths emphasize the grace of God, the differences in how they understand the expression of divine grace are significant. For Christians, the grace of God is focused in the "Christ event," especially the cross; "this grace in which we stand" (Rom. 5:2) is thus bound up with what God is believed to have already done in Christ crucified. Muslims, in contrast, do not link divine grace so closely to any one such moment in sacred history.

Mona Siddiqui's suggestion (included in her chapter in this volume) that "God expects–indeed, wants—human beings to commit sin so that he can forgive" elicited from some Muslim participants the question of whether such an assertion could be corroborated by any text from the Qur'ān or the Ḥadīth. One opined that it may be possible to support the assertion through applying the kind of esoteric distinctions within the divine will described by Ibn ʿArabī, but that mainstream Muslim opinion is that God only wants his creatures to be virtuous, and he desires to forgive them should they sin but does not want them to sin. It was, however, noted that within the Christian tradition there are some echoes of this idea, for example in the famous words of the medieval English mystical theologian Julian of Norwich: "Sin is behovely, but all shall be well." The meaning of "behovely" has been much debated, but perhaps Julian's meaning is that in the sequence of the revelation of God's love the positioning of sin was appropriate in order to lead us to a deeper understanding of God.

The ultimate destiny of human beings in Heaven or Hell has been much debated within both traditions. The idea of eternal punishment has been challenged, particularly in the context of modern Western Christianity, although a participant recalled listening to Catholic "hellfire preachers" in the 1950s, a period when as significant a figure as C. S. Lewis was giving serious attention to the doctrine of Hell in works such as *The Great Divorce*. Muslims have perhaps generally been less troubled by the morality of the idea of Hell; one participant spoke of having no problem with the Qur'ānic language of judgment, which is neither arbitrary nor unjust. However, an important debate within Islam over the centuries has been whether the punishments of Hell continue eternally. It was noted that theologians such as Ibn Taymiyya and Ibn Qayyim al-Jawziyya assert that God can threaten eternal punishment for sinners without carrying out His threat—for, on the one hand, "He does what he will," and, on the other, failing to carry out a threat does not make the one making the threat a liar. By contrast, God's promise to the righteous that they will go to Paradise will be carried out, for one who does not keep his promise is a liar, and God is certainly not a liar. It was also argued that the temporary nature of hell is implied in Qur'ān 11:107–8.

One discussion explored the kinds of arguments proposed by Christians and Muslims in support of the availability of salvation to all people, regardless of their formal religious adherence. Whereas it might appear that the particularity of the Christian emphasis on the salvific significance of the death and resurrection of Jesus limits salvation to those who acknowledge him as savior, this very particularity can be understood to imply the universal applicability of salvation. Appeal has been made to verses from I Corinthians 15 such as 22 and 28 to support an understanding of salvation that is both universal in its applicability but also particular in being grounded in the uniquely salvific and eschatological role of Jesus. However, it was also recognized that much else in the New Testament points away from such universalism. It was argued that Muslims can arrive at a universalist perspective on salvation, but from the opposite route: by explicitly disclaiming the uniquely salvific role of the Qur'ānic revelation. Whereas Christians stress that Jesus alone brings salvation (and then discuss how far that salvation extends), Muslims can argue from such verses as Qur'ān 2:62 that what saves is not the uniqueness of the Qur'ānic revelation but belief in God and the Last Day, and virtuous action in consequence of that belief. Hence, what is unique or particular to the Qur'ānic revelation is precisely its claim to bring nothing unique or new to the universal principles of guidance established by all previous divine revelations. Within this wider discussion of the scope of salvation, there was particular interest in Christian teaching on the salvation of Muslims, and vice versa. Mention was made of the perspective on the salvation of non-Christians in the Vatican II documents (notably *Lumen gentium*, 16). It was also noted that the passages selected from al-Ghazālī included negative references to Christians; a Muslim participant acknowledged a certain "one-upmanship" at work here.

Al-Ghazālī's vivid accounts of the Hereafter raised questions about how these were to be interpreted. Did Muslims take them literally or metaphorically? One Muslim acknowledged that a literal understanding of the descriptions of erotic pleasure in Paradise is widespread, and contrasted the strictly controlled nature of sexual relationships in this life among traditional Muslim communities with the expectation that "you'll have a lot of fun up there." This prompted a Christian to ask whether there was a tension between the attachment to physical appetites encouraged by such eschatological imagery and the ideal of detachment required in this life. Another Muslim commented on the complex relationship between literal and metaphorical interpretations. On the one hand, such imagery should not be taken literally insofar as God tells us (in a *ḥadīth qudsī*) that he has prepared for his righteous slaves what no eye has seen, no ear has heard, no heart can conceive. On the other hand, such imagery should be taken literally insofar as sexual joy on earth, when experienced within a legitimate framework, is a God-given foretaste of the joys of Paradise, just as every positive, noble, uplifting experience is a foretaste of a heavenly fruit. "Every time they are given to eat from the fruits of the Garden, they say: 'This is what we were given to eat before!' And they were given something like it" (Qur'ān 2:25). Furthermore, when one is given the vision of God, all other delights will be forgotten, as we see in the selected texts from al-Ghazālī. The relationship between the various joys of Paradise and the beatific vision in heaven is reflected in an analogous relationship between all good and noble experiences on earth and prayer. The Prophet said that three things had been made lovable to him in this world: the first two were women and perfume, but his greatest delight was in prayer. A Christian asked how Muslim women feel about a Paradise that seems designed more for men than for women. One Muslim response was that this impression derived from extra-Qur'ānic sources and that the Qur'ān itself explicitly promises equal rewards for pious women and pious men (e.g., at 33:35).

The great emphasis in al-Ghazālī's writing on the need to be ready for death led to discussion of preparedness for death and even the desire for death in both traditions. It was suggested that where Islamic spirituality is strong, death is seen as a blessing. In response, it was asked whether we actually want to die, whatever we might believe about the Hereafter. Here reference was made to al-Ḥallāj calling on his friends to kill him—"for in my being slain is my life." It was clarified that the death in question here is the death of egotism, as in the concepts of *faqr*, understood as poverty of spirit, emptiness of oneself, and of *fanā'*, annihilation of the self leading to union with God. A Christian mentioned an interesting passage in which Teresa of Avila says that she had once desired to die but believed that she had to die to her desire to die, reaching the point of no longer desiring death but accepting whatever was given to her, life or death.

The perspectives on "dying well" in the lectures by Harriet Harris and Sajjad Rizvi were explored further with reference to the complex interface between traditional ideas of *ars moriendi* ("the art of dying") and the ideals promoted in modern thinking and practice in this area. Key concepts in this discussion included acceptance, surrender, taking responsibility, and control. If traditional religious approaches emphasized the need for acceptance of the inevitability of death and of surrender to God's will (as in the Islamic idea of one's *ajal* or predetermined hour of death), modern practice tends to emphasize taking responsibility for one's own death and seeking some control or management over the process of dying. The art of dying could today be described as a "tailoring of our freedom to the necessity that faces us."

The interface between tradition and the modern world was also to the fore in discussion of the papers by Musharraf Hussain and Michael Ipgrave on Muslim and Christian funerals, as well as Recep Şentürk's response to Harriet Harris. The impact of the "funeral industry" on Christian practice in the modern Western world was noted; in contrast, it was generally felt that the Muslim world and Muslim communities in the West maintained traditional practices that the "funeral industry" tended to erode. For example, it is usual for the immediate community of a Muslim who has died to take responsibility for preparation of his or her body for burial rather than handing such responsibilities over to professionals outside the community. The considerable expense of funerals in, for example, the United Kingdom was contrasted with the norm of free burial in traditional Muslim contexts. A Christian deeply involved in church policy over funerals was struck by the fact that Muslim practice around death and funerals reveals how cohesive Muslim communities tend to be. Christians had much to learn from Muslims in this regard. However, a Muslim noted that Muslims are not free from the influence of Western society and was concerned about how this might shape attitudes in the future, fearing that, for example, Muslims might drift toward the deeply un-Islamic practice of cremation. Attitudes to preaching about death and the Hereafter seemed to follow similar patterns. A Muslim asked whether the Christian clergy present made much reference to death and the Hereafter in an exhortatory vein in their preaching. "Frankly, no," was the reply, although one Christian noted that while this might be so among most Western Christians today, it would not be true of all Christians around the world—there has been a particular shift in Western Christian attitudes. Interestingly, the same Muslim said that although he was concerned about an apparent evasion by Christians of the reality of judgment, he recognized the influence of Christian friends on his attitude to preaching. Referring to a vivid Qur'ānic text about punishment in the Hereafter, he said he would now avoid use it in addressing children or older people.

A point emerging from time to time in this survey is that while there appears to have been considerable development in Christian theological reflection on death, resurrection, and human destiny, and in Christian practices associated with these beliefs, the Islamic tradition appears to have seen considerably less change. Depending on one's perspective, one might see the developments in Christian belief and the changing nature and huge diversity of Christian practice either, in positive terms, as indicating a capacity for growth and adaption, or, more negatively, as a vulnerability to the spirit of the age, a tendency to be shaped by the latest fashions of the surrounding world. The latter critique, albeit politely phrased, seemed to underlie some of the questions put by Muslims in the course of the seminar. A Christian reflected on whether the apparently much greater variety in both "maps of the afterlife" and funeral practice in Christianity as compared to Islam is a result of contrasting theological dynamics within the two faiths, or is contingent on differences in their historical and cultural contexts. The same Christian, who is deeply involved in the church's pastoral work, wondered to what extent the sheer variety of differing, even competing, narratives in contemporary Christianity inhibits Christians from speaking coherently about death both within the church and in their engagement with the wider world. It should also be noted that for some Muslims, the idea of an unchanging Islamic tradition and practice needed some nuancing. There was development across time in the exegetical trajectory related to some eschatological passages in the Qur'ān as well as shifts in focus and emphasis in theological discussions of eschatology. Muslims, reflecting on their experience in the contemporary West, also spoke of shifts in their thinking and practice, albeit fairly subtle and set within a firm commitment to upholding a given tradition. However, the basic contrast outlined earlier does seem unquestionable.

As with all Building Bridges seminars, this one involved exploration of both shared perspectives and areas of difference. In the final session, a comparison was made with an earlier Building Bridges seminar on the theme of prophecy.[3] In the course of that seminar, it became clear that, however much shared ground there might be between Christians and Muslims in the conviction that "God has spoken through the prophets," it was not possible to develop a deep dialogue without addressing how Islam has understood the prophethood of Muḥammad. Exploration of differences over this fundamental point tended to direct a great deal of the discussion. At Canterbury, we again dealt with a theme that in one sense was solid shared ground—resurrection. Again, however, discussion repeatedly ran up against the particularity of a claim at the heart of one of the faiths—this time the Christian understanding of the resurrection of Jesus. Just as the prophethood of Muḥammad shapes Islamic thought about prophecy in general, so it is ultimately in the light of the resurrection of Jesus that Christians think about the themes that this seminar explored. Muslim and Christian participants thus discovered again that words that seem to overlap need to be attended to carefully. Clarifying the differences is a key part of good and respectful dialogue.

Notes

1. http://berkleycenter.georgetown.edu/resources/networks/buildingbridges.
2. The 2003 Building Bridges seminar focused entirely on the theme of the place of scripture in Christian–Muslim dialogue. For a record of this seminar, see Michael Ipgrave, ed., *Scriptures in Dialogue: Christians and Muslims Studying the Bible and the Qur'ān Together* (London: Church House, 2004).
3. See Michael Ipgrave, ed., *Bearing the Word: Prophecy in Biblical and Qur'ānic Perspective* (London: Church House, 2005).

Afterword

ROWAN WILLIAMS

T alking about death, resurrection, and judgment helps us see more clearly what we really believe about God and about ourselves. The reflections in this book will, I hope, help to explain how and why this is so. If we truly believe that God is (literally) indescribably holy, living in the absolute integrity of love and justice, we shall approach our encounter with him in a spirit that is sober, even somber: "who shall stand when he appeareth?" asks the prophet Malachi (3:2). We cannot but expect the pain of a contact between what is holy and what is compromised, weak, and flawed. If we try to imagine what it is like to be in the light of God's presence, we become more deeply aware of the shabbiness of our humanity and our lack of any claim on the justice of God. One of the recurrent themes in the Qur'ān is that at the Last Judgment we shall all be reminded of what we have always known: God has let his will be made plain, and if we have turned away from it, we bear the consequences of our choice.

Yet Jews, Christians, and Muslims alike trust in the mercy of God. If we acknowledge who and what we are, if we let go of the urge to defend ourselves or prove we were right, and if we appeal only for God to be true to his own nature, we may hope for grace. If we plead for mercy, we do not do so on the grounds of anything except what God has shown himself to be, a compassionate and gracious presence. In the face of God, we encounter inseparably "grace and truth," as the Gospel of St. John has it (John 1:14), the compassionate acceptance that flows from God's very "character" and the truth that we have no place to stand except on the ground of this mercy. The person who is untroubled or indifferent about judgment is clearly someone who has not grasped what the faith actually affirms; but so is the person who approaches judgment in panic and terror. The former has not fully realized what humanity is, we might say; but the latter has not fully realized who God is.

Death is supremely the moment when truth is laid bare. As religious believers, we cannot talk about it clinically or impersonally—which is why (just as in

241

the earlier volume in this series on prayer) it is important that the Canterbury conference included some personal meditations on the experience of encountering mortality and of the pastoral issues around supporting others in their encounters with mortality—with loss and grieving and the complex emotions around death. These bring to light some of the most striking differences in the detail of how we make sense of death, but they share the same air of sober hopefulness with which the person of faith looks toward his or her dying. Again and again in these pages, we have been reminded of how much we need to witness—in a society that is embarrassed, ashamed, or even angry about the fact of mortality—to the possibility of mature confrontation with the fact of death as an aspect of living to the full. In contrast to the caricatures sometimes advanced, the fact is that those who are most vividly alive are often those who are most honest about mortality. Those who seek with ever-increasing anxiety to evade mortality are the ones who miss out on the business of living here and now. A truthful spirituality is not one that allows us to take refuge in consoling feelings of eternity but one that returns us firmly to the present moment, that moment that is oriented inexorably toward death yet is full of God's presence and grace and so can be lived through in joy.

As several contributions have made plain, what exactly happens after death is, unsurprisingly, a matter on which our traditions have much speculation, much (in the broadest and most neutral sense) mythology and pictorial or dramatic imagination. But the strictly theological themes are not obscured: we shall answer for ourselves, yet we are not simply alone in our encounter; in various ways, our two traditions allow some sense of having an "advocate" with God. We die alone, and our death cuts us off from the tangible blessing of a share in the people of God; yet—even in the most austere Protestantism—we are still involved in the same community of faith and prayer. We advance toward communion with God or shut ourselves away from it, yet this cannot usefully be expounded without some understanding of what in us is purged away by the clear vision of God, so that it is not simply that departed souls experience immediate and timeless bliss or immediate and timeless torment. Our hope of communion with God is the hope of endless company with his love and nothing else; yet we surround this hope with extravagant metaphor and prayers for a renewed fellowship with others. There are plenty of paradoxical and teasing elements in all this, and systematization is hard (as many of our discussions in Canterbury illustrated). But at the heart of it all is that clear awareness that we are made to be in God's company and that our life beyond the grave is a homecoming, a movement not away from but deeper into our destiny as *created* beings.

That is perhaps why meditation on death has been so significant for those who have entered most deeply into faith: it is an opportunity to grasp more fully that we are contingent and dependent beings, yet, in all our fragility, we are "held on to" by the freely exercised love of the Creator. If there is one thing utterly distinctive about religious belief in the Abrahamic traditions, it is surely this belief in a God who has promised to be there for us in life and death alike—as judge, certainly, but also as the one who forgives and welcomes and re-creates, who begins our life afresh for us. We mean a good many diverse things by "resurrection," but we are at one in seeing it as the exercise of a divine initiative never defeated by death. Our discussion together in Canterbury left us all with a profoundly enhanced sense of this divine initiative that we celebrate and on which we depend. I hope that the thoughts recorded here in these contributions will have enhanced this same sense in this book's readers.

Personal Reflections on Death

The following contributions by seminar participants, printed here anonymously, were written before the seminar in response to the question: In your experience, what resources has your faith given you for responding to the deaths of others and/or the prospect of your own death?

1

My grandmother sought to teach me her faith throughout her life, but it was her death which finally convinced me. In working through my grief about losing her, I examined the evidence for the death and resurrection of Jesus and I found that brought me a real sense of consolation and hope. As someone studying ancient history, it was good to be able to test out the arguments for the resurrection, but it also affects how we face death. Because Jesus entered into our human existence even to the point of experiencing death, that means that God understands what it is to die, and what it means to lose someone you love dearly. That gives us the chance to grieve ourselves and to help others grieve, to enter into the pain and the hurt, the anger and the tears. But because God raised Jesus from the dead, we do not grieve "as others do who have no hope" (I Thess. 4:13).

Thus, when I officiate at funerals, it is in the "sure and certain hope of the resurrection to eternal life," as the funeral service puts it. In both my personal life and in my ministry, I have had to face good deaths as well as tragedies, but in all cases I have found the Christian teachings about Jesus's death and resurrection to be both intellectually true and personally helpful.

2

God will do for all believers what he did for Jesus at Easter. Believing this provides a framework for facing death. I recently buried my own father; it was a solemn triumph, sending him on a journey, knowing that we would follow and meet eventually in God's new world. A strange kind of joy: we are in touch simultaneously with the sad, often horrible present reality, but also with the extraordinary, glorious reality of God's powerful recreating love. To stand on that bridge, looking both ways, is a glad privilege. I sometimes ask myself whether I really believe this, but at a funeral I always know I do.

This frames what I believe about the "intermediate" state. I am confident that those I have loved and lost are "with Christ, which is far better" (Phil. 1:23), and I pray for and with them, for their rest, refreshment, and celebration of God's faithful love against the day of new Creation. This doesn't diminish grief; it frames, softens, and humanizes it.

The challenge of my own approaching death relates to other vocational questions. God will bring to completion, in the resurrection, all that is here done in faith, hope, and love; I therefore focus not only on the ultimate future, for which I trust God, but also on the present time and its tasks, whose value is not diminished by present transience but rather enhanced by God's promise of new Creation. I fear the process of dying rather than the fact of being dead.

3

We are travelers guided and led by the Most Compassionate and Generous Host through different stations of existence and life. Death is nothing but a passage from one level of existence to another; it is a passage from one form of life to another. This is the good news Prophets gave to their communities over centuries and across countries as expressed in the sacred books in many languages. Like every end, death is a new beginning—this is the hope for humanity. Yet, life is good in all its forms and at all levels of existence because they are different manifestations of God in us. Therefore, praise for Paradise is not a rejection of this life.

Death is the return to Home, Allah the Almighty. It is the union with the Beloved. It is also the return to Paradise from which we descended. It is thus the absolute liberation from the limitations and burdens of the "lower world" (dunyā), which is a temporary guest house in the movement from and to Infinity.

Death is one of the greatest blessings of Allah to His creatures. With it ends the separation from the Creator and longing for the original homeland, Paradise. Paradise is the Garden beyond which there is no garden; life after death is the Life beyond which there is no life.

Death is similar to the longing of the baby in the mother's womb for the time of his birth into this world. Now this world is comparable to the womb from which we will be born with a second birth, but this time to Infinity.

4

A true believer intensely loves his Lord, yearning all day for Him and longing for His beatific vision all night. In prayer and solitude his mantra is "My prayer, my sacrifice, my life and death are all for the Lord of the universe."

The Qur'ān proclaims: "Every soul shall taste death." Here death is not annihilation or extinction but the separation of the soul from the body, a change of state and a move from one house to another. According to a ḥadīth qudsī, God said, "I have prepared for my righteous servants that which no eye has seen and no ear has heard and no mortal's mind ever dreamt." The rewards and the delights awaiting the believer are described vividly in the Qur'ān: "And they will be honored in the Gardens of delight, on couches facing one another." "Lo! Those who kept their duty will be in a safe place amid gardens with water fountains, dressed in silk, facing one another. . . . We shall wed them to fair ones with wide lovely eyes." Death becomes a celebration of the day you arrive in Heaven, liberated from the frailty of bodily form into the home of the ageless eternity.

This opulence and magnificence of Paradise, the beatific vision, and the audience of the Mighty Lord make "death a bridge that unites the lover with the beloved"—hence something to look forward to.

5

I never thought of death until my mother died. I was thirty-three years of age at the time and, although I had older brothers and sisters, none of us were prepared for the suddenness of her death; we did not know how to console each other. Losing someone you love changes you in all sorts of ways, and it changed my faith and my personality. The finality of death and its impact on the living made me more time conscious, and I wanted to do more and more in less and less time. That I too could die at any age was a morose possibility, and when I thought of God, I thought of death; when I prayed, I prayed to live.

Death, the grave, resurrection, the Day of Judgment, and the afterlife are constant themes in the Qur'ān; they remind us not only of earthly transience but of a final destiny with God. But it is how we keep God alive in this world, our ethical framework through faith in him that decides our destiny. The relationship between this life and the afterworld lies in accepting that there is a place in time that has yet to occur; it is often depicted in terms of Paradise or hell or garden and fire, but it is all pervasive; this other world can be imagined but it is not imaginary. For me, both fear and hope are evoked in the Qur'ānic verse, "To God do we belong and to him shall we return."

6

Nearly twenty years ago, I became an Orthodox Christian. One of Orthodoxy's greatest gifts to me that helps me respond to death is its annual cycle of feasts. Its liturgical year—and the same might be said of other churches—provides a moving eternal image of the story of Jesus Christ and His Church. By freely moving within the regularity of its flow, my path can become the same cruciform path leading to resurrection as with Christ Himself. In, through, and with Christ, I can pass over from death to life, from suffering to joy, for in His enduring of the cross, He destroyed death by death.

When my father-in-law died of a brain tumor in the autumn of 2005, I was reminded at the Elevation of the Cross how the "Tree of true life was planted in the place of the skull" and Christ the "eternal King, worked salvation in the midst of the earth." His death could become the soil for a new blossoming. Likewise, when my mother died from cancer just before Christmas 2007, I knew that in the birth of the Savior, she was offered rebirth, a renewed humanity, since by making Himself "utterly poor like us," Christ made "our dust divine through union and participation." Yet this story, although it is an eternal memorial, does not liturgically absorb the world, eliminating tragedy, risk, and human creativity. Rather, the liturgical year is a circular icon of hope pointing to God's secret sanctification of time and death that is a free gift once offered by Christ on the cross.

7

The emphasis on the importance and relevance of death to our lives is undoubtedly among the essential teachings of Islam. The Qur'ān and Sunna, while not ignoring this world, place more emphasis on the Hereafter, and think of death as a gate through which the transfer from this world to the next takes place. The Qur'ān sees the longing for death as a sign of truthfulness (62:6), and being pleased with worldly life and feeling at ease about it as signs of those whose lodging will be in the fire (10:7).

The Qur'ān also emphasizes that every soul tastes death (3:185), and, according to Imam ʿAlī, death is the most certain thing that most people, quite surprisingly, treat as the least certain. According to a ḥadīth, the Prophet said: "The cleverest among people are those who remember death the most and are prepared for it the most." But what are important are the effects of being aware of this undeniable fact in our lives: how death changes our lives. For ordinary believers, the most significant effect of remembering death is that it brings humility and removes conceit and stubbornness. It is the only thing that cannot be conquered. According to a ḥadīth, if there were not illness, poverty, and death, nothing would make humans humble. Therefore, again we read in a ḥadīth that death is the sufficient preacher.

From a more spiritual and mystical point of view, death becomes the means by which the soul frees itself from the bondage of this world. Rūmī likens the situation of the soul to a captive bird for whom death becomes as sweet as leaving the cage. Since its heart is already outside, how will it be when the cage is opened?

8

During a time when I was writing on baptism, prayer, and confession, a friend was dying of cancer. So I became particularly focused on the matter of dying both as a physical reality and as a metaphor for spiritual processes. By engaging simultaneously with physical and metaphorical deaths, I became more aware of the ways in which Christian teaching on dying and rising with Christ, together with accompanying spiritual disciplines, help us to respond to the inevitability of death.

I am grateful for the gift of baptism and the pattern it initiates in us, so that as we move toward our physical deaths we are not dying for the first time. I am grateful for an understanding of prayer as the "manifestation of baptism" (Gregory of Sinai), and as "an abandonment of ourselves . . . because it is a sharing in Christ's abandonment of himself in death" (Herbert McCabe); for Collects in which we ask "continually to die;" and for Offices of Evensong and Compline, which relate our regular pattern of sleeping and rising to the larger reality of dying and rising. I am grateful also to the teaching of St. Paul, that what is mortal is swallowed up in life, and for both letters of Paul to the Corinthians.

9

My most intense encounter with death was at the early age of twelve, when my father died. Apart from shock and the overwhelming feelings of loss of someone I loved deeply, there was also a sense of incompleteness, unresolved issues, and unanswered questions. I had not been able to say good-bye properly, and this was compounded by a common practice at the time of not allowing children to attend funerals. Because of resulting financial and family problems, I also lost my familiar home and lifestyle. We were regular churchgoers, and I was also at a church-related private school. Consequently I was actively involved both in my parish and in school chapel. In the aftermath of my father's death, my faith and prayer were an immense help. Religious language and religious imagery— not least about death and the "world to come"—were simply part of my upbringing. There was a considerable emphasis on the cross and sufferings of Jesus as the result of sin, and sermons sometimes mentioned God's judgment and heaven and hell. Yet, on balance, the overall teaching I absorbed about death—particularly at school—was more humane. The "next world" beyond death was portrayed as more exciting than our present existence. Here we would meet God, our lives would be completed rather than ended, our questions would be answered and our hopes fulfilled. Most importantly for someone who had lost his father, we would also be reunited in eternity with those we loved.

10

Death is the only preacher you need, said the Prophet. There is physical death and metaphysical death. Physical death, that of the body, brings the soul face to face with God in the Hereafter. But metaphysical death, the death of egotism, means encountering God here and now. In the measure that we sincerely intend to purify our souls for God, we can look forward to physical death with confident hope in encountering the mercy of God—mercy which, according to the Qur'ān, "encompasses all things" (7:156). And we can encounter this same mercy, here and now, as we undergo metaphysical death: the process of dying to egotism, through submitting heart and soul to the spiritual and moral disciplines enshrined in the Prophetic paradigm. For one cannot die to oneself by one's own efforts; metaphysical death is not attainable by a kind of spiritual suicide. It is by divine grace alone that any effort to transcend the ego truly succeeds. Death, therefore, can be embraced as a source of mercy, both here and in the Hereafter. ʿAlī ibn Abī Ṭālib famously said: "I am more intimate with death than is the suckling babe with the breast of its mother." To be perpetually aware of death is to be perpetually "imbibing" the mercy overflowing from death; this will be the case for those who have already begun to "taste" the divine mercy as both cause and consequence of their spiritual effort to overcome the most fearful form of death: egotism.

11

Death, as an unknowable certainty (*yaqīn*), is somewhat paradoxical for me. One is enjoined to contemplate the prospect of one's death first as a reminder of the meaning that one's life must acquire, and second as a reminder that death is not "the end." And yet, one can have no experience of death and so it remains distant, even though biologically and religiously we must know that it is an imminent certainty. I think, given this dilemma of not being able to ignore death and at once not being able to conceptualize it means that all I feel I can do is to internalize it somehow by structuring it into my daily worship as much as possible. In this respect, the five ritual prayers (distributed as they are over the entire day and evening) as well as the reading of the scripture (punctuated throughout as it is by frequent reminders of our mortality) are occasions to confront this reality. One also strives to incorporate a reminder of death into one's supplications. There is the Prophet's oft-repeated supplication that one should implore God for a "fair death" (*mīta sawiyya*), gentle and just. But generally the supplications that help me find solace in contemplating the idea of death are mostly not ones in which death is directly mentioned: they involve Qur'ānic formulas that ask for God's grace, mercy, and beatitude in the next life. Reciting the scripture is, I think, key for me. The Qur'ānic enjoinments to lead a good and wholesome life and to hope for God's all-embracing mercy after death help to make death itself seem simply liminal, and so less of an anxiety.

12

Death would be a very grim prospect indeed without my faith in God and the promise of resurrection and continued life in the Hereafter. Our life on earth now as a gateway to the highest fulfillment of our human natures and selves in the next world—should we choose to heed God's guidance and His word—fills me with buoyant hope. Without this hope, life would be chillingly pessimistic and ridden with dark despair—death would spell the absolute end of our existence. We would not then dare to hope to be reunited with our loved ones forever in the Hereafter, mercifully free of disease and want, basking in the divine presence. Must not our earthly relationships and friendships aborted in the midst of worldly vagaries find a chance to fully blossom in a safe and pure haven?

Only God's infinite mercy and justice can vanquish the sting of death and the separation it otherwise threatens to bring about. The Qur'ān says, "We have decreed death for you and We will not be overcome" (Qur'ān 56:60). When I lost my father eighteen years ago—it was the first death of a close family member for me—I am not sure I would have fully recovered without the optimism that my faith engendered in me that I would see him again. I am still fearful of death in unguarded moments; but the hope of resurrection and eternal life in God's presence vanquishes that fear—just as His book promises.

13

It would be fair to say that many of the resources my faith tradition has given me were given rather by osmosis: a sense of hope, which issues from an intuition that death comes in the midst of, and therefore is part of, life rather than just its negation. It has given me music, ritual, and poetry that help make more bearable the real loss and separation associated with death. Though I know that the tradition has filled some good and conscientious Christians with "fear and trembling" before the idea of final judgment, in my experience this has not been the case. I'm prepared to admit that this might just be a presumptuous complacency on my part, but I take very seriously the idea that, as Paul puts it, "If God is for us, who can be against us?" (Rom. 8:31). The reconciliation of God and humanity effected in the Cross is not just a future possibility but a present reality.

On the other hand, there are certain respects in which traditional Christian ways of understanding death and heaven have devalued earthly life, making it seem as though this world and its bodily life are just the disposable "packaging" for a purely spiritual reality that will survive somewhere else—that earth is illusion and only heaven is the real; earth is exile and heaven our home. Fortunately, scholars and pastors of our tradition such as N. T. Wright have helped me to a fuller appreciation of the meaning of death and resurrection as it is proclaimed to us by the New Testament writers.

14

I have been walking mental circles around this dreaded essay for weeks. The question presented to us is precisely posed and thus difficult to dodge. Yet I find myself reluctant to engage it for experiential, existential, and theological reasons. Three recent experiences have been testing the assumption there is any basis for the "resources of faith" I regularly invoke in dealing with death. My brother's sudden and premature death in December 2010, the equally premature death of a beloved nephew in December 2011, and the cancer death of a dear friend in the same month give this question new urgency. Inevitably, aging adds the existential dimension. Both the experiential and the existential converge in the theological, exposing the tension of head and heart. To use a phrase made famous by the sociologist Peter Berger, I live in a continuous state of "cognitive dissonance." The "heart" side holds firmly to a belief in bodily resurrection and of eternal life as a perpetual reunion with those whom we love.

Only the thought that my brother has joyfully joined our parents got me through his funeral. Ancient Christian phrases like "the communion of saints" and "the cloud of witnesses" frequently occur to me in prayer, evoking beloved faces that I hope to see in heaven. But my "head" side finds no way to square all of this with contemporary science. I know Paul's answer—"You fool!"—to the question, "But someone may say, 'How are the dead raised? With what kind of body will they come back?'" (I Cor. 15:35–36), yet I frequently find that my sympathies lie with the questioner.

15

Some years ago, when I was on a sabbatical in Tübingen, I would walk through a graveyard on my way to and from my office. As I entered the gate, I would pass the tomb of the Goes family. The letters were written in capitals, and I could not help myself reading the text in English: "MARIANNE GOES, HEINRICH GOES, OTTO GOES," and then I would add, "And eventually we all go!"

At the other gate, on my way out of the graveyard, I would pass by the tomb of the famous Tübingen theologian of the last century, Ferdinand Christian Baur. During the minute that it took me to walk between the two graves, I would place my work in the light of my own imagined end; I wanted to make sure that I was not seduced by day-to-day pressures or popular concerns to betray what truly mattered. This was my own way of extending to myself the old greeting of the Trappist monks: "Remember that you will die!"

But where is it that I would go when "we all go"? "Enter into the joy of your master!" said Jesus in one of his parables (Matt. 25:23), describing what would happen to those who used their talents rightly. Not "God will make you rejoice!"—by giving a person entering the world to come a mere private joy. The joy of which Jesus speaks will be not merely an individual's state of mind but a state of the world, a state into which one enters, in which one participates, and which one shares with others.

On that journey through the graveyard, every time I remembered that I would die, I was letting *that joy* orient my day's work.

16

My first close experience of death was in my final year of study as a theological student, when a dearly loved aunt, who was my godmother, died. At a time of theological questioning, I realized how important it was to have a theology and faith that encompassed death. That experience led me to explore in my theological research nineteenth-century Christian debates about death, judgment, hell, and heaven and the ministry of Christian funeral services and prayers. The Christian faith is rooted and grounded in the revelation of the creative and redeeming love of God in Jesus Christ, which comes down to the lowest part of our need. The paradox and amazing grace of God who freely gives himself into our human condition, to the very point of knowing our human dying from the inside, mean, as one great English hymn-writer puts it, that "Christ leads me through no darker room than he went through before." We believe that, in Christ, God himself knew the absence of God and the destruction of death. But we believe also that in the resurrection of Jesus Christ death is "but the gate of life immortal" and, as we confess in the Creed "we look for (wait for in longing expectation) the resurrection of the dead and the life of the world to come." It is this faith that gives life in the face of death and hope of an eternal life that is nothing less than participation in the life of God.

17

When my mother was diagnosed with cancer, we spoke on the phone that evening. I was shocked, worried, and felt a deep anguish. She spoke with calmness and said two things that have shaped my thoughts. She said God had been good to her, and if this was the time to return to Him, then she would be glad. Life was in His hands. She also said: "Don't worry, we will all be together again in a more wonderful way. Just make sure your dad is OK if I go." She did not die. But since, I have begun to recognize the deep fears of death in me which have gone unchecked, and in some ways this has made me realize my weak and fragile faith. Since that day, I have felt a growing calmness at the prospect of my own death. It is a tender shoot. Sometimes, I have a hunger for a closer vision of God, face to face, a vision of the reality of a loving relationship to be enjoyed forever, and I feel relief that so much misery, suffering, and pain might after all not be the final word. Sometimes, the very thought of eternity frightens me.

18

My mother and father passed away some years ago, and the moment of mourning was a real consolation for me. The mourning was shaped culturally, shared together in a huge family gathering, and enacted according to our local ritual. In the midst of the cries, songs, and dances, the Christian voices of God's gracious love appeared through a sermon delivered by a pastor. Indeed, both parties, our traditional ritual and Christian voices, are sources given to me to face death faithfully.

We die in community, as death is a very public event. The sad news, once announced, ripples through neighbors, families, and churches as well as Muslim relatives and friends. The person who has died had lived with us for some time; his or her "soul-life" had animated us with great joy and hope but sometimes had also brought problems. That is why, during the lamentation, we sing of the love and care received from the deceased. And after the burial, we gather again, strip away the layer of sadness, and, with water mixed with lemon, we wipe our faces so that no more tears drop. The person who has died is not totally gone and is still part of our daily lives and memories.

Indeed, no one will be lost (Luke 15:3–7). The Triune God is a universal, loving God: creator, savior, connector of every human being. God will reunite us, the beloved, somehow, somewhere. And indeed, the heaven promised by God will be filled with brothers and sisters, and each name will be called joyfully.

19

"All that is on earth will perish, only the Face of your Lord, full of majesty and splendor, will endure" (Qur'ān 55:26–27). This is the Divine command that necessitates the occurrence of death.

Since death is a reality which everything that has been brought to existence after being nonexistent has to face, it makes sense that it be approached in a more or less positive fashion. Many traditions of the Prophet Muḥammad (peace be upon him) in fact exhort Muslims to look at death in such a manner. For instance, the Prophet (peace be upon him) said, "Be in the world as if you are a stranger or a traveler and consider yourself among the people of the grave." The fleeting character of the world is evident in this tradition, and the saying of Sayyidunā ʿAlī (may God be pleased with him) further explains it: "People are sleeping; when they die, they awaken." Thus the world is dreamlike in nature while death is what prepares us to face the Lord of the Universe—the Ultimate Reality. It is perhaps for this reason that remembrance of death and regular visits to the graveyard are highly recommendable acts for Muslims.

In our Islamic tradition, death is a transitory phase between the fleeting world and the ever-lasting Hereafter. Interestingly, however, because death itself is a creation of God, it will be made to perish after Judgment Day, so nothing will have to face death again.

20

As a priest, I am accustomed to ministry to the dying and to the bereaved, and I constantly marvel at the ways in which the Christian story can give people meaning and its promise can give them hope. These issues, though, became much more immediate for me with the death of my parents. My mother died, after a long and painful illness, as a believing Christian. I was able to celebrate a requiem mass for her using vestments that she had herself made for me. I was strongly conscious of her prayers for me, and a sense that after death she was in a way closer to me than before. For my father, faith was much more problematic, and I think he probably died without any expectation of a future for himself; he had found satisfaction in giving of himself for his family and (as a teacher) for his pupils. Thinking of him and praying for him as I do, I am brought back more and more clearly to core Christian affirmations: that there is a God of mercy who knows each of us by name; that in Jesus he has burst through death to a new life; and that through his Spirit we can do the same. And I hope and trust that, however hard it may be for them or for me to believe it, I may come to share with my parents and with all whom I love in that life which is greater than death.

21

Christ's death and resurrection are the life-giving events which lie at the heart of Christian faith, transforming our experience of death. We are all dying from the moment we are born because we are finite, mortal creatures. For me, one of the greatest gifts of the Christian spiritual tradition is learning to live with this fact in the light of the hope we have in Christ. Living well and dying well are the same thing.

Viewed from the perspective of Easter, death has been destroyed. We each still have to face our own deaths, but death can no longer define us or hold us to ransom. Every Christian has to embrace Christ's gift of his life, given in his death. This happens sacramentally and originally at baptism, when we die with Christ to sin and to our sinful desires; our corrupted self has to die. Our true self can then rise with Christ to new life, sharing in his resurrection, with him living in us. This experience is repeated daily: each morning we (as individuals and as communities) are called to repent, to die with Christ and allow him to live in us; each evening, in the *Nunc dimittis*, we pray with Simeon that we might be permitted to depart in peace.

Christian life is a preparation for death, just as it is a preparation for heaven. Part of the reconciliation offered in Christ is this hopeful (not fatalistic) reconciliation with our own mortality. Part of Christian discipleship is bringing this reconciliation to others.

22

Throughout my life, particularly my twenty-five years in ministry, I have often felt anxious, sometimes disorientated, when having to offer pastoral counseling to terminally ill people or those who have experienced sudden or tragic bereavement. Despite believing that through the cross Jesus conquered death and rose again to guarantee eternal salvation for those who believe in him, it has never been easy in real-life situations to reassure people that everything would be "all right." Then, five years ago, I lost my forty-four-year-old sister after a two-year battle against breast cancer. How could I comfort myself? How could I reassure my parents? How could I tell the young children that their beloved mother was in "a better place?" During those very difficult times, my personal approach to life and death was transformed by reflection on familiar biblical passages such as "For to me, to live is Christ, and to die is gain" (Phil. 1:21), and I came to a deeper personal grasp of the Christian hope of eternal life and grew in the conviction that with my personal relationship with God, through Christ and the Holy Spirit, death is not the end but the beginning of a new chapter of my journey.

A Decade of Appreciative Conversation
The Building Bridges Seminar under Rowan Williams

LUCINDA MOSHER

"In the months following that appalling catastrophe," explained Rowan Williams, reflecting on his decade as convenor of the Building Bridges Seminar, "my predecessor . . . believed it necessary to draw together as many as possible of the representatives of Christianity and Islam who were willing to engage seriously with each other about mutual understanding and cooperation in a very fragile global situation."[1] In January 2002, as one response to the catastrophic 9/11 attacks on the United States, Archbishop George Carey, with cohosts Prime Minister Tony Blair and HRH Prince El Hassan bin Talal of Jordan, invited thirty-eight Christians and Muslims to Lambeth Palace (the London home and offices of the Archbishop of Canterbury) for a seminar titled "Building Bridges: Overcoming Obstacles in Christian–Muslim Relations." Thus was inaugurated an ongoing international Christian–Muslim dialogue under the auspices of the office of the Archbishop of Canterbury. The intent was to create an environment for bridge building in the sense of "creating new routes for information, appreciation and respect to travel freely and safely in both directions between Christians and Muslims, Muslims and Christians."[2]

When Carey retired in October 2002, plans were in place for another Building Bridges seminar, albeit somewhat different in character: it would be longer and would have collaborative study of scripture as its core activity. During his tenure as Archbishop of Canterbury, Rowan Williams made Building Bridges a priority. Each year he chose Muslim and Christian scholars to meet with him for three full days of deliberation on some theological theme by means of pairs of public lectures, closed plenaries, and small-group sessions. This essay reviews and reflects on Christian–Muslim bridge building under his leadership.[3]

259

2003: Doha, Qatar

Having accepted the invitation of His Highness Sheikh Hamad bin Khalifa al-Thani, Emir of the State of Qatar, Building Bridges moved to a Muslim-majority context when it convened for a second time. In spite of meeting in close proximity to the US Central Command briefing platform for the invasion of Iraq, the March 2003 seminar remained focused on a topic chosen months earlier: "Scriptures in Dialogue: Christians and Muslims Studying the Bible and the Qur'ān Together." In preparation, participants wrote short responses to the question, "When, where, how and with whom do I read scripture?" Many of these essays are quite moving; taken together, they reveal a range of approach and multiple levels of engagement among members of both communities of faith.

Plenary presentations included an account of how the Bible is perceived by and functions for Christians; an explanation of the prominence of listening as a Qur'ānic notion; a reflection on the Qur'ān as theophany; a consideration of the ethics of gender discourse in Islam; a review of the history of biblical interpretation—with a report on the exegetical approaches of African women theologians; and explication of various challenges of modernism, postmodernism, and fundamentalism.

Williams later would call Doha the "seedbed" of the Building Bridges enterprise. From the Lambeth seminar in 2002 had come the sense that these conversations should be regular, extended, and searching, and should alternate between Christian- and Muslim-majority venues from one year to the next. The Doha meeting had tested these notions and had "encouraged all those who took part in it to believe that it was possible, desirable, and indeed necessary that the conversations which we had begun should be continued."[4]

2004: Washington, DC

Hosted by Georgetown University, the 2004 seminar considered Christian and Muslim perspectives on the nature of prophecy, the calling of prophets and apostles, prophets and their peoples, the place of Jesus and Muḥammad in prophetic religion, and the completion of prophecy. Small-group sessions of "scripture dialogue" involved intensive close reading of preselected, challenging pairs of texts.

On the eve of this seminar, Rowan Williams gave a public lecture proposing that more dialogue be invested in "looking at what is disbelieved in other religious discourses" because "we can learn better how to understand other religious believers if we learn better how to understand unbelievers."[5] The result would then be twofold: the emergence of "a conceptual and imaginative world in which at least some of the positive concerns of diverse traditions are seen to be held in common" but also, the discovery of "the appropriate language in which difference can be talked about rather than used as an excuse for violent separation."[6]

In their public lectures, two participants analyzed the emerging Building Bridges methodology. Miroslav Volf applauded the "great deal of *methodological sophistication*" operative in 2003, in spite of (or perhaps because of) there having been "virtually no reflection on method" by that gathering.[7] Where Volf celebrated the "momentous decision to organize the seminar around reading the sacred scriptures together," Mustansir Mir called it into question.[8] He asked whether the Qur'ān can indeed be said to support "the very possibility of scripture-based dialogue," yet he ultimately asserted that a credible Qur'ān-based "post-prophetic theology of inter faith dialogue" is both necessary and possible.[9]

Reflecting on the Georgetown seminar, Michael Ipgrave stressed that Muslims and Christians alike perceive themselves as communities gathered "around the Word which has been entrusted to them," thus accepting the responsibility it places on them. "For Muslims and Christians, our mutual recognition of one another as people who bear within ourselves the transforming burden of the divine Word is the surest ground on which to build friendship, trust and cooperation."[10]

2005: Sarajevo

In choosing to focus on "Muslims, Christians, and the Common Good", Building Bridges 2005—which was hosted jointly by Catholic, Orthodox, and Muslim institutions in Sarajevo—turned to some of the specific concerns raised at the inaugural London seminar in 2002: "faith and national identity," for, Christian or Muslim, we are all both believers and citizens; "governance and justice," taking into account both majority and minority situations for Christians and

Muslims as well as the implications of secularism; and, "caring together for the world we share"—which attended to global poverty as well as environmental questions.

Again, pairs of lectures were given in open plenary. Closed-door plenaries featured presentations of regional case studies from Bosnian, British, Malaysian, and West African contexts. As in the past, intense discussion was conducted in preassigned small groups. However, in place of close reading of texts, discussion was driven by questions provided by the day's lecturers.

With Sarajevo, more than any other Building Bridges seminar venue, the setting itself was in a real sense a "participant" in the dialogue. A seminar's location is always integral to how attendees think and interact, one participant asserted. In the case of Sarajevo, however, the place dominated the conversation. As they deliberated, recalls one attendee, participants were acutely aware that "Sarajevo had been sanctified by prayer and suffering." As the meeting neared its conclusion, says another, "most participants paid a visit to Mostar, where the destroyed and reconstructed bridge did indeed prove a powerful symbol of the place of religious difference in Bosnia-Herzegovina, especially in light of the title of our project."

2006: Washington, DC

While unapologetically an initiative of the Archbishop of Canterbury, Building Bridges has been intrinsically ecumenical since its inception—a fact made all the more evident in 2006, when, for a second time, the Seminar was the guest of Georgetown University (a Jesuit institution). Christian and Muslim understandings of divine justice, political authority, and religious freedom—concerns marked for further discussion back in 2002—were topics of discussion at the 2006 seminar. This meeting returned to the practice of close reading but with a considerably broader range of texts to be studied than previously. In addition to Bible and Qur'ān passages, the seminar took up writings of Augustine, al-Ghazālī, Martin Luther, and Ayatollah Khomeini as well as the Barmen Declaration and modern Islamic declarations on human rights.

Use of nonscriptural texts proved somewhat problematic. While each item was interesting in itself, most were too long for truly close reading in the time allotted. Furthermore, none of the selected postbiblical Christian texts were indisputably authoritative for all Christians; neither was it likely that all of the Christian attendees would have had deep prior knowledge of them. The same could be said of the relationship of Muslims to the Islamic texts chosen for 2006. Clearly, the discussion of texts other than scripture was a different experience from "scripture dialogue." Some participants found it frustrating; others hoped it would have a place in future meetings.

2007: Singapore

When plans for a springtime session in Malaysia collapsed, Building Bridges 2007 was postponed to December. Meeting in Singapore at the National University, the seminar's focus was Christian and Muslim understandings of what it is to be human. Grappling with scripture remained the primary activity; public lectures and small-group discussions focused on the topics of human dignity, human alienation and human destiny; human diversity; and the relationship of humans to the wider environment. Building Bridges thus provided a rare opportunity for Muslims and Christians to consider together a range of views on these topics. As Michael Ipgrave noted, during this seminar the dialogue often was "as intense between Christian and Christian, or Muslim and Muslim, as between those of different faiths."[11]

2008: Rome

A mere five months later, Building Bridges reconvened—this time at Villa Palazzola, an ancient monastery near Rome—to consider revelation and its interpretation and translation. Lectures and small-group scripture study facilitated consideration of the prehistory of revelation, the historical particularity and universal significance of the ultimate revelation, the possibility of continuing revelation, translating the Word, and passages in which scripture itself reflects on how scripture is to be interpreted.

To consider scriptural interpretation in the context of interfaith encounter, participants studied excerpts from *Generous Love*, a theology of interfaith relations prepared in early 2008 by the Anglican Communion Network for Inter Faith Concerns; and the final section of *A Common Word*, the pan-Muslim call for dialogue promulgated in October 2007. While time did not permit close reading of a pair of classical texts on scriptural interpretation, excerpts from the writings of St. Augustine and Ibn Taymiyya on this topic were provided nevertheless.

Several participants commended the depth of the Rome proceedings. One contributing factor was that, different from all previous and subsequent seminars, this meeting had no public sessions. Another difference was this seminar's attention to "issues around how to handle scripture and . . . the limits . . . of interpretation," as Rowan Williams noted at the time. This, he said, "enabled us to talk very, very frankly about fundamental differences and deep convergences." He added that there had been "a strong air of spiritual intensity about this meeting, partly because it had been held in a place of prayer."[12]

2009: Istanbul

At Bahçeşehir University, Istanbul, Building Bridges 2009 took up the interface between science and religion as approached by Christians and Muslims, past and present. Because 2009 was the two hundredth anniversary year of Charles Darwin's birth, Rowan Williams noted that "questions about the relationship between science and religious faith [had] once again become very current." Many had observed that Darwin's legacy "is by no means uniformly hostile to religious faith, that we need to understand better the whole nature of the challenge that scientific research poses to theology," a position with which Williams concurred.[13] Building Bridges 2009 was an attempt to do just that.

Preparatory study, lectures, and small-group discussions engaged wide-ranging texts from the Bible and Qur'ān and from the Christian and Islamic classical and contemporary periods: excerpts from the writings of Basil of Caesarea, Gregory of Nyssa, Augustine, Thomas Aquinas, al-Ghazālī, and Ibn Rushd; portions of writings of Charles Darwin and Richard Dawkins; and several items from Pope John Paul II, Sayyid Quṭb, Shaykh Muhammad Mitwallī al-Shaʿrāwī, Zaghloul el-Naggar, and others.

"The Christian and Islamic approach to the rational and ordered cosmos is one in which both divine and human freedom have a crucial role, the latter generated by the former," said Rowan Williams in summary remarks for this seminar. "That finite but authentic freedom, the freedom of persons in relation, is something we can and must celebrate and defend together—as we found ourselves doing, with much relish, in our days together in Istanbul."[14]

2010: Washington, DC

Building Bridges came to Georgetown University for a third time in May 2010—clear evidence that a special relationship had been forged between this institution and Lambeth Palace, with the university's Berkley Center for Religion, Peace, & World Affairs now taking up some of the administrative responsibility for the project.

With "Tradition and Modernity" as the theme, public lectures considered changing patterns in religious authority and different conceptions of freedom emerging in the modern world. Closed, detailed discussion took up examples of the writings of outstanding Christian and Muslim modern thinkers: John Henry Newman, Muḥammad ʿAbduh, Sayyid Abū l-Aʿlāʾ Mawdūdī, Lesslie Newbigin, Alasdair MacIntyre, Seyyid Hossein Nasr, Elisabeth Schüssler Fiorenza, and Tariq Ramadan. In reflection, Rowan Williams stressed the importance of avoiding "an assumption that these two words, 'tradition' and 'modernity,' are in all circumstances natural opposites." He noted the paradox latent in several of the seminar's lectures, "that it is modernity of a certain kind that makes it possible to talk about tradition as we do."[15]

2011: Doha, Qatar

Building Bridges returned to Qatar in May 2011, meeting on the campus of the Georgetown University School of Foreign Service and also enjoying once again the hospitality of the Emir. In a memo to invitees, Rowan Williams pointed out that since the topic was prayer, this iteration of Building Bridges, more so than in any previous year, would take up matters of personal faith, practice, and experience alongside academic questions. In preparation, each attendee wrote briefly in response to the prompt, "What does prayer mean to you?" These mini essays became part of this seminar's resource anthology, along with scripture selections and excerpts from a broad range of classical and modern Christian and Muslim writings about prayer.

Theologies of prayer, Christian and Islamic practices of prayer, and mutual perceptions (a Muslim consideration of Christian prayer; a Christian perspective on Muslim prayer) were the topics of public lectures. Closed sessions featured short lectures (with small-group discussion ensuing) on the Lord's Prayer, the Fātiḥa, Romans 8, two Qur'ān passages (3:190–94 and 28:45), learning to pray, and growth in prayer. An added dimension was the setting aside of time on each of two seminar evenings for demonstrations of Christian and Muslim worship practices. For their part, the Christians offered a version of the Evening Prayer rite of the Church of England. The Muslims' evening offering included Qur'ān recitation, an example of *dhikr*, and a lengthy supplication from Imām ʿAlī, among other elements.

A seminar on prayer offered, as Rowan Williams put it, an opportunity to "reflect not simply on one isolated subject in Christian or Muslim discourse" but "on what it is for a human creature to be related to the Creator. . . . As we enter more deeply into that mystery we enter more deeply, surely, into an understanding of all those other topics we have discussed such as justice, human nature, tradition and modernity, religion and science. We put all those discussions into a new and greater context."[16]

2012: London and Canterbury

For his last Building Bridges seminar as Archbishop of Canterbury, Rowan Williams chose "home" as the location. Given this year's theme of eschatology, seminar participants wrote brief essays on resources their own religion had given them for responding to the deaths of others or to the prospect of their own death, for inclusion anonymously in the anthology of texts to be studied.

The seminar convened in late April at King's College London for three pairs of public lectures on death, resurrection, and human destiny in relation to scripture; these themes in the Christian and Islamic traditions; and the notion of "dying well" from Christian and Muslim perspectives. Two days of closed sessions in Canterbury began with a morning of prepared responses to each of opening lectures—a Muslim scholar responding to a Christian paper, and vice versa—with plenary discussion of each. Small-group study periods considered I Corinthians 15, passages from the Qur'ān, excerpts from al-Ghazālī's *Revival of the Religious Sciences*, and portions of Dante's *The Divine Comedy*—each having been introduced by a short lecture. A fifth small-group session responded to a pair of presentations on funerals in the Church of England and in Islamic practice.

Some Observations

Demography

Since its inception, 157 individuals (77 Muslims; 80 Christians) have had the opportunity to participate in Building Bridges, 133 (63 Muslims; 70 Christians) with Rowan Williams. The inaugural seminar of 2002 had 39 attendees; for those since, attendance ranged from 22 to 31 (in 2008 and 2010, respectively). The attempt to keep the number of Christians and Muslims nearly equal at each gathering was fairly successful.

Given the nature of official religious leadership in many streams and hiring patterns of universities and theological schools, it is not surprising that between 2003 and 2012, only 25 Building Bridges participants were women (19 percent). The 2003 seminar in Qatar was the most gender balanced, with 36 percent women. On average, 22 percent of seminar attendees were women—which, in my experience, is typical for academic colloquia. Worth noting, however, is that the list of eight scholars present for at least seven of the ten seminars Williams chaired includes three women. Furthermore, it is significant that, at every gathering, at least two of the formal presentations were given by women; except in 2006, women lecturing included at least one Christian and one Muslim.

Theological and sectarian diversity has always been a feature of Building Bridges. Most Muslim attendees have been Sunnī, but every roster has included at least one Shi'ī. Albeit an Anglican initiative, Building Bridges has been far from dominated by Anglicans. Significant numbers of Roman Catholics have participated from the beginning; as well, participants have come from a range of other Christian traditions—among them, Orthodox, Coptic, Lutheran, Methodist, and Reformed.

Geography

As for the geographic range of Building Bridges, participants' professional affiliations span at least twenty-eight countries.[17] Including countries of origin or previous employment expands the roster's geographic range to perhaps forty countries. Even so, no attendees have come from South America or from South Africa directly—nor from many European countries, for that matter—and the choice of English as the language of the seminar may be a major factor here.

Attendees often have a professional network in their home country as well as the country in which they work currently and may well deliver insights to both. Yet Building Bridges invitees are not asked to represent a geographical or national constituency; rather, they are simply to bring an interesting perspective to the table.

In fact, "representativeness" can become a tool for excluding someone deemed "not orthodox enough." In the end, while a diverse dialogue circle may be valuable, a gathering of some fifteen Christians and fifteen Muslims is small. When a table has only some thirty seats, balancing too many variables will always be difficult.

Continuity and Trust

Building Bridges has been able to take on increasingly "difficult and delicate subjects," Rowan Williams has suggested, because "trust and . . . mutual affection has developed among us."[18] This claim is interesting when we analyze the rosters of the seminar's ten iterations under his leadership.

It is has been the seminar's custom to reserve some seats at the table for scholars from the host country and host institution. A few seats may go to people with special expertise on that year's topic. Thus, each roster has featured a substantial number of newcomers and one-time participants; almost 90 percent of the 133 participants have attended five gatherings or fewer.

With so little overlap, one wonders how the necessary trust and affection has been able to evolve. Yet seven Muslims and seven Christians have been present at six or more gatherings.[19] Repeat participants insist that trust has indeed developed. Some assert that Building Bridges invites complexity and encourages venturing out of one's safety zone, which regulars cherish. Said one Muslim, "I want us to have the intellect as well as the spirit not to feel threatened by an innocent, searching question."

"To talk together about the serious problems that doctrinal and social barriers create among religious groups requires a certain level of knowledge, a lot of trust, and a willingness to be self-critical," another Muslim points out. "It has been quite valuable that the Archbishop has been very careful to select as regular ongoing members people who have depth of knowledge of their own tradition, who also are willing to be self-critical, and are willing to encourage others to be self-critical."

"I think that, as a corporate body, we are quite a lot more than we are as individuals" a Christian veteran explains. "Trust has built in the corporate sense; we're really not starting over each time." The continuity has been sufficient for Rowan Williams to avow that participants have "come to love one another within the context of the Building Bridges seminars. . . . We have simply learned to enjoy one another's company as human beings."[20]

Style

Building Bridges meetings are marked by oscillation, some participants have said, "between public and more private modes of discourse," and "between classic themes from the heartlands of our faith and the contemporary applications of religious teachings and values." Whereas, in her experience, interfaith dialogue is most often a Christian initiative to which Muslims are invited as guests, says one Muslim, Building Bridges takes seriously the imperative to make Muslim participants feel that they are guests-turning-into-friends.

The Building Bridges style has often been described as an exercise in "appreciative conversation" during which one remains rooted in one's background "whilst at the same time reaching beyond it."[21] Distinguished by "courage, grace, imagination and sensitivity in addressing and retreating from painful issues," it is an exchange in which "people listen without judgement, do not seek consensus or compromise, but share the sole purpose of continuing the conversation in order to sustain relationships of mutual respect."[22] So described, appreciative conversation has much in common with David Lochhead's definition of the dialogical relationship: a relationship of openness and trust, which is clear, unambiguous, and has no other purpose than itself.[23] One veteran participant calls "the 'doing it for its own sake' ethos" of Building Bridges "liberating, and . . . very different from many other [inter faith] events."

The Building Bridges style, says Rowan Williams, involves "working together, studying sacred texts together, and above all learning to *listen* to one another speaking to God and also to *watch* one another speaking to God. It is a style that has been patient, affirming, and celebrating."[24] What develops as a result, he suggests, is "a virtuous circle," rather than a vicious one.[25]

Impact

"What has it achieved and what does it achieve, this series of discussions?" Rowan Williams raised the question in 2007, explaining, "We don't meet as political leaders and we don't meet as decision-makers; we meet as people seeking to reflect on our tradition and seeking to reflect together, to learn from the experience of watching somebody else reflect. If it's true, as sometimes has been said, that Christians and Muslims will never understand the possibility of the common future unless they understand something of the common history they have in common, then these seminars are part of that enterprise."[26]

More importantly, he continued, seminar participants have "sought to encounter one another not simply as scholars, but as readers and hearers of the word. . . . Because when that happens, I meet the other person not as a scholar, not as the representative of some alien set of commitments, but as someone seeking to open their mind and their heart to the self communication of God. And to meet another person in that light and in that way is to meet them at a very deep level."[27]

"Dialogue is better thought of as a continuing process rather than a specific event," Michael Ipgrave asserts. "So the 'Building Bridges' dialogue will be carried on not only in any future gatherings but in the ways in which participants reflect on the encounter in their own situation."[28] What, then, has been "carried on" from a decade of Building Bridges?

Several long-term participants affirm that the impact of Building Bridges is broad but indirect. Its impact, Daniel Madigan has suggested, is better understood as a "seeping out" rather than a "trickling down." Attendees have found the seminars transformative, spawning insights and generating relationships that then have their effect on participants' teaching and writing. Thus, suggests one participant, attendance at a Building Bridges seminar is best understood as "an investment."

Given that it began as an initiative of the Archbishop of Canterbury, it is logical to assume, as have some Muslim participants, that its impact would be greatest within the Anglican Communion. But the worldwide Anglican Communion comprises some thirty-eight autonomous and very diverse ecclesial bodies—an estimated 85 million Christians.[29] Family resemblance persists, but there is much internal diversity and a multiplicity of temporal, geographical, and contextual particularities in the relationship between Anglicans and Muslims.[30] To the extent they are aware of the project, Anglicans are as likely to be suspicious or dismissive of Building Bridges as welcoming of its work.

Be this as it may, the legacy of Building Bridges is rich and accessible by means of the website of Georgetown University's Berkley Center for Religion, Peace & World Affairs. Paperback books are available for seminars 2002 through 2012. Several Building Bridges volumes are also available as e-books or as downloadable PDFs. Resource anthologies for some seminars are also available there as PDFs.

Application

Having Web access to Building Bridges material is a great boon, especially for professors who wish to include it in syllabi. Could it enjoy even wider circulation? The 2005 seminar book has been translated into Bosnian. Could all Building Bridges books be made available in other languages—perhaps French and Arabic, and possibly Turkish, Farsi, and Urdu as well?

Some interest has been expressed in establishing satellite Building Bridges dialogues at national or regional levels. More modestly, Building Bridges is a replicable dialogical model for use at local levels. Muslim and Christian congregational leaders could work together with this material quite fruitfully over time. So could Muslim and Christian laypersons with sufficient background, curiosity, and perseverance to form a "reading circle" committed to systematic monthly or weekly discussion of the texts and essays from one or several of the Building Bridges seminars. During Building Bridges' next phase, under the auspices of Georgetown University, questions of pedagogy and practical application such as these will receive a fresh look.

The Claim of Uniqueness

At Georgetown University in 2006, Rowan Williams noted that Building Bridges "was brought into being to fill what was thought to be a gap; a gap not at the diplomatic or political level but a gap of a lack of opportunity for serious, reflective, and fairly loosely-structured encounter between Christian and Muslim scholars."[31] The implication is that Building Bridges is unique. How unique is this project?

Williams has often spoken of Building Bridges' distinctiveness in twofold terms. First, although the Seminar is a high-level project, its goal has never been to arrive at joint positions. Crafting a coordinated statement is terribly time consuming; from the beginning, it has been decided that the Seminar is better spent in free-ranging small-group discussion. Second, the Seminar has maintained profound commitment to "shared study" of scripture and tradition—with participants chosen for their prowess as scholars but also because they are persons committed to, and active in, their respective communities of faith. Thus, Building Bridges falls into the category of dialogical projects marked by both religious conviction and academic rigor. Indeed, what is most attractive to many participants is not that Building Bridges is "dialogue," or that it is "interfaith," but that it is almost always an exercise in "reading scripture sitting side by side with other colleagues." To prepare, one Muslim explains, one must sit with one's Qur'ān or one's Bible; participants owe it to their audience and to each other to do their homework!

Commonalities can be discerned between Building Bridges and the annual International Theology Conference sponsored by the Center for Religious Pluralism of the Shalom Harman Institute in Jerusalem—in which leading Muslim, Christian, and Jewish theologians engage together in mini seminars, public forums, and the traditional Jewish practice of scripture study with a partner; or with The Societies for Scriptural Reasoning—an initiative that describes itself as "circles of Jewish, Christian, and Muslim text scholars and theologians who bring both their sciences and their faiths to the table while they engage together in extended periods of [comparative] scriptural study";[32] or with the work of the Elijah Interfaith Institute in Jerusalem. Several Building Bridges regulars are veterans of one or more of these other initiatives, but Building Bridges differs from all of them in that it limits itself to the Christian–Muslim conversation. In this it is similar to the Groupe de Recherches Islamo-Chrétien. However, that is a dialogue in French, whereas Building Bridges is conducted in English, and all texts are studied in English translation; participants often refer to the original scriptural language (Hebrew, Greek, or Arabic) in their remarks, but few are proficient in all three.

A further uniqueness of the first decade of Building Bridges was the regular participation of the Archbishop of Canterbury himself—a fact that, one Muslim asserts, sent an immediate signal to Muslims that Building Bridges was a serious project. But while the office may have provided gravitas, Williams himself—as exemplar of being knowledgeable of and committed to one's own tradition while being committed to learning and caring about another's—has, without doubt, been instrumental to the project's ongoing success.

If Anglicanism brings a unique charism to interreligious dialogue, it lies in its very nature as a branch of Christianity both Catholic and Reformed. As *communio oppositorum*, it is an experienced hand in holding "difference" together. The Building Bridges project owes a debt to these attributes. However, its progress for a decade under Rowan Williams' guidance and its ability now to go forward under the stewardship of Georgetown University is due as much to the deep commitment made to it by the participants themselves—Muslim and Christian alike—as practitioners of appreciative conversation.

Notes

1. From Rowan Williams's opening remarks at Building Bridges 2012, London. See preface to the present volume.

2. Michael Ipgrave, *The Road Ahead* (London: Church House Publishing, 2002), 1.

3. This essay is informed by the published proceedings of the Building Bridges seminars; David Marshall's digest of a 2007 survey of participants in the first five seminars; input solicited from Guy Wilkinson, Clare Amos, and David Marshall; and my own interviewing of a number of participants. Early versions of this essay include a number of public lectures since March 2002 plus an essay reflecting on the project's first five years.

4. Rowan Williams, preface, in *Prayer: Christian and Muslim Perspectives*, eds. David Marshall and Lucinda Mosher (Washington, DC: Georgetown University Press, 2013).

5. Rowan Williams, "Analysing Atheism: Unbelief and the World of Faiths," in *Bearing the Word*, ed. Michael Ipgrave, 1–13 (London: Church House Publishing, 2005), 5, 12.

6. Ibid., 11, 12.

7. Ibid., 21. Emphasis in original.

8. Ibid., 24.

9. Mustansir Mir, "Scriptures in Dialogue: Are We Reckoning Without the Host?" in *Bearing the Word*, ed. Michael Ipgrave, 13–19 (London: Church House Publishing, 2005), 13, 19.

10. Michael Ipgrave, "Bearing the Word: Prophecy in Christian and Islamic Scriptures," in *Bearing the Word*, ed. Michael Ipgrave, 124–40 (London: Church House Publishing, 2005), 140.

11. Michael Ipgrave, "Introduction: Humanity in Context," in *Humanity: Texts and Contexts*, eds. Michael Ipgrave and David Marshall, xv–xvii (Washington, DC: Georgetown University Press, 2011), xv.

12. See "Archbishop's Reflections on the 7th Building Bridges Seminar" http://rowan williams.archbishopofcanterbury.org/articles.php/1118/archbishops-reflections-on-the-7th-building-bridges-seminar. Last accessed January 19, 2013.

13. Rowan Williams, "Building Bridges in Istanbul," in *Science and Religion: Christian and Muslim Perspectives*, ed. David Marshall, 1–3 (Washington, DC: Georgetown University Press, 2011), 3.

14. Rowan Williams, "Afterword," in *Science and Religion: Christian and Muslim Perspectives*, ed. David Marshall, 173–77 (Washington, DC: Georgetown University Press, 2011), 177.

15. Rowan Williams, "Afterword," in *Tradition and Modernity: Christian and Muslim Perspectives*, ed. David Marshall, 221–26 (Washington, DC: Georgetown University Press, 2013), 221.

16. From opening and closing remarks by Rowan Williams at Building Bridges 2011. See his preface to *Prayer: Christian and Muslim Perspectives*, eds. David Marshall and Lucinda Mosher (Washington, DC: Georgetown University Press, 2013).

17. Algeria, Australia, Austria, Bosnia-Herzegovina, Canada, Dubai, Egypt, Germany, Ghana, India, Indonesia, Iran, Italy, Jordan, Kenya, Lebanon, Malaysia, Nigeria, Pakistan, Qatar, Serbia, Singapore, Switzerland, Syria, Turkey, the United Kingdom, the United States, and the Vatican.

18. Rowan Williams, "Remarks at Dinner to Mark the Fifth Building Bridges Seminar," March 28, 2006. http://rowanwilliams.archbishopofcanterbury.org/articles.php/1275/justice-and-rights-fifth-building-bridges-seminar-opening-remarks. Last accessed: January 27, 2013.

19. Daniel Madigan and Jane McAuliffe were present at nine seminars chaired by Rowan Williams; Mona Siddiqui, eight.

20. Williams, "Preface," in *Prayer*, eds. Marshall and Mosher.

21. The term "appreciative conversation" was coined by Gillian Stamp in commenting on the first Building Bridges seminar in "And They Returned by Another Route," in *The Road Ahead*, ed. Michael Ipgrave, 112–18 (London: Church House Publishing, 2002), 112, 113.

22. Ibid., 112, 113.

23. David Lochhead, *The Dialogical Imperative: A Christian Reflection on Interfaith Encounter* (Maryknoll, NY: Orbis, 1988).

24. Williams, "Preface," *Prayer*, eds. Marshall and Mosher.

25. Williams, "Remarks at Dinner."

26. Rowan Williams, "Remarks at the Opening Session of the 6th Building Bridges Seminar," December 4, 2007, National University of Singapore. http://rowanwilliams.archbishop ofcanterbury.org/articles.php/1145/the-archbishop-of-canterbury-at-the-opening-session-of-the-6th-building-bridges-seminar. Last accessed February 3, 2013.

27. Ibid.

28. Michael Ipgrave, "Reflections from the Dialogue," in *Bearing the Word* (London: Church House Publishing, 2005), 116.

29. Statistics from the official Anglican Communion website: www.anglicancommunion .org. Last accessed January 27, 2013.

30. For a thorough study of classical Anglicanism's engagement with Islam and Muslims, see Nabil Matar, *Islam in Britain 1558–1685* (Cambridge: Cambridge University Press, 1998).

31. Williams, "Remarks at Dinner."

32. See "What Is SR?" *JSR Forum*, http://etext.lib.virginia.edu/journals/jsrforum/writ ings/OchFeat.html. Last accessed: January 27, 2013.

Index